The Man Who
Invented the Computer

The Man Who Invented the Computer

The Biography of John Atanasoff, Digital Pioneer

Jane Smiley

Doubleday
New York   London   Toronto
Sydney   Auckland

DD

DOUBLEDAY

Copyright © 2010 by Jane Smiley

All rights reserved. Published in the United States by Doubleday,
a division of Random House, Inc., New York, and in Canada
by Random House of Canada Limited, Toronto.

www.doubleday.com

DOUBLEDAY and the DD colophon are registered
trademarks of Random House, Inc.

Book design by Michael Collica

Library of Congress Cataloging-in-Publication Data
Smiley, Jane.
The man who invented the computer : the biography of
John Atanasoff, digital pioneer / Jane Smiley. — 1st ed.
p. cm.
1. Atanasoff, John V. (John Vincent) 2. Computer scientists —
United States — Biography. 3. Inventors — United States — Biography.
4. Physicists — Iowa — Biography. 5. College teachers — Iowa —
Biography. 6. Electronic digital computers — History — 20th century.
7. Sperry Rand Corporation — History — 20th century. 8. Patients —
United States — History — 20th century. 9. Intellectual property —
United States — History — 20th century. I. Title.
QA76.2.A75S64 2010
004.092 — dc22
[B]
2010018887

ISBN 978-0-385-52713-2

PRINTED IN THE UNITED STATES OF AMERICA

2 4 6 8 10 9 7 5 3 1

First Edition

Mathematical reasoning may be regarded rather schematically as the exercise of a combination of two faculties, which we may call intuition and ingenuity.

—*Alan Turing, "Systems of Logic Based on Ordinals," 1939*

Contents

The Man Who
Invented the Computer

Introduction

The story of how the computer on my desk got to me is one of the most peculiar tales of the twentieth century, and it demonstrates many tropes often considered merely literary—peripeteia (a sudden reversal in the plot), hamartia (an error in judgment or a mistake), anagnorisis (unexpected recognition), catharsis (strong feelings), as well as significant amounts of tragedy, terror, and pathos, and even some comedy. Many characters took part, and they did, indeed, act in character—some were dedicated, brave, enterprising, and lucky. Others were hotheaded, deceptive, foolish, and unfortunate. All were brilliant, but the story of the computer shows how they were brilliant in different ways. At least one, the most sociable one, turns out also to have been the most mysterious but maybe the most pivotal. And oddly enough, no inventor of the computer got rich off the invention, even though a few tried.

The inventor of the computer was a thirty-four-year-old associate professor of physics at Iowa State College named John Vincent Atanasoff. There is no doubt that he invented the computer (his claim was affirmed in court in 1978) and there is no doubt that the computer was the most important (though not the most deadly) invention of the twentieth century. But on the MIT Inventor Archive, there is

no "Atanasoff" between Barbara Askins (Method of Obtaining Intensified Image from Developed Photographic Films and Plates) and Mike
Augspurger (Handcycle). Where and when did Atanasoff invent the
computer? In a roadhouse in Rock Island, Illinois, while having a
drink. He jotted his notes on a cocktail napkin.

At the time John Vincent Atanasoff conceived of his invention, he
lived in Ames, Iowa, north of Des Moines, and taught in the physics department at Iowa State College (later to be renamed Iowa State
University). He had been attempting to come up with a calculating
machine since the early thirties, and he had tried all sorts of ideas. On
that night in December 1937, frustrated that his work seemed stalled
and baffling, he left his house on Woodland Street after supper and
went back to his office in the physics building, but that was no good,
either. So he jumped in his new car and headed for the Lincoln
Highway—the two-lane road that was the first highway to connect
the East Coast with the West Coast (Times Square in New York with
Lincoln Park in San Francisco). Atanasoff drove east for some sixty or
seventy miles, through the flat prairies of Story County and Marshall
County, to Tama, then he turned southeast toward Marengo. He drifted
past Iowa City on Highway 6. The landscape of eastern Iowa was roll-
ing and forested—decidedly different from the flatlands around Ames.
He drove rather fast, and so his trip demanded concentration and was a
relief from his recent obsessive focus on his computing problem.

Atanasoff later recalled, "I had reached the Mississippi River and
was crossing into Illinois at a place where there are three cities . . . one
of which is Rock Island. I drove into Illinois and turned off the highway into a little road, and went into a roadhouse, which had bright
lights . . . I sat down and ordered a drink . . . As the delivery of the drink
was made, I realized that I was no longer so nervous and my thoughts
turned again to computing machines."

The youthful professor came up with four ideas about how a computer might work. They came to him all at once—four parts of a system
that he had not been able to get a handle on in the previous five to
seven years of concentrated effort. After he finished his drink (or two,

though his son later maintained that more than one drink tended to put him to sleep, and that he had been known to stretch out on the carpet at parties after two), he got back into his car, drove home, and set about working out his ideas in detail. Within two years, he and a graduate student named Clifford Berry had constructed a working prototype at a cost of $650 ($450 to pay his assistant and $200 for materials).

If this sounds like the American dream, it is—Atanasoff's invention of the computer came about as a result of immigration to the United States from a troubled area, internal migration around the United States in search of better opportunities, and a system of general, and inexpensive, public education that was based upon the land-grant universities established by the Morrill Act of 1862. Atanasoff's American dream also included wholesome family values, innovative genius, and, eventually, vindication, but the path from those notes written on a napkin in Rock Island to this computer on my desk was a tortuous one. The story of the invention of the computer is a story of how a general need is met by idiosyncratic minds, a story of how a thing that exists is a thing that could have easily existed in another way, or, indeed, not existed at all.

But although this volume is a biography of Atanasoff and focuses on him, his story can only be told in the context of other stories, because in that December of 1937, others too were pondering the difficulties of calculation. Alan Turing, a visiting fellow at Princeton, was wondering if the Liverpool tide-predicting machine, a system of pulleys and gears used to measure and predict tides on the river Mersey, could serve as a core idea for a general calculating machine. Tommy Flowers, an engineer at the General Post Office outside London, was wondering if vacuum tubes (or "valves" as they were called in England) could be used for telephone system relays. Max Newman, a Cambridge mathematician, was nervous about what was going on in Europe but hadn't turned his thoughts to computers yet. John Mauchly, aged thirty, was teaching at Ursinus College in Pennsylvania—his passion was weather prediction, and he had his students attempting to find mathematical correlations between U.S. rainfall and patterns of solar rotation. J. Presper Eckert, only eighteen, was applying to college at MIT, though in the end he went to business school at the University of Pennsylvania. Konrad Zuse, in Berlin, had already built one computer (the Z1) in his parents' apartment. He later said that if the building had not been bombed, he would not have been able to get his machine out of the apartment. John von Neumann, born in Hungary but living in Princeton, New Jersey, had become so convinced that war in Europe was inevitable that he had applied for U.S. citizenship. He received his naturalization papers in December 1937. Von Neumann was one of the most talented mathematicians of his day, but he wasn't yet involved with computers. It is the weaving of these individual stories that makes up the whole story and causes it to become not merely the tale of an invention, but a saga of how the mind works, and of how the world works.

Atanasoff invented the computer as a labor-saving device. In 1930, when he was studying quantum mechanics at the University of Wisconsin, he decided to do his doctoral thesis on using a quantum mechanical method of calculating the capacity of helium to reduce the intensity of an applied electric field relative to that in a vacuum. His dissertation, only ten pages long, involved weeks of arithmetic on a heavy metal desk calculator with a hundred typewriter-like keys designed to perform addition and subtraction (multiplication and division were performed through repeated additions or subtractions). Atanasoff found performing the calculations extremely laborious, and when he began teaching the following year, he realized that his students were trapped in the same tedious difficulty—by the 1930s, solving mathematical equations with large numbers of variables was becoming a serious obstacle to progress not only in education and science, but also in industry, government, and the military. In 1940, Atanasoff estimated that it would take a person 8 hours to solve eight equations with eight unknowns, 125 hours for twenty equations and twenty unknowns. Another computer scientist for Bell Labs suggested in 1948 that there was "a practical limitation on the size of systems to be solved . . . It is believed that this will limit the process used, even if used iteratively, to about 20 or 30 unknowns." The problem was a product of increasing knowledge about how numbers work, how the world works, and how the one might be applied to the other. It was likewise the product of industrialization and modernization, of hundreds of years of ingenuity and the inventions and the observations and theories that ingenuity permitted.

Each of the inventors I will discuss in this volume had different motives for turning his thoughts to ideas of a new variety of machine, and the genius of each was idiosyncratically formed by temperament, education, family history, by restrictions as well as by opportunities. In some ways, Alan Turing was Atanasoff's precise opposite, drawn to pure mathematics rather than practical physics, educated to think rather than to tinker, disorganized in his approach rather than systematic, never a family man and required by his affections and his war work to be utterly secretive. His figure is now so mysterious and tragically evocative that he has become the most famous of our inventors. The man who was best known in his own lifetime, John von Neumann, has retreated into history, more associated with the atomic bomb and the memory of the cold war than with the history of the computer, but it was von Neumann who made himself the architect of that history without, in some sense, ever lifting a screwdriver (in fact, his wife said that he was not really capable of lifting a screwdriver). It is von Neumann for whom partisans of John Mauchly and J. Presper Eckert reserve their greatest wrath—with some justification—but Mauchly and Eckert have their own story of imagination, ambition, and disappointment, all of which grew out of their characteristic ways of thinking and doing. Perhaps the oddest duck in our gallery of odd ducks was Konrad Zuse, whose work on the computer can only be described as an adventure of the most daring kind. Zuse was two years older than Turing, born in Berlin but reared in a small town in East Prussia and lured into computer design not out of a passion for numbers or a pedagogical desire to advance mathematical computation but through an interest in art and design. Zuse conceived and built his computer without any contact with the world outside of Germany or even Berlin, and under the most adverse of circumstances. It is as if we have several movies running simultaneously—a sunlit-apple-pie-American-progress movie in one theater, a noirish tale of cold war deception, paranoia, and intrigue in the theater next door, a version of *Mrs. Miniver* crossed with a spy movie set in the blacked-out streets of London in a third, and, as a bonus in the fourth theater, a terrifying German resistance film, set in a collapsing Berlin, but with a happy ending.

The great event all these films share is World War II. In his recent volume of essays, historian John Lukacs catalogs the ways in which, seventy years later, World War II is still shaping the world we live in, even though all the power relationships and ideologies then in play, among the Allies and the Soviet Union and Hitler's Germany, have shifted utterly. In the index of Lukacs's book, no mention is made of the computer. But, as we will see, the Second World War was the sine qua non of the invention of the computer and the transformation of the nature of information and the nature of human thought that the computer age has brought about. However, we begin with another war, a small war in a place very far removed from Rock Island, Illinois.

Chapter One

John Vincent Atanasoff's father, Ivan, was born in 1876, in the midst of a period of climaxing political unrest. His parents were landed peasants in the Bulgarian village of Boyadzhik (about eighty miles from the Black Sea and perhaps halfway between Istanbul and Sofia). The Ottoman Empire was breaking up — Serbia had won independence in 1830 and Greece in 1832. Revolutionary agitation in Bulgaria, which intensified in the 1870s, culminated in the April Uprising of 1876, in which bands of Christian resistance fighters attacked Ottoman government offices and police enclaves. The attacks were followed by a campaign of reprisal on the part of the Ottoman government. Ivan's father, Atanas, and his mother, Yana, were forced to flee their village, Atanas carrying the baby Ivan in his arms. In the course of the melee, Yana was knocked unconscious and Atanas was shot in the back. The bullet killed Atanas and creased the baby's scalp as it exited through his father's chest, but Ivan and Yana survived (though American translator Eugene Schuyler estimated from his own observations at the time that fifteen thousand Bulgarians were killed, and five monasteries and fifty-eight villages — including Boyadzhik — were destroyed in these attacks). The revolution was put down for the time being and the Ottoman response was widely publicized and deplored, and then in mid-1877, Russia attacked the Ottoman Empire in the Balkans with the express purpose of liberating the Balkan Christian states and regaining access to the Black Sea that Russia had lost in the Crimean War. The conflict was short—the autonomy of Bulgaria was recognized in the Treaty of San Stefano, signed on March 3, 1878. Among the Russian cheerleaders for the war were Ivan Turgenev, who thought Bulgaria should be liberated, and Fyodor Dostoyevsky, who hoped to unite all Eastern Orthodox churches under the Russian church.

Yana subsequently married a local cattle breeder who could afford to educate little Ivan, while her brother made contact with American missionaries, who helped him get to America. When this uncle returned on a visit to Bulgaria in the late 1880s, young Ivan, now thirteen, decided to go back to America with him. Yana financed the trip by selling a piece of land that Atanas had left her.

At Ellis Island, Ivan Atanasov's name was changed to John Atanasoff. Although he had a bit of money, it was only enough to rent a room in New York City so that he could work at a series of menial restaurant and handyman jobs while he improved his English. Life was difficult and jobs were scarce, though he did manage to keep a chicken in his room for a while. A charitable local minister he met through his uncle found him a place as a student at the prestigious Peddie School, in Hightstown, New Jersey (not far from Princeton), where he worked hard and did well, but upon graduation, his education at first seemed to be of little use—his uncle had returned to Bulgaria, and there were no more family funds forthcoming. He was homeless for a while, working temporary jobs, but then he related his tale to a Baptist minister named Cooke, who encouraged him to seek the aid of various local congregations. Once he had accumulated $200 in savings and gifts, Pastor Cooke helped him find a spot at Colgate, at that time a Baptist-affiliated college.

At Colgate, John met the sister of two brothers who were fellow students, a girl named Iva Purdy, a descendant of early settlers in Connecticut and generations of farmers in upstate New York. Iva, herself a high school graduate with a talent for mathematics, was teaching in a nearby school. After courting Iva, John married her at Christmas 1900 and then graduated from Colgate the following June. John Vincent was born on October 4, 1903.

Although John had taken his degree in philosophy, he found work in industrial engineering at the Edison power plant in Orange, New Jersey. When work at the plant (possibly chemicals used in the manufacture of lightbulbs) seemed to be adversely affecting his health, he moved on to the power plant in Utica, New York, then to the Delaware, Lackawanna, and Western Railroad electrical plant in Hoboken, New Jersey. At night, he took correspondence courses in electrical engineering. Four children had been born by the time John Vincent was nine — two who lived and two who died in infancy. John and Iva came to feel that the family was not thriving because, in addition to John's own respiratory problems, the children were suffering repeated bouts of illness. They decided to move to the newly founded town of Brewster, Florida, on the west coast, some thirty miles as the crow flies southeast of Tampa, where American Cyanamid was in the process of exploiting local phosphate deposits. John got a good job, and the children's health improved. John Vincent attended school at the local two-room schoolhouse.

Iva Atanasoff gave her oldest child considerable freedom, both of action and of thought, in part because other children were born in Florida (eventually there were seven) and she oversaw a large garden in addition to the household. But Iva also retained her interest in intellectual pursuits — according to family stories, she liked to sit in her rocking chair and read while John and his younger brothers and sisters played about her. By the time young John got to school, he already knew how to read and calculate, and at first he was a difficult pupil — he was used to following his own agenda. Since he had no trouble doing his work, he finished ahead of the other children, and once he had done so, he made himself a "pest," according to his younger sister. But he was an inconvenient pupil also because he was inquisitive and knew more than many of his teachers. He was easily offended, especially by teasing and slurs, and he didn't mind getting into fights. Some teachers handled him well and some did not, but however they handled him, his pronounced eagerness to learn persisted—he eagerly explored both the countryside and whatever books he could get hold of.

In 1913, when he was not quite ten, John helped his father wire ·their home for electricity (subsequently, they wired the homes of some of their neighbors, too). In 1914, John mastered the owner's manual of his father's new Ford Model T, and at eleven he was driving it. John read his mother's books, including Ruskin and Spenser, and he read his father's books—including a manual on radiotelephony (wireless sound transmission). When his father ordered an up-to-date slide rule, then decided that he didn't really need it, John mastered it within a couple of weeks and thereupon became, in his own mind, a nascent mathematician. He found his father's old college algebra textbook and began to work his way through it. What he could not understand (differential calculus, infinite series, logarithms) Iva explained to him. During this period, he learned about various number systems other than the decimal system—this unusual familiarity with nondecimal ways of counting and calculating and his practice using them was what would eventually distinguish his ideas about calculators from those of his contemporaries.

John liked to make things and to demonstrate his skills—in sixth grade, because some older girls who had already finished elementary school were gathering in the back of the classroom and crocheting, he learned to crochet. He pursued his project at school, no longer undaunted by teasing but stimulated by it—he flaunted his work and bragged about his skills until the teacher banned crocheting at school. He soon learned to sew. In fact, John Vincent Atanasoff seemed to see every new idea or object as an opportunity to explore and master whatever his world had to offer. Atanasoff's parents gave him plenty of freedom, encouraged his enterprise, and helped him pursue what he wanted to master. They also made a stable life for him in an out-of-the-way spot where there was plenty to do and plenty of space to do it in.

The Atanasoffs' life in Brewster was not untroubled—the Atanasoff family, with its strange name and alien ways, was sometimes harassed and their property vandalized. John Atanasoff encountered resentment at work. The larger culture seethed with prejudice and vigilantism. A local Catholic lawyer was run out of the area. Between 1909, when the Atanasoffs arrived in Brewster, and 1920, more than fifty black people were lynched in Florida—Atanasoff himself remembered witnessing a lynching as a teenager, in Mulberry (about eleven miles north of Brewster), though that one is not attested to in Ralph Ginzburg's *100 Years of Lynchings.*

In 1912, John and Iva purchased a 155-acre farm southwest of Brewster, which included a 30-acre orange grove and 120 acres of timber. For young John, the farm meant more scope for exploration and, in particular, endless chances to not only repair the machinery used on the farm, but to take it apart and improve its design. The boy became interested in farming itself—he subscribed to *Wallaces' Farmer* (the publication founded in Iowa by the grandfather of Vice President Henry A. Wallace) and tried the latest farming techniques. Since John Atanasoff worked full time, young John became the one who organized and ran the farm. In the meantime, he graduated from the high school in Mulberry, completing his coursework in two years, at fifteen. The teachers at the high school did not attempt to control Atanasoff's independence or restrict his education—they encouraged his curiosity and his enterprise. Once he had graduated, Atanasoff got himself certified to teach math classes and saved the money he earned toward his college education, which he already knew would be in math and science. He worked for a year as a phosphate prospector and entered the University of Florida in 1921, just before his eighteenth birthday.

The University of Florida is and was a land-grant university. The Morrill Act of 1862, under which both the University of Florida and Iowa State College were founded, was written for a specific educational purpose: "to teach such branches of learning as are related to agriculture and the mechanic arts, in such manner as the legislatures of the States may respectively prescribe, in order to promote the liberal and practical education of the industrial classes in the several pursuits and professions in life." In other words, the land-grant colleges were intended to focus on the useful. In what is perhaps the paradigm of public higher education, the three state-funded colleges in Iowa are an example of this idea of the distinct (and class-based) purposes of higher education: postgraduate degrees are offered by the medical school, the art school, the music school, the graduate school, the law school, and the business school at the University of Iowa. Postgraduate degrees in engineering, agriculture, veterinary medicine, design, and industrial engineering are offered at Iowa State (though these categories have gotten somewhat less distinct in the last twenty-five years). The third state-funded school was, until 1961, Iowa State Teachers College, a normal school. Although the system of higher education was not as distinct in every state as it was in Iowa (the University of Wisconsin and the University of Minnesota have all types of programs on the same campus), the land-grant colleges retained their focus on disciplines applicable to the health and wealth of the individual states. The Morrill Act promised to fund these colleges by granting each state thirty thousand acres of federal land, the proceeds of which would go to the colleges. The land did not have to be inside the state — New York State was granted land in Wisconsin, for example.

The Morrill Act did not originally cover Florida, because the Confederate states had seceded from the Union before the passage of the act, but the act was extended in 1890 to the former Confederate states. Most of these states used money from the act to fund the useful arts at the main campus and to fund the establishment of separate, segregated black colleges. In 1905, Florida Agricultural College, in Lake City, was moved fifty miles south to Gainesville and renamed the University of the State of Florida. At the time of John Vincent Atanasoff's matriculation, the university was all male and all white — women students went to Florida Female College, in Tallahassee, and black students of both sexes went to Florida Agricultural and Mechanical College for Negroes, also in Tallahassee. Related to the Morrill Acts of 1862 and 1890 was the Hatch Act of 1887, which funded (also through land grants) the establishment of agricultural experiment stations in each of the states. These stations were normally attached to the land-grant colleges, broadening their practical mandate.

By the time he began college, Atanasoff knew he wanted to study physics and to be *a physicist*. He was familiar with and excited by Einstein's theories and by the other work being done in the field, but no physics major was offered at the university, so he went into electrical engineering, the most theoretical scientific major offered. In Gainesville, Atanasoff was surrounded by opportunities to think, but also opportunities to do. Requirements of the electrical engineering major included building models and projects, so Atanasoff took classes in machine shop, forge and foundry, and electrical mechanics. He also pursued his earlier interest in radio communication. He tutored students for money and worked summers—one summer in Jacksonville, he found a lucrative job surveying the city streets. He was, in short, brilliant, eager, enterprising, highly directed, and hardworking. Just as John Atanasoff's life had been almost a paradigm of the classic immigrant story, John Vincent Atanasoff's life was almost a paradigm of the classic ambitious American tale—a Tom Sawyer–like boyhood followed by a Horatio Alger–style self-funded and successful career.

But the elder Atanasoff's life remained difficult—while John Vincent was away in Gainesville, John and Iva decided to sell the farm and move to Bradley Junction, a town between Brewster and Mulberry. One night when John was coming home, he was attacked by a mob clad in white robes and nearly killed. He was saved by the wife of the Cyanamid plant manager, who heard the ruckus and ran outside with a shotgun. The mob was revealed to be made up, in part, of neighbors whose children Iva tutored in math and, in part, men who worked for John at the plant, all apparently motivated by the strangeness of John's name and origins. The attackers broke John's leg and ribs, and there were so many internal injuries that John was bedridden for weeks; John Vincent had to return from college to help take care of him. Although the attack was foiled, the younger Atanasoff children suffered for years from the xenophobia, and probably the envy, of the local population.

Atanasoff's childhood and adolescence constitute a case history of creativity—of the sometimes overlapping psychological characteristics of creative people enumerated in R. Keith Sawyer's *Explaining Creativity*. According to family anecdotes, the young Atanasoff seems to have exhibited every trait Sawyer cites, from self-confidence, independence, high energy, and willingness to take risks, to above-average intelligence, openness to experience, and preference for complexity. In the crocheting, we even see what Sawyer calls "balanced personality"—that is, a willingness to do things that are considered the province of the opposite sex. The key component of a creative mind that Atanasoff consistently showed as a child and a young man is what Sawyer calls "problem finding"—that is, the ability to productively formulate a problem so that the terms of the problem lead to a solution. Young Atanasoff's pleasures on the family farm seem precisely those of "problem solving" evolving into "problem finding." When a fence required fixing or a machine broke down or work needed organizing, he didn't figure out how to return things to their original configuration—rather, his goal was to understand how the original operated and then to streamline and improve those operations, as when he took apart and repaired farm machinery, or when he tried new cropping ideas without consulting his parents, or when he organized his siblings' chores, not forgetting to include a lesson or two for them in biology or mechanics.

In 1925, when Atanasoff graduated from the University of Florida, he had the highest grade average ever recorded up to that point at the university. He applied to master's programs in physics, his true love; the first to respond with offers of admission and aid was Iowa State. Atanasoff accepted the offer and made his plans to go to Ames. Sometime later, he received an offer from Harvard, but he turned it down. He was to remain in the land-grant system, and his tenure there was to profoundly shape his career.

Iowa Agricultural College was founded in Ames in 1856, ten years after Iowa statehood. Ames lies at the southern end of a geological feature known as the Des Moines Lobe, deposited by the Wisconsin ice sheet when the glaciers retreated ten to fifteen thousand years ago. The landscape is open, frequently marshy, and pockmarked by small lakes. For this reason, north-central Iowa was somewhat slower to be settled than eastern Iowa; when settlers first entered the Des Moines Lobe region, they found tall-grass prairie that stretched for hundreds of miles. But the land proved exceptionally fertile, and though the climate was marked by winds and weather extremes, Iowans understood very early that farming was the future of the state—the pre–Morrill Act state college included a model farm. In 1862, the Iowa legislature was one of the earliest state legislatures to accept the terms of the Morrill Act. The first undergraduates, a class of twenty-four men and two women, entered in 1869 and graduated in 1872; the Iowa Experiment Station was set up along with the college in the 1860s (by contrast, the Connecticut Agricultural Experiment Station was set up in 1875 and the University Farm of the University of California was not set up until 1905).

By the time Atanasoff arrived in 1921, Iowa State was already famous as the alma mater of Carrie Chapman Catt, a prominent nineteenth-century feminist, and of George Washington Carver, a botanist and inventor, the first black student at the college and the first black researcher at the Experiment Station. An 1893 alumnus, Bert Benjamin, had invented the Farmall tractor, which was the first tractor that could be used to perform all farm operations.

Atanasoff's stipend for teaching undergraduate math classes at Iowa State for the school year 1925–26 was $800, enough to allow him to find a room on Knapp Street south of campus. The campus was then and is now self-contained but spacious. Although a train ran between the campus and Ames, Atanasoff bought himself a bicycle to get around. At first he did his work and kept to himself—according to his granddaughter, Tammara Burton. "Hurrying toward his destination, he typically wore an expression of severe concentration as he worked to solve the equation that was of greatest interest to him at the moment. With his foreign name, his unfashionable clothes, and his dark unruly hair, he soon earned the nickname around campus of 'The Mad

Russian.'" In addition, he spoke in an alien southern drawl as a result of his childhood in Florida. But he impressed his professors, soon gaining a reputation for brilliance. He taught his math students and took his own courses, and these activities were time-consuming. However, Knapp Street was not far from Fraternity Row on Ash Avenue, and it was there, at a mixer for southern students, that he met Lura Meeks, who had come to Iowa State from Cheyenne, Oklahoma, a place at least as wild, in its way, as Florida. Lura was somewhat older than John but still an undergraduate, putting herself through college. Her personality was in many ways the female counterpart to John's—she had always played the piano, painted, done wood carvings, and written poetry while working on the family farm and doing chores on neighboring farms for cash. At Iowa State, she was on the tennis team and the swimming team, and she was a devoted reader, like Iva. Herself intelligent, energetic, and enterprising, she recognized both John's talent and his ambition. They were married shortly after he received his master's degree in physics, in June 1926. Atanasoff then accepted a position at Iowa State for $1,800 per year, teaching mathematics and physics while taking more classes to prepare for his doctoral studies at another land-grant institution, the University of Wisconsin.

Things did not go smoothly in the early months of the marriage. Lura left for Montana, where she had a contract to teach high school, but not wishing to be away from John, she gave up her job and came home in November; John's contract with Iowa State was not completed in the winter of 1927 until after classes at the University of Wisconsin had already commenced. Money was tight, and Lura got pregnant. John, however, was not much daunted—after he arrived in Madison in the winter of 1927, he began his classwork, knowing that he would soon catch up. The only professor who was offended by this plan was the professor of quantum mechanics, John Hasbrouck Van Vleck. Quantum mechanics is the science that predicts what happens in systems, and in the 1920s it was the most up-to-date and exciting field in physics.

Professor John Hasbrouck Van Vleck was only four and a half years older than his graduate student, but he was from a much different background—his grandfather was an astronomer and his father was a mathematician. He had grown up in Madison and completed his degrees at Harvard at the age of twenty-four. By the time he encountered Atanasoff (and his southern drawl), he had already taught at the University of Minnesota. After the University of Wisconsin, he would return to Harvard. He would eventually win the Nobel Prize in 1977, along with Philip Warren Anderson and Sir Neville Francis Mott ("for their fundamental theoretical investigations of the electronic structure of magnetic and disordered systems"). Though only in his late twenties, Van Vleck already possessed the means to begin a serious art collection. He did not want to allow Atanasoff to enter his class late, and he did not think Atanasoff would be able to do the work. Owing to tight finances, though, John and Lura could not afford to stay an extra semester in order for John to take the course from the beginning. In a replay of his behavior in elementary school, John attended lectures, spoke up in class, asked questions, and, perhaps Van Vleck felt, made himself a pest. At any rate, Van Vleck felt no hesitation about denigrating Atanasoff's performance and often appended remarks to his answers such as, "If you had been here in the first half of the semester, you wouldn't have to ask that question." The course was so difficult that only a few of the students completed it—Atanasoff told Clark Mollenhoff, the *Des Moines Register* writer who wrote *Atanasoff: Forgotten Father of the Computer* in the late eighties, "There were perhaps twenty-five graduate students in the class, and . . . only five even bothered to take the final examination. I wrote for seven hours on that test, and when Dr. Van Vleck called me in later he told me it was one of the best and indicated that it was the best, but made no comment of congratulation." Van Vleck was not the last scientist to fail to appreciate Atanasoff.

Since Atanasoff hoped to specialize in quantum mechanics, Van Vleck was his assigned major professor, but Van Vleck went on leave in 1929–30, so Atanasoff worked under Gregor Wentzel, visiting from Zurich, where he had succeeded Erwin Schrödinger (who was to receive the Nobel Prize in 1933 for his contributions to quantum mechanics) in the chair for theoretical physics. Although he was only a year older than Van Vleck, Wentzel was more sympathetic to Atanasoff and oversaw Atanasoff's dissertation, "The Dielectric Constant of Helium."

Atanasoff's dissertation and his degree were in theoretical physics, his long-standing passion. The "dielectric constant" or "relative static permittivity" is a practical measurement, the ratio of the electric field in a vacuum to the electric field in a medium. He did the calculation by using the governing partial differential equation of quantum physics, the Schrödinger equation. The thesis was concerned only with theory and was not an experimental measurement (this had already been done by someone else). Atanasoff's calculation, accurate to within 5 percent of the measured value, used a mathematical technique called the Ritz variational method. The solutions to the linear equations he had to solve so laboriously were coefficients of the approximate wave functions he used in the variational calculation. The thesis result was important because it showed that the answer was obtainable by theoretical quantum mechanics. His calculations were about the probability that electrons in helium would act in a certain way when subjected to an electric field. But as always, his work pointed in more than one direction: what he was calculating demonstrated the utility of quantum mechanics as applied to atomic structure, but more important, as it turned out, the difficulty of making his calculations forced him to encounter, over and over, the flaws of modern computing machines.

Atanasoff was awarded his PhD by the University of Wisconsin in July 1930. He was twenty-six years old and had been married for four years. His daughter, Elsie, was just over a year old and Lura was expecting a second child. His first job offer—assistant professor of mathematics and physics—came from Iowa State. His salary was to be $2,700 dollars per year, $900 more than he had made as a student teacher after receiving his master's. Jobs in physics were scarce, and Atanasoff once again committed himself to the Iowa State position, only to be subsequently offered a job at Harvard that he once again could not accept.

In 1929, when John Vincent Atanasoff was working on his PhD in physics at the University of Wisconsin, Alan Turing, seventeen (born June 23, 1912), was sitting for his Higher School Certificate examination. The examiner who evaluated his mathematics paper wrote, "He appeared to lack the patience necessary for algebraic verification, and his handwriting was so bad that he lost marks frequently—sometimes because his work was definitely illegible and sometimes his misreading his own writing led him into mistakes." He had to take this examination three times and switch his major subject from science to mathematics in order to gain acceptance (with a scholarship) to his preferred school, King's College, Cambridge.

He was already an interesting young man. Turing's parents, Julius and Ethel, were both born into the English civil service in India. Ethel Stoney's father was in the medical corps; she was born in Madras and lived most of her life (with occasional trips back to England) in Coonoor. Julius served as a peripatetic official, head assistant collector, near Madras. They met on a ship returning to England by the eastern route, stopping in California. Part of their courtship was a transcontinental journey across the United States, with a sojourn in Yellowstone Park. Alan was born in London in 1912, while his parents were once again on leave. Alan had one older brother, John, born in 1908. Alan was born in Paddington, and then the family settled in the southeast, near Hastings. When Alan was nine months old, his father returned to India. When he was fifteen months old, Ethel followed Julius, leaving John and Alan in the care of a retired army couple. Both parents went back and forth between India and England for the next five years, sometimes together and sometimes separately. They never had a house of their own in England.

Alan was quick as a child and eccentric—he taught himself to read in three weeks, and he had no trouble expressing his opinion. He tended to get caught up in observing things—serial numbers, daisies—but failed to grasp other apparently simple ideas, such as the fact that Christmas came at the same time every year. He was not indulged, and his failure to conform to English (and, no doubt, military and bureaucratic) standards of behavior often led to arguments and tantrums. Descriptions of Alan's childhood seem to leap out of the writings of Oliver Sacks. The boy was busy, untidy, inventive, inquisitive, and obviously brilliant, but the Turings were bureaucrats—several generations had served as officials in British India. Alan's mother's family, the Stoneys, was known to be inventive and commercial—one great-uncle designed sluice gates for water-level control on the Thames and other rivers, while his grandfather worked as chief engineer on the Madras and Southern Mahratta Railway and also designed a type of indoor fan. As bureaucrats, they had status but little money. They had expectations, however, and a class identity to maintain. Much of this maintenance depended on conforming to strict standards of behavior and attending the proper sort of school. Even though Alan readily learned such things as long division and also showed an eager interest in the "underlying principles" of every operation (according to his mother), he did poorly on exams and was always more or less unpopular. He was also sloppy. According to his brother, "It was all the same thing to him which shoe was on which foot."

Like the young Atanasoff, Turing was enterprising, opinionated, and inquisitive—in Scotland, at age six, he located a beehive by observing where the flight paths of the bees intersected and gathered honey for the family tea. Like Atanasoff, he did not fit into school very well—he pursued his own projects (such as origami and maps), but unlike Atanasoff, he did not care enough to do the assigned work as well as his own projects (or he found it difficult because of such things as poor handwriting). He was terrible at sports and later said that he learned to run fast in order to avoid the ball.

Like Atanasoff, he learned things on his own. One of his favorite books was one he received at the age of ten—*Natural Wonders Every Child Should Know*, by Edwin Tenney Brewster. In this book, Brewster set out a picture of the natural world that was organized and understandable, as well as scientific and machinelike. Brewster describes the process of evolution and says of the human body, "It really is a gas engine, like the engine of an automobile, a motor boat, or a flying machine." This machine analogy would prove seminal in Turing's later work. About the same time, chemistry became his passion, and his family let him pursue various experiments in the basement of the house they were living in.

As Alan approached the age when it was necessary for the Turings to find a public school for him, the problems posed by his eccentricities became more pressing. He took an entrance exam for the school his brother was attending, and was admitted, but John thought life there would be too difficult for him. Eventually, he ended up at the Sherborne School. It was not a good choice. School was not, in the expressed opinion of the Sherborne headmaster A. J. P. Andrews, a place for learning information or developing one's capacity for critical thinking, but rather where the English class system was to be reinforced and boys to be shown their place within it.

Andrew Hodges writes in his biography that in his first year at Sherborne School, "Alan had no friend, and at least once in this year he was trapped underneath some loose floorboards in the house day-room by the other boys. He tried to continue chemistry experiments there, but this was doubly hated, as showing a swottish mentality, and producing nasty smells." Alan Turing was from long lines of inventive people on his mother's side and his father's side, and he showed a ready and determined fascination with practical things from earliest childhood, but he was repeatedly diverted from these interests by the class system that he was born into and the educational system that was his only route to social respectability. Although, like Atanasoff, and in the manner described by creativity researcher R. Keith Sawyer, Turing persistently looked for problems to solve and then solved them, and also exhibited self-confidence, independence, high energy, willingness to take risks, above-average intelligence, openness to experience, and preference for complexity, his world was not one where he could cultivate these qualities. Iva and John Atanasoff seem to have accepted the fact that, as painful as it could sometimes be to live at the periphery of their society, it was also freeing, and it gave their children valuable experience not only in getting things accomplished, but also in flouting received opinion. The same mode of thinking, and course of action, seems not to have been available to the Turings, and Alan spent his entire youth being balked in his attempts to go his own way. One telling detail is that when he did try his chemistry experiments at Sherborne, they were invariably found and thrown away. The result was that he switched his field, and his thinking, from practical physics to pure mathematics, but he never gave up his interest in machines.

Chapter Two

A tanasoff was now at Iowa State, where his primary responsibility was teaching, not research. Although he might have said that his first love was theoretical physics, or even quantum mechanics, Iowa State did not have a course in quantum mechanics until Atanasoff began teaching one. Atanasoff did have quite a few students, however, and teaching them reminded him over and over of the difficulties of calculation. By all accounts, Atanasoff was a gifted teacher who used an individualized Socratic approach, engaging his students in discussions and questioning them, trying to discover their areas of expertise and ignorance. He saw over and over that all scientific and engineering progress would be retarded until some sort of breakthrough in methods of calculation. He also employed his students in investigating ways of calculating. One of these students came up with an idea for a type of small analog calculator, something like a slide rule, that measured fourteen inches by three inches by three inches. Atanasoff, the student, and another colleague designed it to calculate the geometry of surfaces and called it a "Laplaciometer," after the eighteenth-century French mathematician and astronomer Pierre-Simon Laplace, but its uses were limited.

Most calculators in the 1930s were analog, that is, they were similar to a slide rule in that something is measured in order to ascertain a number. As Atanasoff later explained to Clark Mollenhoff, his first biographer, the thing measured "can be anything: a distance, an electric voltage, a current of electricity, air pressure, etc." Calculating ever larger numbers requires ever more sensitive measurements, so that, for example, a slide rule, which calculates numbers by measuring distance, would have to be enormous ("the length of a football field, or in some instances a mile or more") in order to represent the numbers Atanasoff was interested in calculating.

One famous analog calculator that Atanasoff read about in the thirties was the Bush Differential Analyzer, developed in 1927–31 at MIT by Vannevar Bush, who had already founded the company that was to become Raytheon and would later head the National Defense Research Committee and the Office of Scientific Research and Development (which was in charge of what would become the Manhattan Project from 1941 until it was taken over by the army in 1943). The Differential Analyzer may be pictured as an automobile gearing mechanism used for calculation. It was "in essence a variable-speed gear, and took the form of a rotating horizontal disk on which a small knife-edged wheel rested. The wheel was driven by friction, and the gear ratio was altered by varying the distance of the wheel from the axis of rotation of the disk." What was measured (as the slide rule measures distance) were the various positions of the shaft as it turned. These positions were assigned values like the numbers on a slide rule.

When, in 1936, Atanasoff and his colleagues decided that the possibilities of the Laplaciometer were limited, Atanasoff turned his attention to what might be done with the Monroe calculator, the same typewriter-like machine he had used at the University of Wisconsin when he was doing the math for his dissertation. The solution he thought up was similar to the mechanically based solutions others were trying, such as linking thirty machines and thereby enlarging their capacity. But enlarging capacity did not change the theory behind calculation—adding and subtracting remained the essential operations. Atanasoff did not have access to thirty machines, though.

Instead, he got together with an Iowa State colleague, statistics professor A. E. Brandt, whom he had first met as a student in 1925. Brandt had access to a single IBM tabulator owned by the statistics department.

In the mid-1930s, IBM was a fairly new company, the product of several mergers, but having its origins in the Tabulating Machine Company, which had been founded in 1896 by inventor Herman Hollerith—his first model had been used in the census of 1900. In 1911, several companies joined to form the CTR (Computing Tabulating Recording) Corporation, which offered a wide range of services to businesses—calculating, but also timekeeping and meat-slicing (a product called the Dayton Safety Electric Meat Chopper—the division was sold to Hobart Manufacturing Company in 1934). Thomas J. Watson, Sr., had become president in 1915, and the name of the company was changed to International Business Machines in 1924. In 1928, IBM introduced the standard eighty-column punch card (the Hollerith card) that came to be familiar to students and secretaries for decades afterward. A 1931 model, developed for and used solely by the Columbia University Statistical Bureau to tabulate results of observations and experiments made at Columbia, seemed exciting at the time—one astronomer declared himself thrilled just watching how quickly the machine went through its additions and subtractions.

The less advanced device Atanasoff and Brandt decided to modify looked more like an upright piano than a desk calculator and operated in the customary Hollerith/IBM fashion, by reading a deck of punched cards and adding or subtracting the values represented by holes in the cards. With the help of IBM representatives, Atanasoff and Brandt modified the Iowa State–owned version of the tabulator in several significant ways and published an article about their product in 1936 in the *Journal of the Optical Society of America* entitled "Application of Punched Card Equipment to the Analysis of Complex Spectra." It reads rather dryly, but what Atanasoff and Brandt were really doing was something Atanasoff had been doing since childhood—fiddling with a machine and redesigning it in order to get it to perform in a better or faster or more complex way. At the end of the article abstract is the line

25

"The advantages of the method include high speed, accuracy as high as desired without checking with an adding machine, and the fact that only one simple modification is needed of standard equipment that is available almost everywhere." According to Mollenhoff's biography of Atanasoff, while IBM representatives cooperated with Atanasoff and Brandt in modifying the IBM calculator that they were using, IBM internal memorandums at the time were highly critical of Atanasoff and Brandt for "meddling with the tabulators and using them in ways the corporation officials had not intended that they be used." According to Tammara Burton, who may have heard it from her grandfather, the memo said, "Keep Atanasoff out of the IBM tabulator."

IBM was jealous of its intellectual property, something that another computer innovator was also discovering. If Atanasoff had ended up at Harvard, he might have met Howard H. Aiken (born March 8, 1900), whom he also might have met at the University of Wisconsin. Aiken, too, was eager to develop a calculating machine that would solve differential equations, and Aiken was not unlike Atanasoff in other ways—he had put himself through high school while working at the local electric company in Indianapolis and then through the University of Wisconsin (at precisely the same time that Atanasoff was putting himself through the University of Florida) by working at the gas company in Madison. After earning his bachelor's degree, he worked in the private sector before going to the University of Chicago and then to Harvard for his master's and his PhD. His dissertation, "Theory of Space Charge Conductions," was similar to "The Dielectric Constant of Helium"—it considered "the properties of vacuum tubes—devices in which electric currents are passed across an empty space between two metal contacts." Like Atanasoff, Aiken was exhausted by the calculations required to prove his thesis, or, as his biography puts it, "The mathematical complexities involved in describing space charge conduction made calculating solutions to his problems impossible." While Atanasoff was pondering the Laplaciometer, Aiken, at Harvard, was trying to conceive of a way to improve Charles Babbage's original Difference Engine. Harvard offered Aiken even less support than Atanasoff found at Iowa State College—in fact, President Conant actively discouraged him. Aiken then approached several mechanical calculating machine companies without success.

Most computer inventors in the 1930s, including Vannevar Bush and Howard Aiken, were convinced that the future of computing lay in its past—in the theories of Charles Babbage (1791–1871), who had begun laying out his ideas for a mechanical calculator in 1822 and proposed constructing it to the Royal Astronomical Society. It was an analog device, designed to solved polynomial equations using shafts and toothed gears. Babbage worked on it for twenty-five years, redesigning it at least once, but nineteenth-century machining wasn't up to the precision of the task, and the Difference Engine never really worked. Even so, Babbage grew more ambitious and designed a machine he called the Analytical Engine. All of the twentieth-century computer inventors were aware of Babbage's work (except Konrad Zuse, isolated in Germany). Howard Aiken proposed to update Babbage's ideas with more modern industrial techniques—the machining of gears and shafts had advanced considerably in the hundred years since Babbage's time. His Mark I was to be a relay-switch-based computer. And it was to be huge. It was to be built of

a power supply and electric motor for driving the machine; four master control panels, controlled by instructions on punched rolls of paper tape and synchronized with the rest of the machine; manual adjustments for controlling the calculation of functions; 24 sets of switches for entering numerical constants; 2 paper tape readers for entering additional constants; a standard punched card reader; 12 temporary storage units; 5 units each— add/subtract, multiply, divide; various permanent function tables (e.g. sine, cosine, etc.); accumulators; and printing and card punching equipment. All of these components should be built to accommodate figures up to 23 digits long. Finally, Aiken estimated the speed of the calculator based upon the speed of contemporary IBM machines, 750 8-digit multiplications per hour, representing a vast increase in speed and accuracy over manual methods of calculation.

It used a decimal number system, and even though Aiken had done his dissertation on vacuum tubes, his was a mechanical switching system.

At some point, perhaps reflecting on his efforts to get his computer built, Aiken is said to have remarked, "Don't worry about people stealing your ideas. If your ideas are any good, you'll have to ram them down people's throats." Perhaps in this, too, Aiken would have found a sympathetic listener in Atanasoff.

But Atanasoff was at least in a place where he could gather together the information he needed. Right around the time of the Laplaciometer, he discovered an electronic engineering textbook entitled *The Thermionic Vacuum Tube and Its Applications*, by Hendrik Johannes Van der Bijl, a South African physicist who had studied in Germany before returning to South Africa to design the national power grid and other state-sponsored enterprises. According to Burton, after reading Van der Bijl's book, Atanasoff built some vacuum tubes on his own and began to think about novel ways he could put them to use.

A simple vacuum tube, called a diode, works like an incandescent lightbulb: a filament, called a cathode, is heated and then releases negatively charged electrons, which stream toward a positively charged metal plate, called an anode. The mechanism is enclosed within a tube of glass, which preserves the vacuum and disperses the heat generated by the filament. Numerous improvements in the diode were made throughout the beginning of the twentieth century, mostly for the purpose of improving radio design, reliability, and transmission. In 1936, the vacuum tube was used in radios to amplify transmission and reception of signals, and tubes continued to be used in radios and televisions until the invention of the transistor. The tubes were delicate and expensive to operate because of energy loss through the glass shell. But Atanasoff didn't want his tubes to do much—he just wanted them to turn on and off. The measurement required by an analog calculator would be replaced by counting. Since this is similar to the way a child counts on his fingers, this came to be known as digital calculation.

The difference between measuring and counting, for Atanasoff's purposes, was enormous: counting is precise, infinite, and as portable as an abacus. No quantities such as distance are involved, and no estimation needs to be made (as it does, for example, when the mark giving the result of a slide rule calculation falls between two marks indicating numbers). However, counting had its problems, too, since it is repetitive and mind-numbing. And for most of those attempting to invent the computer, the problem was that they themselves were used to counting in a base-ten (0–9) number system; there was no way to invent a simply constructed calculator that could do that. It is probably also true that the more that the inventors made use of mechanical calculators such as the Monroe, the more the idea of base-ten counting was reinforced, since a Monroe calculator consisted of a hundred black and white keys arranged in a ten-by-ten grid (using the digits 0–9), with red function keys set in two rows, across the bottom and down the right side as the operator faced the machine.

As a young man with a wife and young children, Atanasoff was busy at home as well as at school. Although faculty salaries were cut in the early 1930s as a result of the Great Depression, Atanasoff managed to get promoted quickly and to save up enough money to buy ten acres on Woodland Street, which runs due west from the ISU campus. He chose a plot for himself, designed a brick house, and oversaw its construction, moving his family into the basement in the summer after the February 1935 birth of his third child, a son named John Vincent II. Since Atanasoff believed in pay-as-you-go, progress on the house depended on ready cash. As a result, the family lived in the basement through the winter of 1935–36, protected from the cold and snow at times only by tarps and the floorboards of the partially constructed ground floor. Lura cooked in the laundry room. Atanasoff himself installed the electricity and plumbing, as well as the heating system for the baby's room.

Shortly after the house was completed, Elsie, the older daughter, aged eight, became seriously ill with asthma and allergies. According to Burton, the standard treatment of the day, adrenaline shots, had a negative effect on Elsie's condition, so Atanasoff threw himself into reading about allergies and observing his daughter. He decided that she was allergic to cow's milk, chocolate, and wheat, and he bought two pregnant female goats, which Lura cared for and milked in the backyard of the Woodland Street house. He rigged up a system for circulating fresh air into Elsie's room and became so knowledgeable about allergies that a local doctor used him as a consultant. His daughters also gave him entrée to the grammar school authorities—when teachers complained that the girls were often late because Atanasoff was dropping them off on his way to the college, he got interested in how the teachers were doing their jobs—investigated how school resources were being used and made suggestions about what the science and math curriculum should look like. When the school nurse suggested that one of the girls have her tonsils removed, Atanasoff lectured her on why they should not be removed. His arguments were always complete and forcefully presented, and school authorities soon learned to leave well enough alone. Once, Burton writes, "when the family's enormous vegetable garden produced a large crop of soybeans, he immediately addressed the problem of shelling the beans by rigging the washing-machine clothes-wringer to assist in the task. Whole soybeans were hand-fed into the electric clothes wringer and came out shelled on the other side."

But he worked late at the office, worked at home, and read the newspaper at the supper table. Home, like the office, was an arena for projects and creative thinking, not interaction, familial relationships, or leisure enjoyments—in fact, Atanasoff rather disdained pursuits such as art, music, and literature that Lura enjoyed. Lura understood Atanasoff's pressing commitment to solving the problem of calculating, both as the inner drive to solve a problem creatively and as an essential scientific task. Burton indicates that Atanasoff's frustration with the failures of the solutions he and his colleagues were coming up with in the mid-thirties was making him moody and hard to live with, but also that Lura's own close-knit family of origin had not prepared her for the lonely life she found herself leading. Atanasoff was not happy. He wrote later, "I had been forced to the conclusion that if I wanted a computer suited to the general needs of science and, in particular, suited to solving systems of linear equations, I would have to build it myself. I was leading a full life and had too much to do; I did not want to search and invent, but sadly I turned in that direction." He feared he would be wasting his best years on an endeavor that might prove fruitless. And he had no way of knowing who was inventing what in the world of computing or how his thinking fit into that of others— even if it worked, his invention could easily be preempted by another.

Like all land-grant universities, Iowa State was provincial and local, and intended to be so. Its obligations were to the state of Iowa, not to the larger worlds of industry or intellect. Atanasoff's field was physics— he wanted a tool, and the tool was missing. It was characteristic of both his personality and his education that he decided to invent the tool, but it was also realistic on his part to fear that inventing the tool would be a waste of time he could be spending on other projects—his schedule was full and he had no real confidence that he could come up with the solution he sought.

Atanasoff spent 1936 and 1937 reading as much as he could about every calculator then in existence, and also about what other innovators thought possible. He also moved his office from the mathematics department to the new physics building, which was more spacious and more practically oriented. According to Burton, he felt that mathematics as a field was moving in the wrong direction—toward greater and greater abstraction—while physicists continued to be interested in concrete problems. In the meantime, Alan Turing was wrestling with similar dissatisfactions.

Alan Turing's life at Sherborne was punctuated at the end with tragedy—in the winter of his last year (1930), his dearest friend,

Christopher Morcom, died of tuberculosis. Morcom, slightly older and gifted with the star power that eluded Turing, had won many prizes at Sherborne, and then a scholarship to Trinity College. The two young men shared scientific and mathematical interests, and Turing profoundly respected not only Morcom's intelligence, but also his thoroughness and his broad interests—he could play the piano and he could also do his work legibly without making arithmetical mistakes. Moreover, he was fun—among other pranks, he once sent gas-filled balloons over Sherborne Girls. It may have been Morcom's positive influence that enabled Turing to get higher marks at Sherborne as he got closer to finishing his education there.

In 1931, Turing won his own scholarship to Cambridge, but to King's College rather than Trinity. If, at the University of Florida and Iowa State, and even at the University of Wisconsin, Atanasoff was always more or less at the periphery of both the mathematics and physics establishments, at King's College Turing was at the exact heart, especially of mathematics. He took courses from astrophysicist Arthur Eddington and mathematicians G. H. Hardy and Max Born. He met John von Neumann there—many mathematicians fleeing conditions in Germany and the East passed through Cambridge on their way to settling elsewhere. And it was Max Newman, who was lecturing on topology—the study of relationships between geometric spaces as they are transformed by such operations as stretching, but not such operations as cutting—who introduced him to the Hilbert problem that would make his career. Working on the Hilbert problem was not his first attempt at a dissertation—one professor had suggested he work on the dielectric constant of water, but he got nowhere.

David Hilbert's *Entscheidungsproblem* (one of twenty-three famous Hilbert problems) had been proposed by the German mathematician in 1928. In layman's terms, the *Entscheidungsproblem* asked if there was or could be a procedure (an algorithm) that could determine whether a mathematical statement was true or false—just the sort of question that no longer interested Atanasoff. To many mathematicians of the period, the *Entscheidungsproblem* seemed to point toward concepts that were psychological, epistemological, or even theological. Alan Turing's answer to the problem was no—there was no algorithm that could determine the truth of every mathematical statement. He was preempted by a few weeks by American mathematician Alonzo Church, who was at Princeton. Church's answer to the question was a logical system called lambda calculus. Turing's answer was a different sort of act of imagination, and he came to it in a manner similar to Atanasoff's revelation—he set out on a cross-country run along the river Cam. He was an avid and fit runner who occasionally ran north as far as Ely, some twenty miles from Cambridge. One day, resting in a meadow after a long run, he imagined a procedure, or set of instructions, so simple that a machine could perform it, if the machine could operate eternally.

In the paper he wrote about this idea, Turing describes the psychological process of making a simple but arduous calculation. He imagines that the person making the calculation is given a set of instructions, and if she follows the set of instructions every time she sits down to her work, her mind will always work in the same way, and she will make no mistakes in her calculation (though the work, of course, will be unbelievably tedious). Turing soon makes the leap from the set of instructions to the notion of an ideal machine—it would operate on its own, without human input. It would perform a set of operations forever, and the operations would be clearly defined and of a limited number. As his example, he described a machine that is fed an infinitely long tape. The tape is divided into squares, and each square either has a mark on it or is blank. As the machine scans each marked square or each empty square, it is instructed to perform an operation—to put a mark in an empty square, to erase a mark in a marked square, to shift one space to the right, or to shift one space to the left. When each operation is completed and the machine has moved on to the next instruction, it now scans the new square and performs the instruction for that square. However, the machine does not treat every mark and every blank in exactly the same way—the set of instructions progresses as the calculation progresses. This progression Turing called "the table of behavior."

We would call it the program. Eventually, the machine arrives at the end of the calculation—for example, it is instructed by the table of behavior to stop after erasing a mark and shifting to the left. This operation denotes that the answer has been arrived at—in the case of an addition problem, the series of marked squares now adds up to the sum of the marked squares defined by the problem.

Turing imagined all sorts of machines set up to solve all sorts of mathematical problems, including those considered impossible to solve. The only things necessary for these solutions would be instructions and time (and a binary number system consisting of marks and blanks). What would define a problem as soluble would be that the machine would progress to the end of the problem. What would define the problem as insoluble would be that the machine would get stuck—a wrong instruction sequence could set up the operation of the machine so that it would simply move back and forth, erasing and re-marking the same two squares. Turing then went on to imagine a comprehensive machine, which he called a "universal machine," that, given sufficient instructions, could solve every problem that each of the specialized machines could solve. He showed that, given infinite time and instructions, there could be such a machine. The kicker, though, and in this he addressed the *Entscheidungsproblem,* was that by thinking through how his machine would operate to solve a problem, any problem, he could easily see the way in which a problem could be given to the machine that would stop the operations of the machine— that is, cause it to infinitely repeat an operation without arriving at a solution. And the only way to determine which problems would result in failure and which problems would result in solution was to try to solve them. Mathematics could not devise methods in advance that could predict the solubility of every problem, therefore the truth of a given statement could not necessarily be determined. In addition to this, while the machine could operate eternally, there was no way for the machine to check itself, and so there was no way to know whether every answer was "true" or not.

The lambda calculus "represented an elegant and powerful symbolism for mathematical processes of abstraction and variation," but the Turing machine was a thought experiment that posited a mechanical operation, to be done by either a mechanism or by a human mind. Andrew Hodges, Turing's biographer, points out that Turing's idea "was not only a matter of abstract mathematics, not only a play of symbols, for it involved thinking about what people did in the physical world . . . His machines—soon to be called *Turing Machines*—offered a bridge, a connection between abstract symbols and the physical world. Indeed, his imagery was, for Cambridge, almost shockingly industrial."

In May 1936, Alan Turing submitted his paper, entitled "On Computable Numbers, with an Application to the *Entscheidungsproblem*," to the *Proceedings of the London Mathematical Society* and then applied unsuccessfully for a Procter Fellowship at Princeton. As far as anyone in England knew, only Turing and the American Alonzo Church had come up with answers to the *Entscheidungsproblem*. No mathematician in England was equipped to referee either Turing's or Church's paper.

Atanasoff and Turing, in their different ways, understood that counting was the future of computing, but the differences between them could not have been more clear—Atanasoff had to invent an actual, physical machine that when turned on would perform a useful function. Turing was imagining a process that was repetitive and mechanical, but since he himself was not an adept tinkerer, and he had never been asked to develop whatever engineering abilities he may have inherited from his family, his machine was meant to inspire invention rather than to be an invention. But the third early inventor of the computer, Konrad Zuse, did not think like either Atanasoff or Turing.

Chapter Three

Although Atanasoff made every effort to find out about what calculating machines were being invented, and Alan Turing was as well connected as a mathematician could be, neither one of them was, or perhaps could have been, familiar with Konrad Zuse, an inventor who was working in Berlin. Zuse, born on June 22, 1910, was two years older than Turing and, unlike the others involved in the invention of the computer, he wrote his autobiography, entitled *The Computer— My Life*. Konrad Zuse, born in Berlin, was the son of a Prussian civil servant. Of his ancestors, he writes, "I have traced my ancestry back to my great-grandparents, who lived in the village of Voigtshagen in Pomerania. Many a shepherd is said to be among their forefathers. Perhaps this explains my inclination toward introversion." The elder Zuse's work with the civil service took his family to the small city of Braunsberg in East Prussia, south of Rostock, before the First World War, but even before that departure, the little boy was fascinated with architecture, noticing the railroad bridges in Berlin and the patterns they made as they overlapped one another in his childish gaze. Zuse's earliest strong memories were of the dangers and fears of World War I—of the influx of refugees from the eastern front, where the German armies were fighting Russia, and of fires in Braunsberg itself, especially in the medieval section of the town.

Zuse's earliest aptitudes were not for math or engineering but for performance and visual art. As a child, he loved traveling circus troupes that performed in the post office square in Braunsberg, and he emulated them by perfecting his own routine—doing tricks while balancing on an empty oil drum. His schooling was standard for the time and place—his worst subsequent memories were of eight hours of Latin class every week. Like Atanasoff, he was something of a disruptive influence in class when he was not merely inattentive—the margins of his Latin textbook were filled with drawings, and one teacher nicknamed him "Dozy." His drawing skills were appreciated, though— the art teacher saw some of his work and persuaded his father to give him higher-quality drawing paper. During his teens, the family moved from Braunsberg to Hoyerswerda, not far from Dresden, where the gymnasium provided a more modern education, with younger teachers. Hoyerswerda was in an industrial area of Germany, which piqued Zuse's interest in technology, and his great hobby, in addition to drawing, was his Stabilbaukasten, or Erector Set. At one point, he built a model of a large crane in his room and then sketched a picture of himself lounging underneath it, with his feet on the desk. Like Atanasoff, he graduated early. Around the same time, he acquired a bicycle that was bent to the right side. Zuse attached a string to the left side of the handlebars so that he could ride with no hands, like his friends did. When the bicycle repairman could not fix the gearing mechanism, he fixed it himself with some pieces from his building set.

Undecided about whether to pursue art or engineering, he pursued engineering, but with a continued interest in design—for his senior school project, he had designed a city of the future (à la Fritz Lang's *Metropolis*) based on a hexagonal grid. Like Alan Turing, Zuse was educated in a system that focused on a child's emotional and philosophical life as well as his intellectual life, and at the end of school, like Turing, Zuse found himself to be something of an outsider—to the disappointment of his very conventional parents, he no longer believed in God or religion.

In 1927, at the same time that Turing was making his difficult way through the Sherborne School, Zuse entered the Technische Universität in Berlin and took up residence in the city of his birth, a sociable young man in an exciting and rapidly changing urban environment. He was immediately fascinated once again by the bridge building that was going on, a fascination that was encouraged by the requirement that students at the Technische Universität had to have practical experience in ironwork or carpentry or bricklaying. Zuse's experience in these trades served to break down class barriers somewhat, but he remained a thinker more than a builder—interested in photography, movies, drawing, performance. When he became intrigued by a technological question, such as how to build a rocket that might head to a distant star, it was more often through some form of art, such as science fiction, than it was through science itself. He does not mention taking an interest, per se, in physics or mathematics or cosmology, as Atanasoff and Turing did. He writes, "Given my many detours and by-ways, I am still amazed that I earned a diploma at all." (And then he goes on to recount how he was lucky that his mathematics examiner asked a particular question—as he was eavesdropping upon the questions that the other students were asked, he realized that he could not have answered any of them.)

According to Zuse, amid all the busyness, freedom, and pleasure of his university and postuniversity life, there was not much understanding about what the Nazis were up to. While Zuse himself was reading *Das Kapital* and the autobiography of Henry Ford, neither he nor his friends paid much attention to those who were reading *Mein Kampf*. Zuse, as a son of the Prussian civil servant class, felt more inspired by the writings of Oswald Spengler than of Hitler, especially Spengler's anti-Marxist 1920 political tract *Prussianism and Socialism*. Even so, Zuse found the Marxists he knew friendly and interested in discussion.

Times soon changed, and "on all sides now Germans were being forced into line and marched off," yet Zuse and his fellow students

seem to still have had the feeling that they had some freedom of opinion, some future in terms of working choices. And then, on the night of
June 30 (the Night of the Long Knives), Hitler used his personal bodyguard, the SS, to purge Ernst Röhm, an enemy in the von Hindenburg
government, and two hundred of his allies in the armed forces. When
von Hindenburg died a month later, Hitler made himself president
and head of the armed forces, which were henceforth to pledge alle-
giance to him personally rather than simply to the state. After von Hindenburg's funeral, Hitler assumed the title "führer," but, perhaps as
an indication of Zuse's ongoing focus on other things, he writes, "The
psychological effect was that one assumed the impetuous and hysteri-
cal period would now be followed by a period of common sense and
work." Zuse belonged to a fraternity of long standing at the university.
When the three Jewish members were required by the Hitler government to leave the club, the club decided to disband but ultimately did
not do so, only because the Jewish members asked them not to.

At the end of his university career, Zuse idled about Berlin for a
year, undecided about what to do next, but in 1935, aged twenty-five,
he took an engineering job with the new aircraft division of Henschel
and Son, a locomotive corporation that was to produce several types of
planes for the Luftwaffe. Zuse, apparently alerted by his new job to the
sorts of calculating problems that aircraft design required, quit almost
immediately to begin his own project—a computer.

According to Zuse's account, he started from scratch. "When I
began to build my own computer, I neither understood anything about
computing machines nor had I ever heard of Babbage." Zuse is not
clear about why he decided to build a computer, or the theoretical
basis of the machine, but it seems to have grown out of his talent for
and interest in design rather than the desire to solve a particular kind of
mathematical problem. His first attempt at a machine had nothing to
do with mathematics—it was a skeletal vending machine "which took
money and gave mandarin [oranges], and sometimes, indeed, returned
the money with the mandarins."

Zuse's working space was the living room of his parents' apartment and his capital (amounting to several thousand marks at the most) came from his father's and sister's paychecks and the contributions of his friends who had managed to find jobs or had a bit of money. His collaborators were his friends from the technical school, who received their pay in the form of meals that Zuse's mother provided. His raw materials were bought piecemeal when he had the money, and they were simple ones. One friend describes how he made the mechanical relays—Zuse would draw the pattern on a piece of paper, then the friend "pasted the paper on a small plywood board, then fixed the necessary number of metal sheets between it and a second board that lay under it." He then "screwed the two boards together with threaded screws, and sawed out the form of the relays with a small, electric fretsaw." He "made these relays by the thousand."[1]

Zuse seems to have built on the loyalty he developed in his college fraternity to accrue dedicated student helpers, who, like Atanasoff and his students (and Turing, too) recognized that the sorts of calculations they were required to do normally with analog desk calculators were much easier with Zuse's machine. But the project was secret (Zuse does not say why, but possibly the authorities would have looked with suspicion upon a project that was diverting parts and supplies from war preparations). Those working on it declared when asked that they were attempting to build an aircraft tank gauge, because the German Air Ministry was at the time sponsoring a contest to build such a machine.

The basis of Zuse's original design was electromechanical, akin to telephone relays, with which Zuse happened to be familiar, but, like other pioneers, he soon realized that the number of relays required in even a small-capacity machine was impractically enormous—the machine he was building so filled the family apartment that a friend who was working on it later wrote, "It took up almost the entire living room. It was a permanent fixture in the apartment. I think that it was only after the house was bombed during the war that the first Zuse

---

1. The objects he calls "relays" bear no relationship in either looks or operation to what are now known as relays. They were entirely mechanical.

Universal Computing Machine could be moved into the museum." In his first effort, Zuse had some success with his electromechanical ideas and was able to build a flexible enough device so that he could use it to test his ideas about switching and build his understanding of mathematical logic.

As his work progressed, Zuse decided he needed more reliable financing. In 1937, he got in touch with a Dr. Kurt Pannke, who manufactured calculators. Pannke told the young man, "I don't want to discourage you from continuing work as an inventor and from developing new ideas, but I must go ahead and tell you one thing: in the field of computing machines, practically everything has been researched and perfected to the last detail." When Zuse told Pannke that his prototype could multiply, Pannke was silent for a long time and then came for a visit to the machine. Zuse demonstrated that because (like Atanasoff) he was using binary numbers (only the digits 1 and 0), adding and multiplying amounted (literally) to the same thing. In his autobiography, Zuse demonstrates why this is. When a calculator uses ten digits (0–9), the number of different keys required to represent the multiplication table is unwieldy—$0 \times 1 = 0$, $2 \times 2 = 4$, $6 \times 6 = 36$, $8 \times 8 = 64$, with each digit represented by a key of its own. As we saw in third grade, when we were learning the multiplication tables in the back of our arithmetic books, between 0×0 and 9×9, there are a hundred different numbers. In a binary system, $0 \times 0 = 0$, $1 \times 0 = 0$, $0 \times 1 = 0$, and $1 \times 1 = 1$. Only two digits are needed. The problem for Pannke, as a businessman, was that calculators that multiplied by repeated adding were cheaper to build than calculators that attempted to multiply; there was a limited market for calculators, so adding was good enough. Zuse points out, "To construct large and expensive computing machines for scientists, for mathematicians and engineers, appeared absurd, and above all held no promise of commercial success. These people didn't have any money." But Pannke gave Zuse about 7,000 reichsmarks, and he began to work on his second prototype, the Z2.

———

In his home workshop and at school, as well as in plans and diagrams, Atanasoff was trying this and that. The work was taxing and frustrating mostly because there was no apparent place to begin. Every idea he came up with immediately branched into a tangle of relationships that were complex and contradictory. And he had to factor in available hardware. Like other inventors of the computer, he knew that rods and gears and motors were reliable and much more precise than they had ever been, thanks to advances in machining and production—Atanasoff was tempted by these advances to pursue the analog path. But he was strongly drawn to the speed that the novel, but as yet unreliable, technology of electronics offered.

Atanasoff's interest in binary system was not based on quite the same reasoning as Zuse's interest—IBM had, after all, introduced a multiplying calculator in 1931. What he suspected was that using a binary number system would make it possible to use vacuum tubes for actual calculating. The vacuum tubes would be arranged inside a processing unit and different arrangements of on and off tubes would stand for different numbers—any number could be represented by a row of on-off vacuum tubes. At the same time, although he himself was perfectly familiar with binary counting systems, he knew that not many other people were (something Zuse's experience also demonstrated)—even most mathematicians were uncomfortable operating outside of the decimal system. The prevailing wisdom was that translating from the binary system to the decimal system would pose an enormous difficulty—a decimal number would have to be entered somehow, turning on the tubes and turning them off, then, when the calculation had been performed, the result would have be communicated to some sort of output mechanism that would translate the binary number to a decimal number.

And there would have to be "memory." In the most advanced IBM tabulator of the day, there were two types of memory. The first comprised the set of instructions that the tabulator used to carry out operations. If a byte in today's computer terminology consists of 8 bits of storage capacity,[2] the first type of memory belonging to the IBM tabulator of Atanasoff's day had 266 bits or 33.25 bytes of memory. That tabulator's memory hardly bears comparison with what we are familiar with in 2010—a single page of text saved as a file in Microsoft Word that includes all preference settings, containing 514 words and forty lines of English text in 14-point type, uses 28 kilobytes, or 28,662 bytes, or 862 times the capacity of the IBM tabulator Atanasoff was familiar with. A single 3.2 megabyte digital photograph (3.2 million bytes) uses almost 96,400 times the IBM's memory capacity. The IBM's second type of memory was larger, but external to the machine—it was the record of calculations produced, punch cards that could then be fed back into the machine and used for future tabulations. The punch cards, of course, were kept track of by the operator, not the machine.

Modern computers still have two types of memory. The first type is called the RAM, or random-access memory, which the computer uses while it is turned on for operations, applications, and frequently accessed data. The second type is the storage memory, which the computer has access to and is stored externally to the main operating system on hard disk drives, floppy disks, magnetic tape, and so on. Although today, at least in personal computers, they are both inside the computer, the two kinds of memory follow Atanasoff's (and IBM's) ideas by being separate but communicating with each other.

When Atanasoff jumped in his new Ford V8 that evening in December 1937, he later testified, "I was in such a mental state that no resolution was possible. I was just unhappy to an extreme degree." But he was pleased with his new car (Burton notes that he purchased a new car every year). He enjoyed its speed and maneuverability. He felt himself calm down, and he also felt a sort of suspension of time— "When I finally came to earth I was crossing the Mississippi River, 189 miles from my desk." His next thought was perhaps characteristic of his

---

2. The term "bit" is an abbreviation for "binary digit."

practical and no-nonsense temperament: "Now you've got to quit this damned foolishness."

Then he saw the tavern sign. He went in, sat down, and ordered a bourbon and soda. A radio sitting behind the bar was playing music. Almost as soon as the waitress brought him his drink, the nature of his computing system occurred to him as a logical whole, and he began envisioning both the component pieces and how the pieces could fit together. He jotted some notes down on a paper napkin, but later he didn't need the notes because he was able to visualize and contemplate his machine so thoroughly that he had no trouble recalling what he had come up with. He sat in the bar for several hours, thinking through each of his concepts but concentrating particularly upon ideas for how the memory would work and how an electronically based on-off process would calculate.

Atanasoff's experience is interesting on a number of levels. The way in which a state of effort followed by a state of relaxation induced an understanding of the system he wanted to build is reminiscent of what had happened to Turing and also to Henri Poincaré, the mathematician, as quoted in psychiatric researcher Nancy Andreasen's *The Creative Brain*:

> For fifteen days I strove to prove that there could not be any
> functions like those we have since called Fuchsian functions.
> I was very ignorant: every day, I seated myself at my work table,
> stayed an hour or two, tried a great number of combinations
> and reached no results. One evening, contrary to my custom,
> I drank black coffee and could not sleep. Ideas rose in crowds;
> I felt them collide until pairs interlocked, so to speak, making a
> stable combination. By the next morning, I had established the
> existence of a class of Fuchsian functions . . . I had only to write
> out the results, which took but a few hours.

But what Poincaré really wants to do is to boil his results down into a principle that can be understood in relation to other well-known mathematical principles. When he then takes a trip, he manages to do this without even interrupting his conversation with another passenger: "The changes of travel made me forget my mathematical work. Having reached Coutances, we entered an omnibus to go someplace or other. At the moment when I put my foot on the step, the idea came to me without anything in my former thoughts seeming to have paved the way . . . On my return to Caen, for conscience's sake, I verified the result at my leisure."

Andreasen then goes on to detail recent research (as of 2005) into how the brain is structured and how it works to create. She describes the brain as a system of sending and receiving neurons that are organized into areas that govern different functions. They connect to one another at synapses, where a tiny electric charge jumps over a tiny space. The neurons are embedded in gray matter (the cortex of the brain that contains nerve cell bodies), and the fuel of the brain is glucose. Andreasen distinguishes between ordinary creativity of the sort that is required in talking and the extraordinary creativity required for innovative or artistic thought. She points out that "most of the time that we speak, we are producing a sequence of words that we have not produced before." But the sort of creativity that invents the computer is of a different order. The brain, she argues, is a self-organizing system "created from components that are in existence and that spontaneously reorganize themselves to create something new." An essential part of a self-organizing system is the feedback loop—in the brain, this would consist of electrical impulses passing along neurons back and forth between one part of the brain and the others, contradicting or reinforcing earlier impulses and influencing later ones.

In order to understand how the brain creates, Andreasen distinguishes between episodic memory, used for personal reminiscence and free association of thoughts, and semantic memory, used for information storage and retrieval of thoughts and concepts not related to personal history. Using positron emission tomography (PET) to image her study subjects' brains while they relax and free-associate, Andreasen discovered that the most active regions in her free-associating subjects' brains were the associative regions, that is, the frontal, parietal, and temporal lobes, the most complexly structured regions, the slowest to develop, and the regions dedicated to generating connections among all the other regions of the brain. She notes that in famous recollections of creative moments by poets such as Coleridge and scientists such as Poincaré and chemist Friedrich Kekulé (who dozed off and dreamed of a snake eating its tail and came up with the structure of the benzene ring), there is often a sudden flash of insight, in which previously unconnected ideas combine into a new thing. She explains this often attested experience: "I would hypothesize that during the creative process, the brain begins by *disorganizing*, making links between shadowy forms of objects or symbols or words or remembered experiences that have not previously been linked. Out of this disorganization, self-organization eventually re-emerges and takes over in the brain. The result is a completely new and original thing."

Clearly, Atanasoff began his trip from Ames, Iowa, to Rock Island, Illinois, in a disorganized (and frustrated) state. Like Turing and Poincaré, though, once he was able to forget his mathematical work, ideas that had refused to come together when he was thinking about them (using his semantic memory) succeeded in coming together once he came to earth upon crossing the Mississippi and realized how far he had traveled in a dreamlike state.

What is especially intriguing, and even moving, about Atanasoff's story is that the machine he was trying to create was intended to mimic the brain—it was to be a self-organizing system, with feedback loops. The very mechanism that he pondered most that evening in the tavern was the calculator's "regenerative memory"—the mechanism by which the capacitors and the vacuum tubes would charge one another, in a feedback loop. And without having a concept of how the human brain works, he also understood that electricity would be the medium of memory and thought, as it is in the human brain. Turing was thinking of a machine-like human process. Atanasoff was thinking of a human-like machine process.

Another way of looking at Atanasoff is that he fits into Malcolm

Gladwell's profile of a maven, that is, a person so interested in a particular field of endeavor that he not only drives himself to become an expert in that field but also is driven to communicate what he learns and intuits about that field to others. Atanasoff was widely considered to be a dedicated and effective teacher: he was good at explaining concepts to his students; he was good at probing their depth of knowledge; and he was good at encouraging them to learn what they needed to know. When his students came up with ideas, he helped them work them out, and he learned from what the students did. Atanasoff also had productive relationships with colleagues like A. E. Brandt. First and foremost, Atanasoff wanted to invent the calculator he thought the world of physics and mathematics needed—he seems not to have given much thought at the time to who might own what piece of the equipment, unlike the IBM executives who were offended when he fiddled with their machine. It also does not seem to have occurred to him that people at IBM *could* be offended, just as it seems not to have occurred to him that the authorities at his daughters' school might be offended at his oft-expressed negative views on the science curriculum there. Atanasoff was intent upon innovation.

Through 1938, Atanasoff worked out both the practical and the theoretical implications of the ideas he came up with in the tavern in Illinois. To reiterate, Atanasoff's four linked ideas were:

1. Electronic logic circuits (which would perform a calculation simply by turning on and off)
2. Binary enumeration (using a number system with only two digits, 0 and 1, rather than ten, 0–9)
3. Capacitors for regenerative memory (a capacitor is like a battery in that it can store electrical energy while not connected to a source)
4. Computing by direct logical action and not by enumeration (that is, by counting rather than by measuring; the numbers

represented by rows of 0s and 1s, or the on-off states of the
vacuum tubes, would be directly added and subtracted rather
than being represented by points on disks or shafts)

One important consideration was how to stabilize the electrical supply of the vacuum tubes that would be doing the calculating. Atanasoff
decided to construct the operating memory (CPU, or central processing unit) and the storage memory in different ways, in this case because
vacuum tubes were expensive. He decided to reserve them for the operating memory and use capacitors for the storage memory. The results
(including intermediate results) would be charred onto paper cards—
still another type of memory. Capacitors (also known at the time as
condensers) were (and are) very simple devices that store electricity
like a bottle stores water. They store electricity without converting it to
anything, using two conductors separated by an insulator. If a charge
is applied to one of the conductors, it stays there by electrostatic attrac-
tion but cannot jump across the insulator. The charge can be removed
very quickly by completing the circuit to the other conductor. In terms
of the binary operation of a computer, "charged" can represent a 1
and "not charged" can represent a 0, for example. But insulators leak
slightly, so the electric charge doesn't stay there very long; therefore,
both Atanasoff's design and modern DRAM chips have electronics to
refresh the state of the capacitor periodically by detecting its charge
and restoring it before it fades.[3]

Atanasoff was perfectly familiar with condensers—when he was con-
sidering the dielectric constant of helium in his PhD dissertation, he

---

3. Thanks to John Gustafson, who adds, "Whenever you scuff your shoes on a carpet
in dry weather such that you get a shock when you touch something metallic, you've
made yourself a capacitor. Rubbing shoes on the carpet scrapes electrons from one surface to the other, creating an excess electric charge. The electric charge stays there
because the charge cannot jump through the air, which serves as the insulator. If you
'close the circuit' by touching a metal object, the charge will suddenly discharge with
a painful spark. Or if you stand still long enough, the static buildup will dissipate by
itself, because even air conducts a little electricity."

was calculating the reduction in electric field strength caused by the presence of helium. Alan Turing was familiar with them, too—when he could make no progress finding the dielectric constant of water— that is, in calculating how effective water is at reducing electric field intensity. In the thirties, the most common insulator in capacitors was dry paper, which has a dielectric constant of 2, meaning that it cuts electric field intensity in half. Most modern capacitors now use ceramic insulation.

The idea Atanasoff had that most vexed and intrigued him over the next year was that the passive capacitors could work with the vacuum tubes. He later testified, "I chose small condensers for memory because they would have the required voltage to actuate the tubes, and the plates . . . of the tubes would give enough power to charge the condensers." Atanasoff called this energy reciprocation "jogging," as in "jogging one's memory." He thought that jogging would make both memories more stable while also saving on expense for supplies and on electrical usage. In this context, I think it is important to remember that Atanasoff was by nature and upbringing as frugal as he was ambitious, and also that he had no access to government money or private investment funds. Frugality was part of what drove him to invent a calculator—he didn't want to waste time calculating using the machines of the day. Frugality dictated what he could try—he and Brandt had to experiment with what they had on hand, the IBM, not a Monroe. And frugality dictated the terms of his invention—it had to be cheap to produce, easy to operate, and cheap to run.

The use of electronic components both dictated the use of a binary number system and was dictated by it. If all Atanasoff needed to indicate a number was "on" or "off," he was free of the burden of gears, shafts, measuring, and estimating, but once he was freed of those clumsy parts, he was committed to a binary number system, which he justified in two ways at the time—that his device would prove itself by being accurate, and that his device was intended to solve various sorts of mathematical problems including but not restricted to systems of equations,[4] which meant that it was most likely to be used by scientists, who were more likely to understand a binary number system. It could also be said that using a binary number system is, as Zuse was pointing out to Pannke at the same time, the frugal choice.

Atanasoff spent a good deal of 1938 thinking about a mathematical system that would enable him to understand how to compute by direct logical operation, the way a person computes

$$
\begin{array}{r}
137 \\
-\ 26 \\
\hline
111
\end{array}
$$

by subtracting 6 from 7 and writing 1, then moving to the left and subtracting 2 from 3, and writing 1 to the left of 2, and then moving to the left and subtracting 0 from 1 and writing 1 to the left of 1, then seeing the answer as 111. Although it looks much more complicated to those used to decimals, binary subtraction would work the same way:

$$
\begin{array}{r}
137\ (10001001) \\
-\ 26\ (00011010) \\
\hline
111\ (01101111)
\end{array}
$$

What he came up with was his own form of Boolean algebra (which he, like Zuse, later said that he was unaware of at the time). Here again, Atanasoff and Turing were thinking along the same lines, but Turing, as a mathematician among mathematicians, did not have to devise his own system.

Boolean algebra is a logic system invented by George Boole (1815–1864) that posits that there are only two values in the universe. They are

---

4. The list he eventually came up with was: (1) multiple correlation, (2) curve fitting, (3) method of least squares, (4) vibration problems including the vibrational Raman effect, (5) electrical circuit analysis, (6) analysis of elastic structures, (7) approximate solution of many problems of elasticity, (8) approximate solutions of problems of quantum mechanics, (9) perturbation theories of mechanics, astronomy, and the quantum theory.

zero and one. On these two values, four operations can be performed: (1) "no-op" (also called identity), (2) "not" (the value is changed into its opposite), (3) "and," and (4) "or." The first two operate (i.e., do something to and then return a single outcome value) on a single value. The second two operate on a pair of values and then return a single outcome value.

The values do not have to be read as numbers—they can be read as "true" or "false," or "green" or "not green," for example. For the purposes of the computer, both Atanasoff and Zuse realized that large numbers were easier to calculate using a 1 and 0 system, but Boolean algebra also has philosophical implications about the nature of reality and how to discover if something is true or not true that Turing brought to bear on not only breaking German codes, but also on his theory of how the mind works, and how, therefore, a mind-like machine might work. Working out his own form of Boolean algebra showed Atanasoff, as it showed Zuse, that his system was manageable and would not require rooms full of hardware.

Atanasoff didn't have the money or resources to try to build any of his components, so most of the work he did was on paper and in his head. However, in March 1939, fifteen months after the revelation in the roadhouse, Atanasoff turned in an application for a grant of $650 to hire a graduate student and attempt to build what he had conceived of. In May, his grant request was approved: $450 was salary for the student and $200 was to go for raw materials.

Chapter Four

Perhaps Atanasoff's greatest piece of luck in inventing the computer was that Iowa State College, unlike Cambridge, Harvard, or Princeton, had an excellent college of engineering, and from his years as a student and as a professor, Atanasoff was familiar with and on good terms with the engineering faculty. One day, walking across campus, Atanasoff ran into a friend, engineering professor Howard Anderson. The two started chatting about the sort of graduate student Atanasoff was looking for—intelligent, motivated, handy, and able to think for himself, as well as familiar with electronics. Anderson suggested a young man named Clifford Berry, who had just completed his bachelor's degree. He was twenty-one. Anderson thought he was uniquely gifted.

Clifford Berry's background was not unlike Atanasoff's own. He had been born in Gladbrook, which was northeast of Ames, about halfway between Ames and Cedar Rapids. His father had owned an appliance store and was an accomplished tinkerer who repaired appliances and built the first radio in Gladbrook. Berry himself built a ham radio when he was eleven. In 1929, Berry's father went to work for a power company (as Atanasoff's father had done, and Howard Aiken himself had done) and the family moved to Marengo. Violence, too, had figured in Berry's life—his father was shot and killed by a disgruntled worker when Berry was fifteen. Although the murder of Berry's father resulted in hardship for his family, Berry's mother recognized her son's talents and sacrificed to give him the opportunity to go to Iowa State, where his abilities were recognized immediately—once again, we see the land-grant system at work, as it had been in Florida with Atanasoff and at Iowa State with Lura.

Physically, Berry could not have been more different from Atanasoff—he was short, slight, and wore thick glasses; his demeanor was self-effacing. When the two met in the summer of 1939, Atanasoff, the experienced teacher, questioned and probed the young man and found himself more than impressed. Berry was knowledgeable, enthusiastic, enterprising. When Atanasoff outlined his ideas, Berry was not shy about making good suggestions. He seemed to grasp Atanasoff's concepts with no trouble, and the two men began to get excited about the project, though because of financial considerations they could not begin actual construction until September, the start of a new academic year. Temperamentally, Atanasoff and Berry complemented each other. Berry was neither intimidated nor overwhelmed by Atanasoff's rush of ideas, and he was not subject to mood swings. He combined exceptional intelligence and mechanical dexterity with a steady work ethic and a mild demeanor. He was not the sort of boy who had ever been a pest—at twenty-one, he was only a few years past being an Eagle Scout.

In Berlin, Konrad Zuse was pressing forward in his magpie fashion: the German showing of the film *King Kong* inspired Zuse's fraternity to put on a King Kong skit with paper skyscrapers. It starred a young man Zuse had never met, named Helmut Schreyer, as the ape. Schreyer made such an impression on Zuse that Zuse invited him to have a look at the computer. He writes in his autobiography, "I . . . was of the opinion that whoever was capable of such despicable deeds could also be of use in my workshop." As soon as he walked into the room where the computer was, Schreyer, who was an electronics engineer, asserted, "You'll have to make it with vacuum tubes," but Zuse was hard to convince. He writes, "I never pursued the idea seriously, which may be attributed chiefly to my visual approach to the world. Things that could not be seen were always difficult for me to grasp." It was during this time, when Zuse and Schreyer were hard at work (sometimes eighty hours per week) on their computer that they discovered Boolean algebra (or, as Zuse calls it, "propositional calculus"). The task was to come up with a mechanism that would switch the relays—or, once Schreyer had convinced Zuse, the vacuum tubes—on and off according to these operations (as Atanasoff also realized).

Zuse and Schreyer managed to build a vacuum tube switching prototype and demonstrate it (sometime in 1938) to a group of people who knew about and were interested in the computer at the technical university. Even as they watched the demonstration, though, the audience felt that what Zuse and his team were attempting to do was impossible. Zuse proposed a machine that would require two thousand vacuum tubes and several thousand of what he called glow-discharge lamps—almost ten times the number of vacuum tubes that the typical electricity transmitting station of the time employed (at least as far as Konrad Zuse knew), and so acquiring so many vacuum tubes would be difficult, if not impossible. He also says in his autobiography that when pressed to think of facilities that used as much power as the computer they were designing, he mentioned high-speed wind tunnels in the aircraft industry—the local power station had to be notified before one of these was turned on. After the demonstration, Zuse and his team decided to resume their former secrecy—they realized that they appeared, at least, to be attempting something that no one believed possible. Schreyer did complete his doctoral thesis about the project, but the computer itself seemed to have no future.

Zuse, not in sympathy with the Nazis and used to secrecy, focused on building his machine. Of the coming of the war, he writes, "It is not true that virtually all news in a totalitarian state is false. On the contrary, most news is completely correct, albeit tendentiously slanted; it is just that certain information is suppressed. One can adjust for the political slanting of the news, but there is virtually no way to fill in the omissions." If we wonder how Zuse and his friends failed to understand the Anschluss, the takeover of Czechoslovakia, the pact with Mussolini, and the pact with Stalin, well, they were not alone in assuming that Hitler's intentions were not particularly aggressive and could be ignored, especially since they managed to meet up with some young British men who traveled to Germany in August 1939. All of the German young men felt warm friendships toward the visitors, but when Germany invaded Poland and Britain declared war, the visit was cut short. Soon Zuse was drafted. He expected to be in the army for six months.

Things were quieter in Ames. Once Atanasoff and Berry were ready to build, they had another piece of luck that at first looked a bit like a slight. When Atanasoff sought a workspace in which to build his computer, he was sent to the basement of the physics building because the first floor was taken up by projects already in progress, and possibly considered to be more important. The basement was full of junk, and Atanasoff and Berry had to set up their workspace in an out-of-the-way, windowless corner (walls with doorways were added later—to the detriment of the computer). Atanasoff appreciated the privacy—later he would also appreciate both the space's proximity to the machine shop and its steady, cool temperature. In Atanasoff's life, frugality had often meant that making do was making better. But space limitations and financial limitations also meant that Atanasoff and Berry had to reconfigure their plans into something smaller and more buildable. As Atanasoff later put it, "We did not dare to build everything into our plans. Our skill as inventors depended on how well we chose between these factors, the indispensable and the impossible." What Atanasoff thought was most crucial were the instructions—that is, how he would set up the sequence of steps, or algorithm, that would perform the mathematical operation he wanted. He was still not quite clear about them when they went to work.

While they were getting ready, Atanasoff did what he could to find out what other computer projects were under way around the country. As far as he could tell, no one was trying what he was trying, in terms of concepts or hardware. Someone he might have heard about was

George R. Stibitz (born April 30, 1904, though some sources say April 20). Stibitz had grown up in Ohio, gone to Denison University, and then to Union College. In 1930, at the same time Atanasoff was working on his dissertation at the University of Wisconsin, Stibitz was working on his at Cornell University. Stibitz's dissertation, like Atanasoff's, involved extensive and tedious calculations. But Stibitz went to work for Bell Labs in New York City. Bell Labs, a joint enterprise belonging to Western Electric and AT&T, was in both the discovery business and the invention business. In 1932, Karl Jansky had detected radio noise that originated at the center of the Milky Way; in 1933, Bell Labs scientists had managed to transmit stereophonic sound over telephone wires (a symphony recorded in Philadelphia was transmitted to Washington, D.C.). Stibitz, whose doctorate was in applied mathematics, was surrounded by equipment as well as engineers.

Like Atanasoff, Stibitz was known as a tinkerer. It was therefore not surprising to his colleagues that when in November 1937 he built his Complex Number Calculator, he named it the "Model K"; "K" stood for kitchen, because, he said, it was based on electromagnetic relays (not the same as the devices Zuse calls relays)—flashlight bulbs, a dry cell battery, and some metal strips he cut from a tin can—that he found and put together in his kitchen. The relays Stibitz was using were ubiquitous in telephone technology, and Stibitz's calculator operated by triggering relays representing different decimal numbers—the activation of a 3 and a 4 triggered the activation (switching to "on") of the switch representing 7. Stibitz also figured out how to use the telephone system to activate his relays from a distance—in 1940, he would use a teleprinter (similar to a teletype machine) at Dartmouth College in New Hampshire to send a calculation to his computer in New York and to receive the solution. The most ambitious attempt was Howard Aiken's developing project at Harvard, with IBM, but Atanasoff knew that it was completely different from what he was attempting.

Once Atanasoff and Berry began, they moved right along—they had a "breadboard" prototype ready to test in October 1939—that is, it consisted of a breadboard-sized piece of wood on which Berry had built an electrical system of eleven vacuum tubes and fifty capacitors (or condensers, as they were called). According to Atanasoff, "It could just add and subtract the binary equivalents of decimal numbers having up to eight places" (anything up to 99,999,999 depending on the placement of the decimal point) but it worked, and it worked in accordance with Atanasoff's four original principles. And it was frugal in every way. Atanasoff demonstrated the prototype for college officials a few weeks later and received further funding—$110 for more materials and $700 for other expenses.[1]

Even so, and this would prove the world's boon and Atanasoff's bane (and also prove Aiken's precept about having to ram good ideas down people's throats), Iowa State officials and Atanasoff's own colleagues didn't show much understanding or enthusiasm. The machine itself was unprepossessing, and no one was as familiar with its innovative nature or its limber technological possibilities as Berry and Atanasoff were. Those who wandered down into the basement to have a look sometimes made dismissive remarks, and the college was "supportive" in terms of hundreds of dollars, not thousands of dollars (IBM was soon spending half a million dollars on Aiken's prototype). At the same time, Atanasoff owed his ideas to no one—there was no government agency or corporate committee that he had to explain his ideas to, no one he might offend by throwing out decades or centuries of common wisdom about calculating. Because he was frugal, he was free to think in innovative ways. What Atanasoff's fellow professors could not see was that the breadboard calculator incorporated seven innovations:

1. Electronic computing
2. Vacuum tubes as the computing mechanism and operating memory

---

1. According to Alice R. Burks and Arthur W. Burks, "The model had two storage bands, each with twenty-five condensers, on the outerfaces of a large disk. One brand represented the abacus . . . or the counter drum, the other that of the keyboard drum. It had an add-subtract mechanism, served by a single carry-borrow condenser . . . and also a mechanism to perform the restore but not the shift function" (p. 22).

3. Binary calculation
4. Logical calculation
5. Serial computation (each step followed a previous one)
6. Capacitors as storage memory
7. Capacitors attached to a rotating drum that refreshed the power supply of the vacuum tubes and maintained (or refreshed, jogged, regenerated) the operating memory

Since he was well aware of Babbage's Analytical Engine, and thought that the English mathematician had foundered because he was too ambitious, Atanasoff's next decision was to limit himself to devising a machine for the solution of linear equations rather than to attempt to invent a universal machine. It was the differential equations that had made Atanasoff's dissertation so tedious in 1930, but more important, even though both Atanasoff and Berry saw the grander implications of the breadboard calculator, they had money only for the next step. The differential equations were converted to "finite difference" equations—these were the equations their computer would be able to solve, equations containing up to twenty-nine unknowns. Such a capacity would almost triple the limit of ten unknowns that was then considered possible in solving systems of equations.

The construction of the new prototype began in January 1940, when Clifford Berry started cutting the angle iron to be used in the larger machine. In the meantime, Atanasoff himself took on a second, war-related project, which was to invent a method of predicting the movement of artillery targets and to invent a device that could perform such accurate tracking. Atanasoff hired another graduate student, Sam Legvold, and took over an area near the computer area in the basement of the physics building. What enabled Atanasoff to take on this extra work (in addition, of course, to his exceptionally energetic nature) was the fact that Berry fully understood the computer they were building, and he had assumed not only most of the construction work, but also responsibility for many of the adjustments and improvements that had to be made. The most important thing, though, was that the vacuum tubes had to work reliably. After Atanasoff and Berry ascertained this by testing in January 1940, the project moved quickly and the machine was constructed and ready to test within a few months.

Once his paper "On Computable Numbers" was completed and published in the spring of 1936, Alan Turing's world expanded again—by the end of that September, he was at Princeton, enjoying (or not) a graduate fellowship there and meeting some of the best mathematical minds in the world. He wrote home in October with a list of those who were around: John von Neumann, Hermann Weyl, Richard Courant, G. H. Hardy, Albert Einstein, Solomon Lefschetz, and Alonzo Church. He regretted having missed Kurt Gödel, who had been there the year before, and perhaps Paul Bernays (of whom he was a bit disdainful—Turing was feeling more and more self-confident). Hardy, whom he knew from Cambridge, was friendly, but Turing found the way Americans talked unpleasant and Princeton disconcerting—casual and familiar, if sometimes fun (an impromptu hockey team of which Turing was a member went to Vassar and played an entertaining game with another impromptu team of girls). "On Computable Numbers" was published in January, but the response was disappointing—only two people asked for offprints. In many ways, even though he was at the most important nexus of mathematics in his time, he was too shy to push himself forward and make connections. Even Alonzo Church subsequently remembered very little about him. At the end of the year, Turing applied for an appointment at Cambridge but failed to get it, so he applied for another fellowship at Princeton—John von Neumann was one of his referees and gave him an excellent recommendation, but in his letter he gave no sign that he had read or even was aware of "On Computable Numbers." Turing spent the summer of 1937 back in England and returned to Princeton in the fall, and there he went into the Princeton workshop and built a small binary calculator.

Although he had written "On Computable Numbers" in binary terms (the marked and unmarked squares on the infinite paper tape fed into the computer could be 1s and 0s), he had not done so as part of the theory of the imagined computer, only as part of its mechanism. In the Princeton workshop, though, he saw the possibilities of binary numbers (and Boolean logic) in the use of relay switches for calculating multiplication problems (as Zuse also saw), and he even made his own relays, since they were no more available in Princeton, New Jersey, than they were in Berlin. Andrew Hodges writes, "The idea would be that when a number was presented to the machine, presumably by setting up currents at a series of input terminals, the relays would click open and closed, currents would pass through, and emerge at output terminals, thus in effect 'writing' the enciphered number." He also addressed the Riemann zeta function, a problem in mathematics that is still unsolved, which concerns very large numbers. What Turing thought of was the movement of waves—and he remembered a device he had seen called the Liverpool tide-predicting machine, an analog machine invented first in the 1920s and then subsequently improved several times in the late 1930s, that used strings and pulleys to predict tides in the river Mersey. It worked by measuring, not counting, but its measurements added up as the machine operated day after day, year after year. Turing wondered if a machine built according to similar principles could be used for zeta-function calculation.

Most important, Turing wrote his PhD thesis, which addressed Gödel's incompleteness theorems. His thesis adviser was Alonzo Church, who seems to have felt some rivalry with Turing stemming from the nearly simultaneous appearance of his lambda calculus and Turing's computable numbers paper. Gödel's incompleteness theorems amounted to a pair of rules that limited the aspiration of mathematics to make an understandable system out of the world of numbers. The first theorem states that no system can be both consistent and complete. The second states that any theory that contains basic arithmetical truths and also certain truths about formal provability will include a statement of its own consistency if and only if the theory is inconsistent. Turing's thinking on this subject was an extension of his thinking in "On Computable Numbers," and he passed his PhD examination at the end of June

1938. According to David Leavitt, the problem for pure mathematics at this time was to limit the implications of Gödel's theorems, so that they "should interfere as little as possible with the practice of mathematics." Turing's ideas supported Gödel's theorems, and subsequently Gödel seems to have approved of them more than he approved of Church's similar but differently formulated lambda calculus. Twenty-six when he took his PhD exam, Turing was gaining a reputation as a mathematician. John von Neumann, who by now appears to have read "On Computable Numbers," was impressed enough to offer Turing a lucrative position ($1,500, about $22,000 in 2010 dollars) as compared to the $800 Atanasoff had received ten years earlier at Iowa State) as his assistant at Princeton for the academic year 1938–39, but Turing missed England and went home, even though he had no position waiting for him (as far as we know).

By 1937, British Intelligence knew that the Germans were using an encoding system called Enigma that, except in minor ways, they could not break. When Turing returned from Princeton, he enrolled in a course about codes and code breaking given by the Government Code and Cypher School. How long he had been in contact with British intelligence, who initiated the contact, and what Turing's motives for enrolling were remain unclear, but by 1938, after the union of Germany and Austria, it was clear that the world was a dangerous place, and England had to begin to act to protect itself. The dangers were brought home to Turing in a very personal way after he got back to England, when a friend of his was contacted by a woman the friend had known in Vienna. In the fall of 1938, the woman's two sons turned up in a refugee camp at Harwich. Turing went with his friend to meet the boys and decided to sponsor the schooling of another boy he met there, Bob Augenfeld, who was sent to a boarding establishment in Lancashire. He also continued with the code-breaking school, and in the spring of 1939, he went back to Cambridge to give a lecture course himself for undergraduate students preparing for their final exams and to take a course from Ludwig Wittgenstein, during which they discussed, and disagreed upon, the idea that mathematics could be a logical system

whether or not it was a "true" system. Wittgenstein persisted in thinking that there was value in a logical system even if it did not work
in the real world; Turing disagreed. Turing also began thinking again
about the Liverpool tide-predicting machine. The machine Alan Turing was thinking of (and received forty pounds sterling to develop)
would use weights and counterweights attached to rotating gears to
set up problems. Their solutions would be measured by a comparison
of weights—an analog idea. Turing and a colleague worked on this
machine in their office at Cambridge through the summer of 1939,
but in the fall, after the German invasion of Poland, Turing went to
Bletchley Park to aid in the breaking of the Enigma.

Yet another, and still more obscure, inventor of the computer, one
whom Alan Turing would soon know very well, was Tommy Flowers.
He was an engineer at the General Post Office Research Station at
Dollis Hill in northwest London (not far from Hampstead Heath). At
the end of August 1939, Flowers was in Germany. In an eerie paral-
lel to Zuse's experience with friendly English students just before
the outbreak of the war, he recalled, "I was in Berlin on laboratory
business only days before hostilities began. A telephone call from the
British Embassy made me go home at once, and I crossed the border
into Holland only hours before the German frontier was closed."
Flowers was the engineer Turing would work with during the war,
and the fates of the two men, with regard to the invention of the computer, were deeply entwined, but no biographies or plays have been
written about Flowers, nor did he write his autobiography, so how he
viewed his career has to be inferred from a very few sources. His obituary on the BBC website is somewhat detailed:

Thomas Harold Flowers was born in London on 22 December,
1905. He seems to have been a practical child, when told of the
arrival of a baby sister he declared a preference for a 'Meccano'
set. After school, he embarked on a four-year apprenticeship in
Mechanical Engineering at the Woolwich Arsenal and went to

night classes to study successfully for a degree in Engineering from London University.

After graduating, he joined the General Post Office (GPO), which was then responsible for all telecommunications within the UK. He worked at Dollis Hill, the GPO's research station, on experimental electronic solutions for long-distance telephone systems. In the 1930s, that meant thermionic valves [known as "vacuum tubes" in the United States], which were seen more as analog amplifiers than electronic switches. These would replace or enhance the electro-mechanical switches then used. These experiments formed the basis for modern direct dialing, but that was some way off. His work also drew the attention of others with quite a different purpose in mind.

With easier access to such tubes than either Atanasoff or Zuse, Flowers did an experiment in 1934 in which he wired together three to four thousand vacuum tubes that controlled a thousand lines, and communicated by means of tones. Like Zuse, Flowers encountered resistance from his superiors on the score of reliability, but in 1939 his system was introduced in a limited fashion.

Flowers later expressed strong opinions about the essential value of what he invented and built to the British war effort. It is also clear that he was the very engineer that Turing needed to realize his own computing ideas, but it was not until 2006 that even the outline of Flowers's work came to be generally known. In the fall of 1939, he was just a thirty-three-year-old engineer with some insights into vacuum tubes who happened to escape from the Third Reich at the very last minute.

A reconstruction of Atanasoff and Berry's second prototype is now on loan to the Computer History Museum near San Jose (as of summer 2010), though it normally resides in Atanasoff Hall at Iowa State University. The original was junked in 1948, with the permission of the chairman of the physics department, by a physics graduate student look-ing for office space (the replica was built in the 1990s by a team headed by computer scientist John Gustafson).[2] Atanasoff and Berry worked on it through 1940, and Berry worked on it until June 1942. The frame of the computer (now known as the ABC, or the Atanasoff-Berry Com-puter) was seventy-four inches long, thirty-six inches deep, and about forty inches tall (including casters). Berry used the angle iron to con-struct a table with two levels, one about four inches off the floor that contained the boards holding the vacuum tubes and capacitors, which stood upright and faced front, along with several other components, including two transformers and a power supply regulator. Above that, at the back of the top table were two drums, each about eleven inches long and eight inches in diameter, several mechanisms for transposing binary numbers into and out of decimals, and a mechanism for char-ring holes in cards and feeding them back into the drums.

Solving twenty-nine linear equations with twenty-nine unknowns was still a lengthy process (taking some thirty hours) and required sys-tematic inputs by the human operator, but it could be done, and the machine was accurate. In the first step of the process, the binary input unit converted each of the equations from decimal form to binary form and entered the equations on the input memory drum. Atanasoff had decided to use a variation of the punch-card system to input his equa-tions and to read out the results of the computer's calculations, but he wanted to use an electronic method to mark the punch cards. The punch-card systems then available were based on decimal numbers, so he had to devise something new. What he decided to do was have the output component use an electric spark to burn a mark onto the card in a manner similar to a hole being punched — a spot charred into a space on the grid represented a 1. An empty space represented a 0. This mechanism proved more unreliable than the other mechanisms he had come up with for the calculating operations themselves —

2. Yet another irony of Atanasoff's story is that the student who dismantled the com-puter, Robert Stewart, later served as chairman of the computer science department.

producing an inaccurate result (on a card) less than once in every ten thousand times, but more than once in every hundred thousand times. The ABC itself was successful, though, and demonstrated that Atanasoff's ideas with Berry's tweaks and construction could perform many more sorts of calculations than the one Atanasoff and Berry had designed it to do. Apart from the card issue, the ABC was operational by mid-1940.

In a thirty-five-page manuscript that Atanasoff completed in August, he described the ABC in detail. He listed the nine sorts of linear algebraic equations he thought a larger machine would be able to solve (see page 50, footnote) and outlined their practical applications in physics, statistics, and technology. They ranged from problems of elasticity to approximate solutions of quantum mechanics problems. He expected the machine to be powerful and versatile, but he always conceived it as a machine for solving mathematical problems. In this, his ideas came to diverge, inevitably, from those Flowers and Turing would soon be contemplating.

Atanasoff's thirty-five-page paper was intended to do what merely watching the ABC work could not do—to demonstrate to the Iowa State College Research Corporation that the computer was innovative, powerful, and successful. The goal was more money—Atanasoff and Berry estimated that they needed $5,000 to go on to the next step. The original and three carbon copies were made of the paper. Atanasoff sent one to the research corporation, one was retained by Berry for his use in overseeing the construction of the next prototype, and the third was set aside for the patenting process that Atanasoff thought the machine was ready for.

In December 1940, Atanasoff took his family east for a vacation, which would include his attending the annual meeting of the American Association for the Advancement of Science, held in Philadelphia. According to Burton, Atanasoff's intense concentration on his teaching, on the ABC, and on his defense project had taken a toll on his marriage, but Joanne Atanasoff, the second daughter, and John Vincent II did feel comfortable riding their bikes to the physics building to see their father—they often played around in the basement there while he worked.

The automobile trip to the East Coast would be a long one, with stops in New York City and Washington, D.C., as well as Philadelphia. Atanasoff planned to do some work—mostly patent research in New York and Washington. Berry intended to meet them. John and his family celebrated Christmas in a hotel in New York, just a little dazzled by the urban world they were not accustomed to.

Chapter Five

Throughout the Second World War, the Germans used a mechanical encoding device that they called the Enigma machine. It had been patented in 1918 or 1919 and put to use by the German army and navy by 1929. In 1931, a German working in the Cipher Office began selling information about the machine (including photographs of the instruction manuals) to the French, but neither the French nor British could break the code. It was a Pole, Marian Rejewski, who first cracked the German Enigma code in 1932 and built a replica of the machine. The Poles were then able to decode Wehrmacht radio messages until the late thirties—advances in Enigma technology foiled them as of 1937 for naval messages, and as of December 1938 for the rest of the German messages. The decoding machines Rejewski constructed were called "Bombas" (named, some said, after the ticking sounds they produced while working). The Bombas operated according to Rejewski's insight that German intelligence operators signaled the day's encryption key by typing in the same three letters twice in a row (for example NGHNGH) followed by the new settings for the three rotors of the Enigma machine. Knowing what these double letters signified, Rejewski then inferred the entire structure of the Enigma and its operation—the Bombas were built to sift through strings of code and find those that were likely to be messages. Through mid-1939, the Poles kept their knowledge to themselves. When the Germans introduced more rotors into the Enigma, the Poles quickly figured out how the rotors worked, but five rather than three rotors raised the number of possible combinations tenfold, outstripping the capacity of the Bombas to quickly sort through encoded messages. At the same time, the political and military situation in Poland was rapidly deteriorating, so the Poles communicated what they had discovered about the decoding of the Enigma to English and French intelligence. Rejewski and his fellow cryptographers spent the war sometimes in France, sometimes in Gibraltar, and sometimes in England, working with Allied intelligence.

Cracking the Enigma code was especially crucial for the British, since it was the code used by the German navy, and Britain was dependent on ocean traffic for every kind of supply, and therefore especially vulnerable to naval disruption or blockade. When Turing first arrived shortly after the invasion of Poland and the British declaration of war, six Bombas at Bletchley Park sifted through intercepted messages for matching letters that would reveal the settings of the German positions encoding the messages, and most of the code breaking was done by linguists, not mathematicians. The prized form of cryptanalytic intelligence was the sort that solves puzzles through a combination of linguistic sophistication and intuition. Turing was an enthusiastic puzzle solver, but since he was also a mathematician, he understood both large numbers (as in the number of combinations of letters that had to be tested in order to break a code) and probability (which combinations were likely to lead to dead ends and which were likely to be productive). It was Turing and an associate, Gordon Welchman, who were to address the problem of the extra rotors that had been added to the Enigma machine. The new "Bombes," as they were rechristened, were designed using relays. Andrew Hodges maintains that Turing "was the right person to see what was needed, for his unusual experience with the relay multiplier [he had built at Princeton] had given him insight into the problems of embodying logical manipulations in this kind of machinery." For his part, Welchman redesigned the wiring that constituted the instructions for the machines.

Andrew Roberts points out in *The Storm of War* that code breaking was not the only form of intelligence that the Allies were using even at the beginning of the war—more traditional methods such as spying, interrogating, and eavesdropping were also employed, but to break the codes meant they could listen to exchanges of information and instruction in real time, and so throughout the war, the code breakers were considered, in Churchill's words, "the geese who laid the golden eggs" and "never cackled."

When Turing went to Bletchley Park in September 1939, Germany seemed to have all the advantages: Stalin had signed a nonaggression pact on August 23, and the Russian army invaded Poland from the east two weeks after Germany invaded from the west. At the end of November, the Russians invaded Finland. Just after the declaration of war, the Germans had attacked an English ocean liner, the SS *Athenia*, killing 112 or 117 passengers (depending on the source). With the declaration of war, U-boats began steadily harassing English ships—on September 17, an aircraft carrier, the HMS *Courageous*, was sunk by two U-boats and went down in fifteen minutes, losing five hundred men. Historian Andrew Roberts notes that "by the end of 1939, Britain had lost 422,000 tons of shipping" by means of attacks and mines and was in danger of being isolated, without resources or even food if the German navy could manage it. The first half of 1940 was worse in every way: Finland fell, Norway fell, the first because of the passivity of the Allies, the second in spite of the Allies' efforts. In May, the Dutch surrendered and English troops were driven back to Dunkirk, only to be evacuated, according to Roberts, because Hitler overruled the wishes of his generals, Kleist and Guderian, with a "halt order" that prevented them from pursuing and wiping out the retreating armies. France fell at the end of June, and the Battle of Britain began in July. Since the United States had declared its neutrality, the situation for Britain was desperate.

Turing's Bombe (the first went to work in March 1940) was constructed like a large, heavy bookcase, six and a half feet high, more than seven feet long, and two and a half feet deep. The "books" were rows of motorized rotating drums, ends facing outward, twenty-six letter positions inscribed around the circumference of each. These were meant to simulate the operations of Enigma rotors. The Bombe worked as a sorter, trying out likely combinations of letters supplied by the operator to see if any German words were created as the patterns of letter correlations were changed. Most of the time, according to Turing's mathematically based insight, sets of letters supplied by the operators (known as "cribs") would proceed by logical substitutions to a state of self-contradiction. If the operator would suspect that A = K, for example, when it arrived at a position in which A = A, it would be self-replicating and not correct, since the decoders knew that for Enigma, a letter could not be encoded as itself. As the rotors tested the positions, they could throw out any self-replicating positions they arrived at. The greatest number of positions that had to be tested for any letter was twenty-five, the fewest, one. Each Bombe contained stacks of rotors that tested the letter combinations simultaneously. The Enigma in Germany was operated by hand, but the Bombe was motorized, so that even though Enigma encoding positions were changed every night at midnight, the Bombes (eventually there were 211) could sort through probable encoding patterns very quickly. When combinations that looked fruitful were found, the code wheels on the English replica of the Enigma machine were set to mimic what had been found, and either a message came up or it didn't. The code breaking was painstaking and tedious work that was aided by captures of German equipment or mistakes on the part of German personnel, as well as the tendency of the German military to use set phrases and clichéd expressions. In December 1939, Turing was instrumental in deciphering five days' worth of five rotor codes from 1938, thus demonstrating that the codes could be broken and showing how. In January 1940, Turing was dispatched to France to meet with Rejewski and his colleagues. On January 17, Turing and the Poles succeeded in breaking codes from the previous October. Throughout 1940, the code breakers made progress, aided by the capture of code wheels from a U-boat in February and another set in November. Fortunately for the British, though the Germans knew that the U-boats had been destroyed, they did not realize that the code wheels had been salvaged.

Once the Bombes had proved successful, Turing had another idea—a machine that would take the output of the Bombe and bypass the work of human decipherers by automatically translating that output from code into understandable German. It was in order to implement this idea that Tommy Flowers came to Bletchley from the General Post Office. But Flowers and Turing never succeeded in putting together that particular machine, in large part because as the war progressed, it turned out that Enigma was not British intelligence's biggest challenge.

Konrad Zuse, now an enlisted man in the German army, was still pursuing his own interests. Early on, Kurt Pannke wrote his commander a letter, asking that Zuse be relieved of duty because the invention he was working on would be valuable to the war effort, especially the Luftwaffe. This letter succeeded only in offending Zuse's commanding officer, who did not believe that the Luftwaffe needed any help. Zuse used the army as a place to take up chess and think about his computer theory and offered himself to work on coding and decoding, but the Germans considered that that problem had been solved by Enigma and the other machines they had devised (see chapter 6). Then Zuse's friend, Schreyer, attempted to get authorization to work on the computer for air defense, but when he suggested that research and development might take two years, the official in charge exclaimed, "What do you mean, after we've already won the war!" Finally, Zuse was put to work as a structural engineer working on weapons at Special Division F, with Henschel Aircraft. The task was to develop remote-controlled bombs. One type was to be dropped from an airplane and controlled by radio until it reached its destination. Another was to be dropped into water, where it would act as a torpedo. Toward the end of the war, the division worked on defensive surface-to-air missiles.

Zuse continued to develop his computer in the evenings and on weekends, managing to bring the second version of his computer, the Z2, to the demonstration stage in 1940—though it wasn't always reliable. Zuse reports in his autobiography that only hours before the planned demonstration took place, the Z2 could not be made to work, but then, once the audience for the demonstration had arrived, it "performed flawlessly," only to become temperamental again once the demonstration was over. He remarks that "afterwards, I hardly ever got the Z2 to run smoothly." The problem, he felt, was not necessarily the design, per se, but that all available relays were secondhand parts from different manufacturers that had to be reconfigured to work in the way Zuse wanted them to, and that in reworking them, he overlooked details of how they would function together. But the single flawless demonstration aroused the interest of the technical director of the Aeronautics Research Institute, which was enough to gain Zuse a contract to develop the Z3. The contract meant money, but the war effort meant that he still had to use secondhand parts.

The Z3, which was completed in 1941, did work reliably. It incorporated the following principles and design ideas:

1. Electromagnetic relay technology (not vacuum tubes)
2. Binary number system
3. Floating point (a system of locating the decimal point)
4. Word length: 22 bits
5. Storage capacity: sixty-four words
6. Control by means of eight-track punched tape
7. Input by means of specially designed keyboard
8. Output by means of display of results on a row of lights, including proper placement of the decimal point
9. High speed: 3 seconds for multiplication, division, or square root

John Gustafson, who constructed the replica of the ABC and is an expert on early computers, writes:

> It was a jaw-dropping accomplishment to invent floating-point arithmetic back then and get it to work at such high speed. It wasn't just a way of adjusting the decimal point: he could represent positive and negative infinity, undefined numbers like 0/0, and a number of other ideas that did not become standardized until the 1980s. Not many computer engineers today, given a pile of electromagnetic relays, would have the faintest idea how to build a floating-point unit out of it, especially not one that can take square roots. He was very far ahead of his time. It is also worth noting that the 64 words of memory were addressable; the computer could pick out a particular one to use by its number. The ABC didn't have anything like that—the ABC had memory in the two drums, but the operator selected which one to use, while on the Zuse machine, it was controllable by the program tape. It was like a modern computer in almost every way except that it couldn't do conditional branches, which is testing a number and then jumping to a different part of the program depending on whether the test was true or false.

Gustafson adds, "This is why I admire Zuse every bit as much as I admire Atanasoff . . . and why I'm thankful that the arrogance of the German military didn't see the merit of Zuse's work, since the world might be a very different place now if they had."

Zuse continued to make do with what he could find—since he could not get hold of a tape-punching machine, he punched strips of celluloid film with a manual hole punch; since his relay coils were secondhand, they were not uniform, so he had to adjust the voltage of each one in order to get them to work together.

Even though Zuse was making progress, and he could demonstrate the usefulness of his machine for certain calculations having to do with wing flutter in airplanes, he could not prove that his computer work was valuable to the war effort. He was put back into the army again in 1941 but managed to establish that his work with Henschel was worth a deferment. His work on the computer progressed, still on his own time.

Wartime rules and regulations favored Zuse's machine in some ways. After persuading Henschel to let him work part-time, he set up his own company to develop the computer. He writes:

> Available were unskilled, mostly female workers, who had made themselves unpopular elsewhere, or who did not fit into the normal working world. So, at one time I was able to hire an excellent technical designer who had had a lengthy stay in a mental hospital. In a normal company, his eccentricities probably would have gotten on everyone's nerves, but we didn't have any problems with him . . . My book-keeper had done something very foolish when he was a young man, and he had been prosecuted for it. But he fit in perfectly with our small company . . . There was also the great added advantage that neither of these workers could be drafted.

One of Atanasoff's goals in attending the meeting of the American Association for the Advancement of Science in December 1940 was to find out what other inventors were doing—he still feared that some larger, more prestigious, and better financed entity might be onto ideas similar to his. He was not giving a presentation himself, though.

One scholar, a man named John Mauchly, gave a talk about correlating weather patterns with solar phenomena such as sunspots, a subject that Atanasoff was interested in (as he was interested in allergies, soybeans, goat milk products, and home construction). In the course of his lecture, Mauchly, who was the only physics professor at Ursinus College in Collegeville, Pennsylvania, mentioned that he had devised a calculator, which he called the "Harmonic Analyzer," to do the correlations. He detailed his design ideas and talked about his plans for building a more powerful machine. Although the Harmonic Analyzer was an analog machine, Mauchly said in his talk that he thought the future of computing was electronic, and he expected to have an electronic machine in about two years.

John Mauchly was about four years younger than Atanasoff. His background was middle-class academic, more like that of John Hasbrouck Van Vleck than like that of Stibitz, Aiken, or Atanasoff. Mauchly's father, Sebastian, was a principal at a high school in Cincinnati, Ohio, until 1916, when John was nine and Sebastian received his PhD in physics and moved to Chevy Chase, Maryland, to become chief physicist specializing in "electricity and earth currents" at the Carnegie Institute in Washington, D.C. One thing he was interested in was the physics of lightning strikes (presaging John's interest in weather prediction). John Mauchly was something of a prodigy and a pest, like the young Atanasoff. According to Scott McCartney in *ENIAC*, he had a sign over his bed that read, "What should I be doing now?" In 1919, Chevy Chase was a fairly new suburb, home to many men employed in scientific fields around the Washington, D.C., area. Twelve-year-old John, who as a five-year-old had rigged a flashlight out of a battery and a lightbulb, laid intercom wires in the trenches that workmen were digging for water lines. He was also a night owl who concocted a switch that turned off his reading light if one of his parents stepped onto the landing outside his door. In high school, he was an impressive student who planned to follow in his father's footsteps as a physicist. By the time John was ready to go to college in 1925, though, Sebastian Mauchly had come to understand, possibly from his own experience, that there was more money in engineering than in physics, so John applied for and received a prestigious scholarship to Johns Hopkins University in engineering. But he got bored with that after about two years and transferred to the physics department, where he so impressed his professors that they decided to put him directly into the PhD program. He completed his doctorate in 1932, writing his dissertation on carbon monoxide. Here, his experience, and the conclusions he drew from it, also mirrored Atanasoff's experience two years earlier—the calculations, which he performed on a Marchant desk calculator, proved onerous and inspired the ambition to invent a more powerful calculator.

Mauchly was just far enough behind the economic downturn when he got his PhD that he had a difficult time finding a job (Atanasoff, who found his job at Iowa State in 1930, had to take a pay cut along with all the other faculty members as the Great Depression worsened in the early thirties). Mauchly spent one year as a research assistant at Johns Hopkins and then was hired by Ursinus College, a four-year liberal arts school outside of Philadelphia founded by the German Reformed Church. At the time Mauchly taught there (and his teaching responsibilities were heavy), the college was associated with the United Church of Christ. Mauchly's students were, for the most part, not planning to be engineers or physicists. Mauchly was the only member of the physics department—his job was to give his premed students their required course in physics and to bring returning high school teachers up to date. His salary was comparable to Atanasoff's—$2,150. He also had a wife and two children—he had married a mathematician, Mary Walzl, in 1930.

Like Atanasoff, Mauchly engaged his students in his research interests—he put them to work correlating rainfall with the rotation of the sun, but the calculations were stupefyingly tedious and time-consuming. In 1940, while maintaining a full teaching load, Mauchly had constructed the Harmonic Analyzer.

After Mauchly's lecture, Atanasoff hurried to the front of the room. The two scientists, both talkative and enthusiastic by nature, hit it off, and they discussed their projects for about half an hour, Mauchly describing his Harmonic Analyzer and Atanasoff describing the ABC. Mauchly showed so much enthusiasm that Atanasoff invited him to visit Ames and have a look at the machine. But Atanasoff was cautious about disclosing technical details because back in Ames, Iowa State was already beginning the patenting process, and Atanasoff was well aware that he could run into trouble if he divulged too much. Patenting was on his mind—the Atanasoffs were to meet Clifford Berry in Washington, D.C., a day or so later. After chatting with Mauchly, Atanasoff and his assistant spent four days looking through patent documents, reassuring themselves that their ideas were new and had never been patented before.

Atanasoff felt that the ABC was such a success that a significantly larger investment on the part of Iowa State was warranted and would pay off in the future. After the Christmas break, he met with college officials in order to persuade them to hire Richard Trexler, a patent attorney from Chicago with an excellent reputation. Iowa State officials balked, but Atanasoff talked them into it, and Atanasoff sent Trexler the third and last copy of his thirty-five-page description of the machine. Trexler seemed to think there would be no trouble patenting it, but Iowa State officials still did not understand the possibilities. It was only after Atanasoff received a $5,330 grant from the Research Corporation of New York at the end of March that Iowa State began to realize that the machine in the basement of the physics building might have a worthwhile, and lucrative, purpose. College president Charles E. Friley was impressed by the size of the grant—about double Atanasoff's yearly salary and equivalent to almost $85,000 in 2010 dollars (although it was still only about 1 percent of what IBM would ultimately spend on the Aiken Mark I).

For the next six months, Friley and Atanasoff negotiated the terms of an agreement to divide up profits that might accrue to Atanasoff's ideas. The college was stingy, to say the least—Friley wanted 90 percent of any income and, following college policy, did not want to give Clifford Berry any portion of the profits. The penalty for Atanasoff of refusing to sign would be that the college would withhold the Research Corporation of New York grant. Atanasoff, never one to be bullied, persisted until the college agreed to give him half of the profits, after expenses. From Atanasoff's portion, Berry would receive 10 percent. The parties signed a final contract in July 1941.

There were other naysayers—Howard Aiken, having begun to work with IBM, was committed to the Mark I and not enthusiastic about the ABC. Warren Weaver, from the University of Wisconsin, who visited concerning Atanasoff's war-related project, also reaffirmed his belief that analog was the way to go. Samuel Caldwell, of MIT, also visited the defense project, and though he was impressed by Atanasoff's machine, he was himself working on Vannevar Bush's Differential Analyzer (soon to be called the Bush-Caldwell Analyzer).

In the meantime, Mauchly had access to various projects that were progressing around Philadelphia and Washington, D.C. According to Scott McCartney, Mauchly took his students on one or more field trips to nearby Swarthmore College and was shown a vacuum-tube system for counting cosmic rays. What impressed him was the speed with which the vacuum tubes reacted—he observed that a vacuum tube could distinguish between two inputs only a millionth of a second apart. He saw that vacuum tubes could be much faster than switches or keys in counting, but he still had the model of a desk calculator in mind. The vacuum tubes were for input speed; he had not conceived of a binary system, in which the states of "on" and "off" would produce a logic system.

In 1939, Mauchly had seen an IBM encryption machine at the New York World's Fair that "used vacuum tube circuits for coded messages." Like Atanasoff, Flowers, and Schreyer, he began tinkering with various bits and pieces; he ordered tiny neon bulbs from General Electric as an experimental substitute for vacuum tubes—they were cheaper to buy and cheaper to run. But there is no evidence that he had a larger system in mind, and his only product was the Harmonic Analyzer, which may be thought of as similar to Atanasoff and Brandt's Laplaciometer. By the time Mauchly drove to Ames, his ideas do not seem to have jelled into a systematic theory about how an electronic calculator would have worked. Although Mauchly's biographer declares that he was a "ferocious record-keeper," he offers no citations of records that Mauchly kept during this period, or for any date before 1943.

Faced with repeated evidence that Iowa State did not understand or particularly value himself, his assistant, or his invention, and that other well-known inventors were committed to their own ideas, Atanasoff reacted with pleasure to Mauchly's enthusiasm. Mauchly first planned to make the eleven-hundred-mile trip west from Philadelphia in the spring but then put it off until summer. In a letter dated May 31, Atanasoff welcomed his imminent visit and suggested that he drop a line giving a date. Mauchly did drop that line, saying he would arrive either the evening of the thirteenth of June or the evening of the four-teenth, but Atanasoff failed to communicate this information to Lura, so when Mauchly arrived on the evening of the thirteenth, just as Lura was cleaning up after dinner, Lura was both surprised and put out—she had expected to get ready for the visit the next day. And to top it off, Mauchly had his six-year-old son with him. He rather impolitely asked for food and then unceremoniously handed the child over to Lura to take care of for the next four days. Lura was put on alert, and she did not like what she saw.

Atanasoff did like what he saw, though, because Mauchly was eager for information and seemed receptive to Atanasoff's ideas—just what a man who was enthusiastic about his project and underappreciated would be looking for. In the four days that Mauchly and his son were in Ames, Mauchly, Atanasoff, and a revolving set of onlookers spent hours in the basement of the physics building. The rest of the time, especially at home, Atanasoff and Mauchly talked incessantly about the machine—how it worked, what the principles behind it were, what Atanasoff's system consisted of. Mauchly seemed impressed—he car-ried the green-covered thirty-five-page description around with him and asked to borrow it and take it back to Pennsylvania. Atanasoff would not allow this, but he did allow Mauchly full access to it while he was in Ames and also allowed him to investigate the computer carefully with Clifford Berry. Sam Legvold, who was working in the next room on Atanasoff's defense project, later remembered that Mauchly had hands-on access to the ABC and even helped Berry do a few repairs—Legvold saw him touching parts and carrying parts around.

At one point, Mauchly also asked Lura for a stack of bond paper. Lura may originally have been offended by Mauchly's insensitivity as a houseguest, but she became alarmed by some of his other activities. Lura was a busy seamstress who often stayed up late sewing. She noticed that Mauchly was up late, too, because the light in his room was on, and she suspected that he was writing. She feared that he was not only taking an interest in the ABC but planning and working to steal her husband's ideas. While Mauchly was in Ames, she warned Atanasoff not to talk as freely and in such detail as she witnessed him doing, and Atanasoff acknowledged her caution. But he did allow Mauchly free access to the computer, and he did answer his questions. He later said that his impression at the time was that Mauchly had neither the background nor the knowledge that would make him capable of stealing the ideas, or understanding them well enough to be able to reproduce the ABC back in Philadelphia. For Atanasoff, the temptation to show off his invention was too great, certainly in part because even while the president of Iowa State was attempting to secure the future profits of the ABC, Atanasoff's colleagues there were almost universally either skeptical about or indifferent to what he was doing.

Subsequent controversy about whether Mauchly or Atanasoff should be given credit for the invention of the computer (or, to be precise, the invention of the calculating device that led to the invention of the computer) has revolved around the question of whether the ABC was operational at the time Mauchly visited Ames. Those who give the credit to Mauchly say that it was not. Those who give the credit to Atanasoff say that it was. But one thing that John Gustafson and his fellow reconstructors discovered when they built the replica and delved into the history of the ABC was that Atanasoff's friend in the statistics department, Professor George W. Snedecor, "would send problems over to Atanasoff and the ABC would solve them. Then the secretary, Clara Smith, would check the results on a desktop calculator. And they would be correct." The ABC was functional.

In the summer of 1941, Mauchly entered a course at the Moore School of Electrical Engineering at the University of Pennsylvania, a much more prestigious and well-connected institution than Ursinus College. The course was given at the behest of the Department of War and was designed as a cram course in electronics for young scientists in other fields. Mauchly, thirty-six, was hoping that he would learn some things that would move his weather project forward. It was there that he met his partner-to-be, J. Presper Eckert, age twenty-two, just graduated from the Moore School in engineering. Like Atanasoff, Berry, and Mauchly, Eckert had a long history of high-energy fiddling, but unlike the others, he was a child of privilege. His father was a Philadelphia developer who hobnobbed with such celebrities as Ty Cobb and Douglas Fairbanks, Jr. Young Eckert went to school—the William Penn Charter School—in a chauffeur-driven limousine. Father and son were both well traveled—Pres, as he was known, had already visited the Pyramids, among other exotic locales. At an amusement park in Paris, he got the idea for a project that won the Philadelphia Science Fair when he was twelve—a four-by-six-foot pond-like tub with magnets resting in the bottom. He steered a model sailboat across the surface of the water using a steering wheel connected to the magnets. He built radios and music systems and installed them around Philadelphia, including a system for a cemetery that, according to Scott McCartney, "masked the unnerving sound of gas burners in the nearby crematorium." His connections around Philadelphia gave him access to such innovative communications companies as Philco, RCA Victor, and others. He was a member of the Engineer's Club of Philadelphia and spent time with Philo T. Farnsworth, an inventor of the television who settled in Philadelphia in 1931.

In 1937, according to Scott McCartney in *ENIAC*, Pres Eckert scored second in the nation on his math SAT and was accepted to MIT, but his mother and father prevailed on him to stay home and go to the Wharton School. Within a few months, he transferred from Wharton to the Moore School, to study engineering. But he was not a good student—he did only what he wanted to do and occasionally fell asleep in class. According to McCartney, upon being awakened by the dean of the Moore School and asked, "If you're going to come to class, why can't you stay awake?" Eckert responded, "Why?" Every day, he wore a clean, pressed, monogrammed white linen shirt to class. After he graduated in the spring of 1941, Eckert joined the same ten-week cram course as Mauchly, and the two were assigned to be lab partners. Mauchly was the oldest student in the class, and one of two PhDs. Eckert was the youngest. At the end of the summer, Mauchly was hired away from Ursinus by the Moore School to teach physics, a replacement for other faculty who were leaving to join the war effort. According to McCartney, Mauchly's hiring was not a sign that the University of Pennsylvania was impressed by him or considered him promising, only that he was the only available candidate.

The other PhD in the course was Arthur W. Burks, originally from Duluth, Minnesota, whose PhD, from the University of Michigan, was in philosophy (though his BA was in physics and mathematics). He had completed his dissertation, "The Logical Foundations of the Philosophy of Charles Sanders Peirce," on a brilliant but troubled and even tragic contemporary of William James whose work is much better appreciated today (in part thanks to Burks) than it was during his own lifetime. In the summer of 1941, Burks was twenty-five. He was hired to teach at the Moore School that fall, like Mauchly. He eventually joined the ENIAC team (ENIAC stood for "Electronic Numerical Integrator and Computer"—Mauchly added "and Computer" after visiting Ames), and, like Mauchly, found a wife, Alice, among the women mathematicians who were computing firing tables. Alice had gotten her BA from Penn in 1944 in mathematics.

The teaching load at the University of Pennsylvania was lighter than that at Ursinus and left Mauchly time that he planned to use improving his Harmonic Analyzer. In October, he wrote Atanasoff, specifically asking, "Is there any objection, from your point of view, to my building some sort of computer which incorporates some of the features of your machine? For the time being, of course, I shall be lucky to find time and material to do more than make exploratory tests of some of my ideas, with the hope of getting something very speedy, not too costly, etc." Mauchly was also looking toward the future—he asked in the same letter whether "in the event that your present design were to hold the field against all challengers, and I got the Moore School interested in having something of the sort, would the way be open for us to build an 'Atanasoff Calculator' . . . here?" And he reported that Irven Travis, the man who had designed an analog "analyzer" on the model of the Bush-Caldwell Analyzer at the Moore School had entered the navy and departed. Mauchly was quite familiar with Travis's machine and had discussed it in depth with Travis. Travis later reported that he had discussed his variation on the Bush-Caldwell Analyzer with Pres Eckert when Eckert was his student. Before leaving for the navy, Travis had already considered the idea of building a computer on the scale of Aiken's at Harvard—he had done a study for General Electric that estimated the cost at about half a million dollars. GE did not want to spend that kind of money, but Travis did give Mauchly a bibliography of material about it. Atanasoff responded cautiously, more cautiously than he had acted in June. He wrote, "Our attorney has emphasized the need of being careful about the dissemination of information about our device until a patent application is filed. This should not require too long, and of course I have no qualms about having informed you about our device, but it does require that we refrain from making public any details for the time being." He went on to say that with these considerations in mind, he had refused an invitation to describe the machine at the meeting of the American Statistical Association.

By the summer and fall of 1941, Turing's work on the Bombe and the Enigma code (which the British referred to as "Ultra") had profoundly impressed his colleagues at Bletchley Park, and he had also impressed Winston Churchill. The code breakers had been successful: so many German supply ships were sunk in the late spring that the British authorities worried that they had handed the Germans irrefutable evidence that the cipher was broken. As Konrad Zuse had seen, though, the Germans simply decided that such a thing was impossible and continued using Enigma. After May, the work at Bletchley Park met with a few small obstacles, but by the autumn of 1941, the British were confident that they could decode any German naval communication, and if the British navy used their knowledge wisely, they could severely limit the vulnerability of British forces to German naval operations.

There was, however, another more complex encoding system that the Germans were working with, which the English decoders at Bletchley Park called "Tunny." When Alan Turing grew famous in the 1980s, almost all of the information concerning the importance of Tunny and its solution at Bletchley Park was still secret. These secrets were finally revealed in 2006 with the publication of *Colossus* by B. Jack Copeland and colleagues. While Enigma was used by the German navy, Tunny was used by the German High Command, including Adolf Hitler. After June 1941, Tunny was produced by a more complex encoding machine, the Lorenz *Schlüsselzusatz* ("Extra Keys"). The security surrounding the breaking of the Tunny codes at Bletchley Park would shape computer history but would remain top secret until the 1990s, long after the death of Alan Turing and long after most historians and students had come to what turns out to be a misunderstanding of the progress of World War II.

Certain details and images of Turing at Bletchley Park have remained a part of the cultural image of him—as recently as September 2009, in discussing the possibility for posthumous honors for Turing, Geoffrey Wansell referred in the *Daily Mail* to some of his well-known habits: "Notorious for his idiosyncrasies—he would tie his tea mug to the radiator so that no one else could use it, and ride his bicycle wearing a gas mask simply to avoid hay fever—Turing was, nevertheless, keen to 'fit in' . . . Despite his high-pitched voice and increasingly odd behaviour—he would sometimes run the 40 miles from Bletchley to London to attend meetings." Wansell points out, "Turing was critical to the war effort." In his spare time at Bletchley Park, Turing, like Zuse, was also thinking about chess, partly because the workforce at Bletchley played a lot of chess in off hours. As a result, Turing's imagination, which seems always to have had a philosophical bent, turned to another thought machine—one that would use probable outcomes to extrapolate the relative benefits of various chess moves. The idea was to create a machine that could simulate human decision making. He also thought about mathematical problems, saying, "Before the war, my work was in logic and my hobby was cryptanalysis, and now it is the other way round." In October 1941, right about the time that Mauchly was feeling out Atanasoff about whether he could use some of his ideas, Turing and a few of his colleagues were writing to Winston Churchill to request additional typists and other staff. In 1941, the war was going better than it had in 1940, partly because Hitler broke with Stalin and attacked the Soviet Union in late June of that year, giving himself only about three months to take the major Russian cities before the onset of winter—according to historian Andrew Roberts, if he had attacked two months earlier, as originally planned, he might have had a chance of prevailing. Germany did manage to take Kiev, Minsk, Kharkov, and Rostov, though just before Pearl Harbor they had to call off the attack on Moscow. The Allies were making progress in Africa, too, but at Bletchley Park, those working on the Enigma cipher were wondering about the Americans. They were certain that Roosevelt would enter the war fairly soon and were nervous about whether the secrets of their methods could be entrusted to the American navy. As it turned out, the Germans declared war against the United States on December 11, 1941. According to Turing's biographer Andrew Hodges, when British intelligence then attempted to share information derived from the operations at Bletchley Park about German U-boat locations in the Atlantic with the U.S. Navy—in particular, "the operation of fifteen U-boats off the American coast at the declaration of war"—the navy ignored the information, resulting in huge losses in the Atlantic at the same time the United States was deploying many vessels to the Pacific. The war in the Atlantic, which had been going well, suffered serious setbacks.

In Ames, the entry of the United States into World War II brought work on the ABC, particularly the electric spark card-marking mechanism, to a halt. Though Atanasoff and Berry felt that if they could find the right card stock, they could make the charring mechanism work, the start of the war in America made supplies and parts of all kinds scarce, and Atanasoff had to turn his full attention to his defense project. Berry had to turn his full attention to looking for a job in the defense industry—he was due to receive his master's degree in May. In their spare time, both men assembled and polished the information needed for the ABC patent application, which, Iowa State continued to assure Atanasoff, would be filed any day. In the summer of 1942, Berry married Atanasoff's secretary and departed to take a job in California. In September, Atanasoff himself left Iowa State for a job at the Naval Ordnance Laboratory in Washington, D.C., though he retained his full professor position at Iowa State with the plan of returning after the war. He had done well in Ames—his salary was $5,800 a year, more than twice his starting salary in 1930, which meant that his salary for defense projects would also be a high one. And he was convinced that between them, the patent attorney in Chicago and the administrators at Iowa State had the patenting of the ABC well in hand. The machine itself he left in the basement of the physics building.

Chapter Six

The John Vincent Atanasoff who worked at the Naval Ordnance Laboratory for the next seven years, through the war and then on several projects afterward, was the same man who had made his self-confident, energetic, innovative, and sometimes abrasive way through school, college, graduate school, and a successful teaching career. He worked unceasingly and impressed everyone who knew him, but he did not always fit smoothly into the navy's way of doing things, nor was he always happy at the way projects for the navy started and stopped according to what seemed to him to be whims on the part of the admirals in charge.

Lura and the children stayed behind in the house on Woodland Street in Ames—Atanasoff commuted throughout the war, a thirty-six-hour train trip each way on top of a weekly work schedule that could run as much as sixty hours. At first, he was put to work on developing mines and depth charges that would operate acoustically rather than magnetically. At the beginning of the war, especially in the Atlantic, mines were used that detected ships by sensing magnetic waves. When they then exploded, the shock wave of the explosion would damage the hull of the passing ship. These mines could be cleared or disarmed by minesweepers dragging electrical cables through an area and passing a large pulse of electric current through the cables, a method called the Double-L Sweep. The navy wanted a mine that could be triggered by the sound of a nearby propeller or the clanking of the metal plates of a ship's hull.

Atanasoff had never specialized in acoustics, but as always, he mastered the material with a few months of intensive reading, and soon he was in charge of the entire acoustics division at the NOL, supervising about a hundred men. He directed projects on the acoustical properties of explosives, acoustical detection, acoustical location, and numerous other topics. He was so inventive that he was later cited for, among other things, "his unusual imagination and exceptional mechanical ingenuity, his enthusiasm and indefatigable energy and zeal." Part of his citation might have easily described the invention of the computer: he "has succeeded in conceiving of the solution to an urgent military problem which had been considered insoluble. Having conceived of the answer to the problem, he saw it through design, production, and test to the final timely adoption despite almost insurmountable obstacles." Some of the men Atanasoff hired he knew from Ames—almost all research not related to the war effort had been shut down by mid-1942, so there was a large talent pool to draw from. In the midst of all of this, he still had time for hobbies, one of which was a comparative study of alphabets. On his visits to Ames, he tried to keep track of the progress of the patent application for the ABC, but his efforts proved frustrating—he was never able to find out exactly what the college was doing about the patent or to persuade them to move more quickly.

Atanasoff's desk was in the Naval Gun Factory—it is an index of his powers of concentration that he got so much work done in the midst of a constant din. Atanasoff held a very high security clearance, so one day in the late spring of 1943, he was surprised to look up and see John Mauchly standing in front of him. Mauchly sat down and lit a cigarette, and, as far as Atanasoff was concerned, they had a pleasant conversation in which they first discussed what they had been doing since they'd last met almost two years before.

Mauchly had a lot to tell. He had become involved in a project at the Moore School, calculating trajectories for aiming large pieces of artillery. The proper aiming of a cannon had to take into account all sorts of factors: the elevation of the cannon and the elevation of the target, wind speed, wind direction, air temperature, humidity, and numerous others things. The variables were organized into firing tables, which were calculated by women employed by the Moore School working on Monroe calculators, but, as with Atanasoff's calculations for the dielectric constant of helium, the calculations were tedious and time-consuming—the army was inventing and producing weapons faster than they could be put to use. At the Aberdeen Proving Ground, the Bush Differential Analyzer—the analog machine based on Babbage's Differential Analyzer and invented by Vannevar Bush, the man who was now the head of National Defense Research Committee—was making some headway on the necessary calculations, but the Bush Analyzer could only solve differential equations with up to eighteen variables. Mauchly was aware of the army's problem and now told Atanasoff about his new colleague, Eckert. He explained that the two of them were attempting to devise a machine that the army could use to make the necessary firing-table calculations.

Mauchly had submitted two proposals. The first, seven pages entitled "The Use of High-Speed Vacuum Tubes for Calculation," was submitted in August 1941 and described "an electronic device operating solely on the principle of counting." He suggested that it would do the same jobs as analog machines, but do them more quickly. The army authorities in charge of research at the University of Pennsylvania apparently did not understand what he was getting at and also did not consider him a serious contender for research funding—one man, Carl Chambers, is quoted by Scott McCartney as saying, "None of us had much confidence in Mauchly at that time"—a sentiment Atanasoff would have agreed with.

The pivotal figure in Mauchly's career was a twenty-eight-year-old lieutenant, Herman Goldstine, who happened to have a Phi Beta Kappa BA in mathematics and a PhD in ballistics from the University of Chicago. Before being drafted into the army, he had taught at the

University of Michigan. Once he was drafted, a former professor found him a position at the Aberdeen Proving Ground. Goldstine was put in charge of the firing tables. When he took over, each table took a month to produce. Goldstine's first thought was to hire more women to do the computations, but when his wife, Adele, also a mathematician, set out to find more female math students (female math students could do the calculations and were not as essential to actual combat operations), she could find only a few. The Bush Analyzer was too slow and hard to maintain in working order. It was Goldstine who heard of Mauchly and his idea, and Goldstine who found Mauchly and asked him about it.

But neither Mauchly nor John Grist Brainerd, the Moore School's liaison with the army, could find a copy of Mauchly's seven-page proposal, now eight months old. At Goldstine's behest, Mauchly, Brainerd, and Brainerd's secretary put together as good a new proposal as they could come up with and took it to Aberdeen.

A major Allied setback that was not understood until after the war was the fact that the Germans also managed to crack English codes, specifically the code that routed convoys, Naval Cipher No. 3. Even though they did not have the benefit of a machine like the Bombe to do so in real time, they could often figure out the "size, destinations, and departure times," according to Andrew Roberts, but "instead of recognizing the danger, the Admiralty put the U-boats' remarkable success in intercepting convoys down to the advanced hydrophone equipment they used . . . Naval Cipher Code No. 3 was not replaced with No. 5, which the Germans never cracked, until June 1943." The spring of 1943 saw the sinking, between March 16 and March 20, of twenty-seven Allied ships on their way from New York to Liverpool; 360 seamen died in the battle. Captain H. Bonatz, of the Beobachtungsdienst, a German naval code-breaking organization, later recalled, "The Admiral at Halifax, Nova Scotia, was a big help to us. He sent out a Daily Situation Report which reached us every evening, and it always began 'Addressees, Situation, Date.'" The rote repetition of the first words of the communication enabled the Germans to break the English codes every day in the same way that the repeated three-letter signal had helped the Enigma decoders. At Bletchley Park, the decoders could tell by what they were decoding that the Germans had access to Allied coded information. But code breaking in Germany was fragmented among various services and commands—there was never a well-funded center for deciphering Allied messages like Bletchley Park.

Turing, at this time, was in the United States. He spent a while at Bell Labs, working on a method for enciphering speech, where he discussed his paper "On Computable Numbers" with Claude Shannon. Shannon, himself a graduate of MIT, had written his master's thesis in 1937 on using relay switches to solve Boolean algebra problems. He also had the insight, like Atanasoff, that the binary arithmetic that relay switches represented would simplify information systems. His master's thesis, written when he was twenty-one and published when he was twenty-two, is considered to be one of the most important, if not the most important, master's thesis of the twentieth century. Shannon had studied neurology, too. According to Hodges, when Turing and Shannon shared their ideas about "thinking machines" in March 1943, "they found their outlook to be the same: there was nothing sacred about the brain, and if a machine could do as well as the brain, then it *would* be thinking—although neither proposed any particular way in which this might be achieved." At the end of March, Turing returned to England on *The Empress of Scotland.*

It was in this context that Mauchly submitted his second proposal to Goldstine and Goldstine sought authorization from the army to fund the project—conditions seemed dire and the army was desperate enough to grant $61,700 (the equivalent of $750,000 in 2010 dollars) to Mauchly and Eckert.

According to McCartney, Mauchly and Eckert discussed their ideas casually—sitting around the Moore School and spending time drawing on napkins in a restaurant nearby. "A machine could be designed to do nothing but count the pulses of electrons, with the pulses representing numbers, and to crunch numbers in different ways to solve different problems. Instead of moving gears and wheels in a conventional calculating machine, Mauchly thought he could build a machine with no moving parts: only the electrons would course through the machine." Eckert agreed with and was inspired by the idea of electronic calculation—he had already devised a method of calculating smokestack emissions that sent a beam of light through a cloud of emissions. The amount of light that got through was then measured, giving a reading on the density of the emissions. There is no evidence that Mauchly and Eckert kept a record of their deliberations or that they elaborated on the theory behind the ideas that they passed back and forth between their meeting in June 1941 and the submission of the first proposal in August 1942.

It was with his authorization in his possession that Mauchly came to visit Atanasoff at the gun factory in April 1943, but he said nothing about it. After chatting amiably for a while, he did ask Atanasoff a few questions about the ABC and about Atanasoff's computer design ideas. Atanasoff, still underestimating Mauchly in several ways, was as forthcoming as he had been before. He felt, after all, that he and Mauchly were friends and that they were on good terms. He also had few opportunities to discuss his passion for electronic calculation. It was only later, after thinking about their meeting, that Atanasoff wondered how Mauchly had gotten security clearance to visit him—to just show up. Though he asked around, he never got an answer to this question more satisfactory than the vague supposition that possibly Mauchly had connections, since his father was a Washington, D.C., scientific eminence.

After the first visit, Mauchly stopped by off and on, always chatting in a friendly way about personal matters before asking a few specific computer questions. At one meeting, he asked about the progress Iowa State was making toward patenting the ABC, but Atanasoff couldn't answer that question with any certainty—he was working so hard at the NOL that he had neither the time nor the energy to keep after the college. Nor could Atanasoff say that he had kept on top of recent developments in computing—he was simply too busy. It seems clear from these conversations that Mauchly was using his access to Atanasoff both to probe him and to gauge whether the computer he was developing with

Eckert might turn out to be profitable. The visits went on for three years.

Frugality was never a feature of ENIAC, which began to take shape in a large unused room at the Moore School in July 1943. At first the engineering team numbered twelve—Goldstine, Eckert, and Mauchly oversaw the general design (with Eckert in charge). Other members of the team were put in charge of individual components and, since the army was in desperate need of the firing tables, the Moore School team worked with seven-day-a-week dedication. Eckert's most controversial decision was to use vacuum tubes—at first five thousand, a number that grew to eighteen thousand (in part because the army, in its desperation, pushed Goldstine to expand the capacity of the machine). Such a number was unheard of, not only because vacuum tubes themselves were considered unreliable, but also because wiring so many together would amplify the malfunction of any single one. But Eckert was determined to use the tubes and decided to make them less prone to burning out by obtaining only the best tubes and then operating them at a much lower voltage than recommended, as well as never turning the machine completely off—the current could be reduced to a trickle to keep the tubes warm and to guard against the potential danger of thermal shock.

Eckert was dedicated to testing every part. According to Scott McCartney, in order to choose his wiring, "Eckert acquired some mice in cages and starved them for a few days. Then he put different kinds of wire in their cages to see which kind they enjoyed eating. The least appetizing brand was used in ENIAC."

Eckert and Mauchly also decided to use a decimal counting system, sort of an electronic version of the Monroe calculator—if the number 345,679 was entered into the calculator, the counter in the ones column would flash nine times, the counter in the tens column seven times, the counter in the hundred column six times, and so on. But the tubes were much faster, of course, than a person tapping a calculator—a number would register in two millionths of a second. The advantages of speed were balanced by the dangers of unreliability, and so the machine, which was huge, had to have repairability built into it—it was so important that every tube be accessible in case it burned out that the machine was designed in discrete units with doors that opened into the mesh of wiring and tubes, and it took so much power to run the machine that Eckert had to include safety switches on every door to prevent electrocution. In addition, because the machine was decimally based, it could only add and subtract, not multiply, but Eckert's idea was that it would be so fast that a binary number system would not improve overall performance and would require an extra piece of input-output hardware.

Like Zuse, Goldstine found help where he could—moonlighting telephone workers assisted with the wiring, Bell Labs supplied telephone parts and help with those parts, IBM designed a card reader for input and output. Goldstine, Mauchly, and Eckert seemed to work together quite well—Mauchly came up with the ideas but was considered by the others to be easily distracted. Eckert followed through, realizing the ideas in the machine and making sure that his designs were properly executed—he was noted for his perfectionism (and appreciated, in light of the expense and the danger of what he was putting together). Goldstine found the money, organized the personnel, and was the liaison with the army. He got along well with Eckert, but not well with Mauchly, who seemed like "a space case" to him. Eckert, it was clear to everyone, depended on Mauchly, but no one knew exactly why, even Mauchly. Since Mauchly was teaching at the same time, he wasn't present at the building site as much as the others were. In 1944, when his teaching load was cut back so that he could work full time on ENIAC, his salary was cut from $5,800 to $3,900, leading to even more anxiety on his part. But he still felt that the project was his because he had originated it. It was at this point that he applied for a part-time job at the NOL, in the statistics department, and used Atanasoff as a reference. Atanasoff later said that he gave Mauchly a good recommendation more out of friendship than out of faith in his talents or expertise, but Mauchly got hired.

Mauchly mentioned his machine the first time in early 1944 — according to Tammara Burton, "He looked Atanasoff in the eye and told him that he was building a new computer. The new computer, Mauchly claimed, isn't 'anything like your machine'; but is 'better than your machine.'" When Atanasoff had asked about the new computer, Mauchly put him off, saying that it was top secret. Though Atanasoff's security clearance was higher than Mauchly's, Atanasoff knew he would not get anywhere by pressuring the other man. Atanasoff still believed at this point that Iowa State was likely to have filed the patent application. He knew that he himself would not have stolen another man's ideas, so he didn't suspect Mauchly — indeed, Mauchly assured him that the principles behind the ENIAC were entirely different from those behind the ABC. A few months later, in August 1944, Atanasoff met J. Presper Eckert for the first and only time, when Mauchly brought him to the gun factory in search of help with quartz transducers. Since Eckert did not have a high security clearance, the two men had to have a military escort, so the visit was brief and unrevealing. Although Atanasoff had agreed to help with the quartz transducers, he didn't see Mauchly again. It was only later that it occurred to him that quartz transducers could be used in a computer to regenerate memory.

When it was completed, ENIAC was huge. It weighed twenty-seven tons, was eight feet long, eight feet high, and three feet deep. In addition to the 18,000 vacuum tubes, there were 7,200 diodes, 1,500 relays, 70,000 resistors, and 10,000 capacitors for memory storage. It required 150 kilowatts of power, the equivalent of 1,500 100-watt lightbulbs. Because of potential failure of the vacuum tubes, the machine was rarely turned off, but it did malfunction — Eckert said in 1989, "We had a tube fail about every two days and we could locate the problem within 15 minutes." ENIAC was not a programmable computer — its switches had to be set and it had to be wired to perform its task; if the task changed, it had to be rewired and the switches reset. This could take weeks. The fact that ENIAC was not programmable was a by-product of the speed with which it was built. In his 1943 progress report, Brainerd rejected the added complexity such a feature would introduce—like Atanasoff, he didn't want to fall into the trap Babbage had fallen into.

As the war progressed in Germany, Konrad Zuse continued to exercise his special genius, which was not just working hard on innovations to his machine, but also making and using all sorts of social connections to circumvent the increasing difficulties of finding materials and developing new ideas. As he began putting together the Z4, he cultivated acquaintances at the telephone exchange who had managed to avoid being drafted into the armed forces by making themselves appear more essential to the operation of German communications systems than they actually were. These "young, energetic, and enthusiastic" friends had access to junk bins, where over and over they turned up parts that Zuse could make use of. And Zuse's own day job contributed to his understanding of what a computer might do—at one point, he devised a machine for Henschel that calculated optimum wing dimensions for innovative aircraft, a machine that worked fairly reliably for two years. This machine led to another machine designed to "mechanize dial gauge reading." Although this machine was completed, Zuse had to abandon it almost as soon as he constructed it—he never learned whether it was blown up at the end of the war, or whether the Russian forces captured it. He writes, "Even as I was putting it together, the order came to dismantle the just-completed factory . . . But I went on working like a madman, driven solely by the ambition to see this interesting machine actually work at least once. Finally, it was created—the first process controlled computer. Even if not a single person had been interested, I had the pleasure of solving a difficult problem once again."

Zuse and his colleagues began on the Z4 in 1942, building the machine in Berlin in the midst of air raids and fire bombings. On one occasion, Zuse was climbing the stairs in his office building and had just come to a landing when he heard "a crackling sound overhead." As soon as he ducked into a nearby doorway, the staircase crumbled away. He managed to get down to the cellar and attempted to put out fires with a portable fire extinguisher, but the building burned to the ground anyway. All told, the Z4 had to be moved three times within the city limits of Berlin during the war. Even as Zuse persisted, he writes, "I didn't always reach the cellar in time" to find safety—sometimes the air raid warnings would sound at just the time he was ready to test some function. But Zuse was dedicated—when he writes about building the Z4 during the war, he suggests that he was more fearful of the computer not functioning than he was of more mortal outcomes:

> So, of course, when after weeks or months of work, I know
> that the time has come for the device to perform without a
> hitch, then the moment when the start button is to be pressed
> is especially tense. I always had a pronounced fear of such
> moments . . . It takes good nerves to withstand something like
> this for years on end.

Zuse was not entirely cut off from the outside world, but communication channels were idiosyncratic. At one point, Zuse's bookkeeper told his own daughter about what Zuse was inventing. The daughter, who worked for German intelligence, responded by reporting that a similar machine was being developed in the United States. Zuse concocted the ruse of sending two assistants to the intelligence offices, where they presented what looked like an official document from the Air Ministry, asking to see the information. They were turned down, but since they had been told which drawer the photo was in, they managed to find it and bring it back to Zuse. The photo was of Howard Aiken's Mark I. Zuse could not infer many technical details from the photo, but he became further convinced that computer development would have many, many applications in the postwar world. Unfortunately, in Germany, "hardly anyone could imagine commercial applications for our machines. Civilian production would also have been out of the question; it was officially forbidden."

But Aiken's Mark I, a machine that looked sleek and elegant (and huge) in the photograph Zuse saw, had a history in some ways as troubled as any of the other machines. Like most of the other scientists working on computers, Aiken joined the war effort (the Naval Reserve) once his PhD was completed. When IBM began building the Mark I (and, subsequently, Mark II–IV), IBM engineers began modifying Aiken's design. The result was that Aiken became less and less involved with the final design features—the machine was taken over by the institutions that financed it. As the computer approached completion, IBM and Harvard made elaborate plans to unveil it in a joint ceremony. IBM, having spent half a million dollars ($6 million in 2010 dollars) building the machine, was eager to fully share the credit for its design and implementation. Aiken, however, seems to have done something—possibly contacting the press—that shifted the emphasis away from IBM and toward Harvard. Thomas J. Watson, Jr., later said, "If Aiken and my father had had revolvers they would both have been dead." Hard feelings lingered for years afterward.

Alan Turing is now a famous man—the subject of biographies, papers, an opera, and at least one play, but his work at Bletchley Park breaking the Enigma code did not come to light until the 1970s, and then, at first, only by means of popular books that did not actually mention him, or mentioned him in cryptic ways (F. W. Winterbotham, *The Ultra Secret*, 1974; A. Cave Brown, *Bodyguard of Lies*, 1975), or in specialized publications that did mention him directly (Brian Randell, "On Alan Turing and the Origins of Digital Computers," 1972; Brian Randell, editor, *The Origins of Digital Computers: Selected Papers*, 1973). Various accounts culminated in an episode about Turing and Enigma in a 1977 BBC series called *The Secret War* (other episodes concerned radio beams, radar, magnetic mines, and the V-1 and V-2, prototype German cruise missiles). Turing's genius then captured the popular imagination, but so did his life, which was idiosyncratic, dramatic, and tragically short—he was not only a genius full of charming eccentricities and in some ways a paradigmatic Englishman, he was also an unashamed homosexual. Andrew Hodges, Oxford mathematician and gay activist, published his dense biography of Turing in 1983, which focused equally on Turing's life and on his work. But there was much more going on at Bletchley Park between 1941 and 1944 than the cracking of the Enigma code.

The essential difference between Enigma messages communicated to German ships and Tunny messages was that Enigma messages were hand encoded, then communicated by radio broadcast, then hand decoded, while Tunny messages, also communicated by radio broadcast, were machine encoded and decoded, therefore not as subject to the human errors that allowed the English decoders to break the Enigma. The Tunny messages were also much more complex. The German army set up a radio network between Ukraine in the east, Brittany in the west, Tunis in the south, and Oslo in the north. Some stations were fixed, but most consisted of two equipment-carrying trucks, one with a sending Lorenz machine, a receiving Lorenz machine, and a teleprinter, the other with radio equipment.

Although in the early 1980s Tommy Flowers was given permission to describe the workings of the code-breaking machine named Colossus that he and his team of engineers built at top speed in 1943, he was forbidden to say what the machine had done or how it had been used in the war. It was only toward the very end of Flowers's life, when the United States declassified some communications by American liaisons at Bletchley Park that mentioned Colossus and described its function, that the importance of the machines began to emerge (there were ten of them, the first Mark I that Flowers designed and built in 1943, and the nine Mark 2s that were larger and faster, built in 1944). In 2000, the British government finally declassified a long report on Colossus, written by code breakers in 1945, that revealed not only the complexity of Colossus but also its importance—and it was dramatically important.

The job of the Colossus team was the same as that of the Bombe builders—to infer by means of technical and theoretical deduction what the mechanical Lorenz encoding machines were doing and how they worked, and then to build a machine that mirrored that structure. In a teleprinter machine, upon which the Lorenz was based, a long strip of paper about an inch and a half wide passed through a slot the way a piece of paper passes over the roller of a typewriter, short end first. It was advanced by means of a line of tiny sprocket holes about three-fifths of the way between the left edge and the right edge. The pattern of holes standing for each letter of the alphabet and other essential characters according to the Baudot-Murray code, which had been invented by Emile Baudot in 1870, ran across the strip, three holes to the left of the sprocket holes and two holes to the right. The five positions in each row, some punched and some unpunched, represented a letter of the alphabet. For example, the letter M was represented as hole/hole/hole/no/no (or x x x . .) while the letter N was no/hole/hole/no/no (or .x x . .). A message communicated by a normal teleprinter (or teletype machine, as it was called in the United States) consisted of a long blank strip of paper to indicate that a message was beginning, followed by a strip riddled with lines of holes, the length of which depended on the message, which was followed by another empty strip that indicated the end of the message. Since every letter consisted of five positions (hole or no), a six-letter word, such as "letter." would consist of six lines. The words of the message ran down the strip: the word "colossus" would have looked like this:

. X X X .

X X . . .

X . . X .

X X . . .

. . X . X

. . X . X

. . X X X

. . X . X

Obviously, such a way of representing letters is time-consuming to generate by hand but easy by machine, easier than Morse code because the machine can punch an entire line at one time.

The job of the Lorenz machine was to take the principle of teletyping and encode the message so that it would be indecipherable except by the target Lorenz machine set to the same key as the originating machine. Since a teletype machine is based on the binary principle that a letter consists of five positions, some of which are punched ("1") and some of which are not punched ("0"), then the machine used a binary arithmetical process to create the code. In *Colossus*, Jack Copeland calls this "the Tunny Addition Square" (appendix 3). The letters and symbols in the coded message were passed through the machine and "added" to letters in what was called the "keystream," or the entirely different order of letters and symbols produced by the machine. The rules of addition were that $0 + 0 = 0$, $1 + 1 = 0$, $0 + 1 = 1$, and $1 + 0 = 1$ (note that this addition square is like Boolean algebra, but the values assigned to the results are specific to the rules of the Lorenz machine — it was not a mathematical machine and was not designed to solve math problems). The products of the addition of the coded letters to the keystream letters were systematic, and because the system was binary, if the Tunny receiving machine was set to the same keystream, all it had to do was take the coded message and add the letters and symbols of the keystream to the coded message, and the original message was retrieved. The Tunny Addition Square has 1,024 possible results (just like a base-ten multiplication table has 100 possible results). The more levels or "wheels" the machine employed, the more shifts were possible, and the German encoders employed the twelve wheels of the Lorenz machine in different ways, all of which were organized by headquarters. What the English eavesdroppers soon realized was that part of decoding the message was getting hold of the key (often transmitted between operators by hand) and using it to sift through the messages (transmitted by machine). However, what Turing understood was that with twelve different wheels, the number of possible variations was more enormous than human decoders could manage. Wheels 1–5 operated together (the code breakers called these the "psi" wheels after the second-to-last letter of the Greek alphabet). Wheels 8–12 also operated together (the "chi" wheels, after the third-to-last letter of the Greek alphabet). Wheels 6 and 7 were called the "motor" wheels. Each wheel had a number of positions—wheel 1 had forty-two positions, wheel 2 had forty-seven positions, for example. The job of the code breakers at Bletchley Park was to decipher the patterns in each set of teleprinted letters so that each shift of each wheel could be peeled away to reveal the original message. Intercepted encoded paper tapes were the raw material that Colossus had to process. Uncovering the shift pattern of one of the encoding wheels of the Lorenz machine was the key—once the position of the first wheel was ascertained, the positions of the next wheels became progressively easier to ascertain through Boolean logic. But while Enigma had three wheels, and then four, which was difficult enough, the Lorenz machine's twelve wheels hugely enlarged the number of possibilities that had to be tested. And though sometimes with Enigma, the German operators encoding and sending the messages made mistakes that gave away the pattern, the mechanization of the Lorenz encoding process gave rise to fewer human errors, which was a large part of the reason Tunny was more difficult to decode.

In order to gain some idea of the work Colossus had to do, let's imagine a message of five hundred holes and spaces representing one hundred letters (a very short message). It was the job of German intelligence officers to designate the positions and of the Lorenz operators to set the positions. Until the summer of 1944, the position of the psi wheels was set monthly and the chi wheels quarterly, then monthly. The motor wheels were set daily. As the war heated up in 1944, the positions of all the wheels changed daily.

The Dollis Hill communications research laboratories were located about eight miles northwest of central London, in an area that had originally been farms, then the estate of a politician who was a friend of William Gladstone and who had served as governor-general of Canada and lord lieutenant of Ireland. As close as it was to central London, the area retained its rustic feel into the twentieth century. But by the First

World War, the team designing the Liberty tank, Mark VIII, was based there, and in 1921 the English government established the Post Office Research Station there. By 1933, a large brick factory and offices had been built, and at the beginning of World War II an underground bunker called Paddock was installed (though Churchill didn't like it and wouldn't stay there). The parts of the Colossus were shipped to Bletchley Park (about an hour's drive farther northwest) and assembled there.

It was Tommy Flowers who conceived and built Colossus at Dollis Hill, where he had worked since 1926. Even though because of his prewar vacuum-tube experiment Flowers knew how much faster the tubes were at such work, in 1943 he could not at first persuade the authorities at Bletchley Park to try the new technology. He decided to construct a prototype on his own, commandeering a post office factory in Birmingham to make the parts. He had a sixteen-hundred-tube processor by the end of 1943 but saw immediately that though it worked, it was not fast enough, and he began on an improved version in February 1944. He was told that the machine had to be installed at Bletchley and functioning by the first of June, the planned date for the invasion of Normandy by the Allied forces. He succeeded. According to Jack Copeland, "Despite the fact that no such machine had previously been attempted, the computer was in working order almost straight away and ready to begin its fast-paced attack on the German messages." Not long before he died, Flowers did write enough about the history, the purpose, and the features of Colossus so that we may understand its main features:

> Colossus was a special-purpose machine designed primarily to perform processes devised by Bletchley Park for discovering the settings of the code wheels made by the [German] machine operators before the messages were sent. Much of the Colossus was an electronic analogue of the Lorenz Tunny machine. Bletchley Park also eventually found ways of using the machine to discover the Tunny wheel patterns when they were routinely changed. (Colossus did not itself decode intercepted messages.

This was done by other machines, specially modified teleprint-
ers, also known as Tunny machines.)

The Colossus operated on two data streams simultaneously—one was
the strip of paper from the teleprinter, carrying the message, and the
other was a data stream that mimicked various wheel combinations
that a Lorenz machine would use. The strip of paper carrying the hole
pattern that was the message was made into a loop, then the loop was
passed over and over through a photoelectric reader that registered hole
or no—each recognition registered as an electric impulse to the logic
unit (the "processor"—the part of the machine that eventually would
be made up of 2,400 vacuum tubes). Each pass of the loop through the
scanner included a blank section that defined the beginning and the
end of the message. The tape passed through the scanner over and over
"until every possible combination of digits" that appeared at the beginning of the message had been read—once the beginning of the message had been worked out, the rest of the message could be decoded.
The electric impulses that passed through the holes in the tape registered on a counter; the code breakers soon discovered that a scan
that did not reveal a message always contained fewer impulses than
a scan that revealed a message—that is, the word "colossus" contains
eight letters, and so, eight lines of holes and nos; in "colossus," there
are eighteen holes versus twenty-two nos. No eight-letter word could
contain, say, three holes and thirty-seven nos. According to probability,
every eight-letter word had to contain more than a certain number of
holes, so Colossus was set to throw out results that contained fewer
than that number. Colossus allowed the code breakers to concentrate
on only the strips of letters that were more likely to resolve into the
actual message.

One flaw in the Lorenz machine, as a system of rings, was that somewhere in every message was a spot where the wheels returned to the
start position. This meant that the encoding, though large and complex, was not perfectly random. Since the machine that the Germans
were using was made of wheels and gears, it, according to Flowers,

"generated and processed numbers" rather slowly—five every second. Colossus, because of the vacuum tubes, was a thousand times faster, its speed limited by the passing of the paper strip through the reader, not by the speed of the vacuum tubes. Since the Colossus was essentially a sorter, Flowers wanted it to sort as quickly as possible—and five thousand times per second was not fast enough, so a shift register was invented that read, counted, and kept track of five different readings of the holes each time the tape was passed through the machine. Colossus read and counted the holes so quickly that the code breakers could usually narrow in on the telling spot fairly quickly. Once they had done that, the pattern of the code was revealed, and the message could be broken. Colossus also had a mechanism for detecting and discounting spots where a message might have been incorrectly received.

D-Day was set for June 1, 1944, but as it happened, the invasion was postponed because of the difficulty of moving troops and materials in bad weather. According to Andrew Roberts, when the chief meteorological officer, James Stagg, was handed the list of weather requirements that suited each faction of the invasion force, he said, "When I came to put them together I found that they might have to sit around for 120 to 150 years before they got the operation launched." But there were concerns other than weather—principally the question of what the Germans thought the Allies were planning. On June 5, Eisenhower was interrupted in a staff meeting by a courier bringing the first Colossus-decoded German communication from Bletchley Park. Flowers writes, "Hitler had sent Field Marshall Rommel battle orders by radio transmission, which Bletchley Park had decoded with the aid of the new Colossus. Hitler had told Rommel that the invasion of Normandy was imminent, but that this would not be the real invasion. It was a feint to draw the troops away from the channel ports, against which the real invasion would be launched later. Rommel was not to move any troops. Eisenhower read the paper silently, then announced, 'We go tomorrow.' And on the morrow, 6 June, they went."

With the help of Colossus, the decoders at Bletchley Park then decoded Hitler's subsequent messages to his armed forces and preempted his attempt to foil the invasion. According to Flowers, "The result was a defeat of the German Army so overwhelming that the Allies were able to sweep rapidly eastwards across France." According to Roberts, Eisenhower also remarked to his staff, "I hope to God I know what I'm doing." But Allied intelligence and counterintelligence worked so well that "even up to 26 June half a million troops of the German Fifteenth Army stayed stationed around the Pas de Calais, guarding against an invasion that would not come."

Flowers felt that he was the pivotal man in the success of Colossus because of his familiarity with vacuum tubes. He writes, "If I had . . . spent the war interned in Germany, Colossus would not have been built, because there would have been no one at Dollis Hill with sufficient knowledge of the new technology to make it. If Dollis Hill had not made Colossus, some other organization may have made something similar, but we now know that none could have done so by D-Day. Those chance events changed the course of the Second World War. If they had not, history would now record the devastation of Europe and a death toll much greater than actually occurred." One key feature of Colossus's success was that Flowers, like Eckert, realized that the vacuum tubes, which were seen as unreliable when he first began to use them, were much more likely to fail at the moment of thermal shock when being turned on. For the fifteen months that Colossus was at work, a machine was only turned off if it was malfunctioning.

Flowers and his fellow inventors were not only proud of their machine, they were thrilled by it. The engineers who authored the report on Colossus at the end of the war (the report that was declassified in 2000) wrote:

> It is regretted that it is not possible to give an adequate idea of the fascination of a Colossus at work; its sheer bulk and apparent complexity; the fantastic speed of thin paper tape round the glittering pulleys; the childish pleasure of not-not [sic], span, print main header and other gadgets; the wizardry of purely mechanical decoding letter by letter (one novice thought she was being

hoaxed); the uncanny action of the typewriter in printing the correct scores without and beyond human aid; the stepping of the display; periods of eager expectation culminating in the sudden appearance of the longed-for score; and the strange rhythms characterizing every type of run: the stately break-in, the erratic short run, the regularity of wheel-breaking, the stolid rectangle interrupted by the wild leaps of the carriage-return, the frantic chatter of a motor run, even the ludicrous frenzy of hosts of bogus scores.

Flowers invented Colossus, but he also gave credit to Alan Turing for his contribution. At a conference in 1980, Flowers saw a young man reading the book that grew out of the BBC series *The Secret War*. The two struck up a conversation, and Flowers recalled, "You'd be working on a problem and not able to solve it, and sometimes someone would look over your shoulder and say, 'Have you tried doing it like this?' and you'd think, 'Of course, that's how you do it!' With Turing, he'd say 'Have you tried doing it this way?' and you'd know that in a hundred years you would never have thought of doing it that way. And that was the difference."

In the course of the eleven months between D-Day and the German surrender in May 1945, the General Post Office built and the intelligence services made use of ten Colossus machines. According to Flowers's obituary by Alan Blannin in the *Daily Telegraph*, "At the end of the war, all but two of the Colossus machines were destroyed. Flowers was ordered to destroy all evidence that they had ever existed. The two surviving machines were taken first to Eastcote, west London, the first home of the new Government Communications Headquarters, and then to its present base at Cheltenham, where a Colossus was still operational in the early 1960s." Flowers, however, did not have access to them.

The code breakers at Bletchley, even with ten Colossus machines, did not break every message, but the Germans did not expect them to be able to break *any* messages, and so they continued to use the Lorenz machine for high-level army communication even after they should have deduced from the failure of certain operations that something was wrong—in fact, Thomas Flowers worried about being too successful and thereby undoing all of his own work. There were other machines and other methods of encoding that the Germans used and the English did not break, but since the Germans chose to use the Lorenz machine for army communications at a time when the war was an army war across France and into Germany, Colossus was, in the eyes of its creators and others, the key to victory. It was this euphoria that led Thomas Flowers to accept the destruction of the Colossus machines and the ban on discussing either how the machines worked or what they had done between June 1944 and May 1945. The obituary in the *Telegraph* pointed out a further irony: "Flowers received very little remuneration from the government for his invention . . . barely sufficient to pay off the debts that he had run up while developing Colossus." According to most sources his insufficient remuneration amounted to about £1,000 (some $40,000 in 2010 dollars, or about five times what Atanasoff had been granted for the development of the ABC).

Chapter Seven

With his family in Iowa, Atanasoff's work in Washington was not favorable to his marriage, and then, in 1944, his daughter Elsie's asthma took such a turn for the worse that it seemed essential that she be taken from Ames and moved to a more healthful climate. Atanasoff suggested Florida, which had worked for his father and siblings forty years earlier. Lura sold the house, packed up the children, and moved to Miami, but the move was not a success—Elsie did not improve, and marital relations did not improve. After living in Miami for about a year, Lura packed up the children again and drove west, looking for a livable climate for her seventeen-year-old daughter. By this time, the war was coming to a close and Atanasoff had to choose whether to return to Iowa State. He considered that his defense work was both essential to the war effort and well paid—he was making about $10,000 a year in salary (the equivalent of about $125,000 in 2010 dollars). His pay grade was above the congressional pay grade because his work was so productive. And his work fascinated him—always a prime consideration for Atanasoff. And then the navy asked him to develop a computer for them, a project that he of course could not resist. Lura and the children ended up settling in Boulder, Colorado, beautiful and neither hot nor humid. Elsie seemed to benefit, and Lura, inspired by the local scenery and by the colors of the native American art that she saw there, rediscovered her long-standing interest in painting. She set up her easel and was soon selling her work in local galleries. But Boulder, Colorado, was much farther from Washington, D.C., even than Ames, Iowa; the Atanasoffs drifted apart.

It was at this time that Atanasoff made the acquaintance of perhaps the most mysterious but also the most famous contributor to the invention of the computer, mathematician John von Neumann. Von Neumann was a personable and charming man (even his biographer calls him "Johnny"). He would show up in the Naval Ordnance Laboratory to chat, and Atanasoff seemed to hit it off with him. Indeed, they had more than a few things in common. They were almost exactly the same age—von Neumann having been born at the end of December in the same year that Atanasoff was born at the beginning of October. Von Neumann's father, Max, only a few years older than Atanasoff's father, had moved from the small town of Pecs in Hungary to the cosmopolitan city of Budapest around the same time that Ivan Atanasoff had departed Bulgaria for the cosmopolitan city of New York. Just as the elder Atanasoff had married into the long-established Purdy family in upstate New York, Max von Neumann had married into a wealthy and established Jewish family in Pest. Both Atanasoff and von Neumann (whose name as a boy in Hungary was Neumann János Lajos) had been voracious students and enterprising learners, able, above all, to formulate pertinent questions and to see hidden connections among apparently disparate concepts.

But in other ways, their lives could not have been more different. Von Neumann's boyhood had been ferociously urban and cosmopolitan. In the Jewish community in Budapest, von Neumann had grown up in a period and in a place remarkable for prosperity, education, talent, and exposure to a world of ideas and sophistication. Norman Macrae, von Neumann's biographer, relates that in the late nineteenth century, enterprising Jews from all over Russia and eastern Europe flocked to Budapest, where changes in the culture meant that they could get ahead in the professions, if not in government, faster than they could in other, more conservative parts of Europe. In Budapest, Jews were welcomed—and educated, thanks to reforms instituted by a man named Maurice von Karman at the behest of Emperor Franz Joseph. But men like von Neumann's father also went to Budapest instead of New York because it was more expensive for middle-class people to go to America than it was for poor people, who were content to travel in steerage. Macrae writes, "More steerage-class Jewish families settled on New York, and more upper-class strivers settled on Budapest." Von Neumann's generation of mathematicians and scientists from Budapest included Michael Polanyi, Leo Szilard, Edward Teller, and Eugene Wigner, but Budapest also produced great musicians (Antal Dorati, George Szell, Eugene Ormandy), moviemakers (Adolf Zukor, Alexander Korda, Michael Curtiz), photographers (André Kertész, Robert Capa), and writers (Arthur Koestler).

In 1914, when eleven-year-old John Atanasoff was attending a one-room schoolhouse in Florida, helping his father rewire the family house, learning to maintain, repair, and then drive the new Model T, as well as frustrating his teachers by surpassing them, Neumann Janusz (called "Jancsi") was delighting his teachers, who were some of the best mathematical minds in Europe. Nobel Prize winner Eugene Wigner recalls, in Kati Marton's *The Great Escape*, that "he was one grade below me, but in mathematics, two classes ahead. He already had an astonishing grasp of advanced mathematics . . . The way he described set theory and number theory was enchanting. The beauty of the subject, his intensity and facility of description made me feel we were close friends." One well-regarded teacher tutored von Neumann without compensation, according to Wigner, for the sheer pleasure of "the brush with a special kind of mind." There were other tutors, too. According to Macrae, "Before he finished high school [he] had been accepted by most of the university mathematicians as a colleague." Jancsi was not a pest. He naturally and willingly fit in with his fellow students (Wigner recalled, "He joined in class pranks just enough to avoid unpopularity") and pleased his teachers. He was so adept at mathematics that he could do difficult problems in several ways and gear his solution to the educational level of his associate if he had to. Perhaps we may say that whereas Atanasoff was a natural fixer and improver, von Neumann was a natural game player, always aware that the moves in any game could be made in more than one way and that each possible move would lead to a different outcome, which would in turn lead to other, different outcomes. And game playing, too, as demonstrated by Turing's fascination with chess, was an aspect of computer innovation.

In 1920, when Neumann Janusz was seventeen, educational circumstances changed for Jews in Hungary. In a place where the vast majority of educated professionals (50 to 80 percent) were Jews, the post–World War I government instituted anti-Semitic quotas for university places—no more than 5 percent. By June 1921, when Atanasoff had saved enough money teaching and working so that he could attend the University of Florida, von Neumann was taking his exams (and worrying so much that as a result his papers were not perfect). In Gainesville, Atanasoff wanted to be a physicist, but the university offered electrical engineering, so he studied that. In Budapest, von Neumann wanted to be a mathematician, but conditions in Hungary made that impractical, so his father pushed him toward chemical engineering. Ironically, when, in September, Atanasoff left Brewster for Gainesville, von Neumann left Budapest for Berlin. But in this, too, he fell into the center of the world, or at least of the mathematical world. Marton writes, "From all over the globe, theoretical physicists gathered in Berlin, and in the medieval university town of Göttingen, three hours away. In those last years before the darkness fell on Germany, a revolution was taking place in the way we understand space and time." This revolution was quantum mechanics, the very subject that Atanasoff was taking from John Hasbrouck Van Vleck at the University of Wisconsin at about the same time, and proving that he could comprehend in spite of a late start and missed classes.

By the time von Neumann encountered Atanasoff, he had exceptional connections, not only because he was a genius, and not only because he had been born and educated at the center of things, but also because he was worldly, charming, and personable—a connector as well as a maven, in Malcolm Gladwell's terms. After completing his degrees at Berlin and Zurich (where a paper he wrote was sent to David Hilbert, the man who posed the problem that Turing addressed in "On Computable Numbers," and so impressed him that he assiduously cultivated the young man), von Neumann went to the University of Göttingen in 1926, just about the same time that Atanasoff was first at Iowa State (and Flowers first went to work at Dollis Hill). In 1930, von Neumann was invited to Princeton, and two years later he was given a professorship at the Institute for Advanced Study, along with Albert Einstein and Kurt Gödel. It was there that he met Alan Turing, to whom he offered the job as research assistant in 1938. Clearly, von Neumann's personality and biography meshed to produce a man who was perhaps preternaturally political in a way that was unusual in a mathematician or an inventor—he was not only completely at ease in all sorts of social situations, he was extraordinarily aware of the ramifications of larger sorts of politics. He was, after all, the man who was assigned to do the calculations at Los Alamos that were to estimate exactly how much damage an atomic bomb might be made to inflict upon the Japanese. His specific task was to calculate at what elevation the detonation should take place in order to achieve the greatest possible destruction. Other Manhattan Project physicists, notably Leo Szilard, von Neumann's slightly older compatriot, preferred an intimidating demonstration of the weapon, but von Neumann was willing to make a list of good targets—according to Norman Macrae, he was instrumental in steering the air force away from the Imperial Palace, but, according to Kati Marton, he thought the Japanese holy city of Kyoto was a good target (of course, the final targets were Hiroshima, a shipping center and supply depot, and Nagasaki, a ship-building center).

Physicist Stanley Frankel, who performed many of the Manhattan Project calculations that predicted whether or not an atom bomb could be made to explode, and what would happen then, later said that von Neumann was aware of "On Computable Numbers" by 1942 or 1943 and made sure that Frankel studied it (Frankel went on to be a computer consultant after the war). With his experience on the Manhattan Project, von Neumann was one of the most influential scientists in the world.

But of course, although everyone knew that von Neumann was a genius, and an important man, in the summer of 1944 the Manhattan Project was highly classified, and in 1944, although one type of bomb had been developed (Little Boy), the method for detonating a more powerful bomb had not been worked out. Just about this time, von Neumann was approached by a young man on a train platform. The young man was Herman Goldstine. Goldstine went up to the famous mathematician (whose lectures he had once attended) and introduced himself, but von Neumann got friendly only when Goldstine began to chat about his (highly classified) work on a computer. A month later, in August, von Neumann visited ENIAC in Philadelphia for the first time. Von Neumann may have been a famous genius, but according to Norman Macrae, Pres Eckert, then twenty-five, viewed von Neumann's visit as a test—for von Neumann. Eckert said to Goldstine that he would find out if von Neumann was really the genius he was supposed to be "by his first question. If this was about the logical structure of the machine, he would believe in von Neumann. Otherwise, not." Forty-one-year-old von Neumann passed the test.

By the time of von Neumann's visit, work on ENIAC had been moving at a fever pitch for fifteen months, but the speed of construction demanded by the army because of the difficulty of creating the firing tables meant that real innovation in every aspect of the machine (Mauchly's and especially Eckert's goal) had not been possible. They had to use parts that were already in existence (and because the machine was a low priority to the military, a percentage of these parts were defective, though not actual discards, like Zuse's parts) and at least some ideas that derived from machines that were already familiar to the army, including Irven Travis's machine at the Moore School that Mauchly was already familiar with by the time he met Atanasoff. Von Neumann grasped that the really new machine would be the next version, and Eckert grasped that, too—he had already begun making drawings for it.

After meeting Goldstine, Eckert, and Mauchly, and chatting with Atanasoff at the NOL (and, no doubt, with anyone else who seemed to know about computer theory), von Neumann went back and forth to Los Alamos, where he worked on the Manhattan Project—it wasn't until December of that year that the detonation device for one of the bombs (Fat Man) was successfully tested. Work continued on the bomb, but in June 1945, von Neumann was not so busy at Los Alamos that he did not have time for other things—under his direction, Herman Goldstine wrote a description of an idea for the second version of ENIAC. The paper was 101 pages long and was entitled "First Draft of a Report of the EDVAC, by John von Neumann." EDVAC stood for "Electronic Discrete Variable Automatic Computer." Mauchly and Eckert were told that the paper was "an internal summary of their work," and Goldstine also told another concerned party that it was meant for internal use only; therefore it did not constitute classified material and could be reproduced. The fact that von Neumann was given sole authorship at first seemed to Mauchly and Eckert insignificant. The purpose of the paper, and its achievement, was that it expressed the logical and overarching theory of what the creators of ENIAC were trying to do, something that Eckert had hardly had time to attempt, and Mauchly had not been inclined to do, even though he had the time. Eckert had written a three-page memo in February 1944, describing a system for storing electrical impulses. A notable feature of Goldstine's paper was that even though Eckert had described what he was building to von Neumann in August 1944 and subsequently, there was no mention of Eckert and only one mention of Mauchly (though Howard Aiken was mentioned several times). Partisans of von Neumann make the case that, as with everything else von Neumann did, he took the raw material of another man's ideas and immediately transcended it, or, as Macrae says, "Johnny grabbed other people's ideas, then by his clarity leapt five blocks ahead of them, and helped put them into practical effect."

The most important contribution of the "First Draft" to computer design was that it laid out what came to be known as "von Neumann architecture"—that is, that the computer could contain a set of instructions in its memory like the set of instructions that Turing's human "computer" would have been given and would have to follow day after day forever. The instructions would be stored in the memory, which the electronic computer could readily access (not like a paper tape or a deck of punch cards). This set of instructions in the memory would be called a stored program. Von Neumann described these ideas in terms of physical structures that had access to one another—the control unit was a self-contained space that could communicate back and forth with the memory. Separate from the control unit was the logic unit (conceived as a place where mathematical calculations were performed), which also communicated back and forth with the memory. The control unit and the logic unit communicated back and forth with each other. The problem to be solved, the input, was fed into the logic unit, and the solution, the output, emerged from the logic unit. But really these "places" were not physical structures—they were sets of instructions, an idea that von Neumann may have (or seems to have) gotten from "On Computable Numbers." According to Macrae, "The primary memory would be fairly small, with rapid random access. Behind it would be a secondary memory. It should be able to transfer information into the primary memory automatically, as needed. The computer should be able to move back and forth through the secondary memory. Individuals should be able to enter information directly into the secondary memory."

Although ENIAC was an army project and the war was still on when Goldstine wrote the paper, over the next few months Goldstine sent von Neumann's report to twenty-four of von Neumann's colleagues and friends in the United States and England. Their response was enthusiastic and included requests for more copies. Goldstine eventually sent out hundreds. It was this that finally alarmed Mauchly and Eckert, who wrote their own paper in September, describing their ideas for EDVAC and more carefully ascribing particular ideas to particular participants in the ENIAC project, but they hadn't the gift—their report was neither as detailed nor as eloquent as Goldstine and von Neumann's in conceptualizing the larger implications of the project. Nor did they have the connections or the reputation. Most important, they did not have the cooperation of the boss, Herman Goldstine. Goldstine, who was in charge of security classification for the project, marked Mauchly and Eckert's report confidential, thereby ensuring that, unlike von Neumann's report, it would not be widely read or, perhaps, read at all. There is no evidence that, even though von Neumann was in contact with Atanasoff because of the navy project, he gave Atanasoff a copy of the report or told him about it. Nor did Mauchly and Eckert send Atanasoff a copy of their report, even though his security clearance was higher than theirs.

Although Atanasoff was invited to the February 1946 unveiling of ENIAC at the University of Pennsylvania, and attended, the demonstration of the machine did not clear up any mysteries for him about how the machine worked or the principles behind it. And Mauchly and Eckert were not present. The purpose of ENIAC was to accomplish what Mauchly had originally proposed—the calculation of artillery trajectories. It was so enormous and so expensive that Atanasoff was intimidated. Even so, not long after he saw the ENIAC, Atanasoff called Richard Trexler, the patent attorney in Chicago. Trexler told him that Iowa State had never paid to file the patent application, and so he had not filed it. Atanasoff knew that his moment to patent his ideas was lost—ENIAC convinced him that computers had progressed. Either his ideas were obsolete or they were irrelevant. Computer technology, it was readily apparent, was now established and developing apace.

In Germany, in 1943 and 1944, Konrad Zuse was still hard at it, still undaunted in attempting the impossible. Even the small prototype using vacuum tubes that Herbert Schreyer wanted to build seemed to be impossible—the type of tubes they needed were not being manufactured in Germany. But while a friend at the Telefunken company made ten tubes in his spare time and smuggled them out of the lab, they discovered that they had another sort of access to materials:

> Dr. Schreyer was able to get [the German Aeronautics Institute] assigned the task of examining the intended uses of mysterious devices found in shot-down American and British aircraft . . . After such an examination, a huge number of completely modern components, resistors, small cylindrical capacitors, variable capacitors, the most modern miniature tubes and small batteries, etc. were left over. Never again did we lack parts which we needed ad hoc for developing the computing machine; we had so much left over, we were able to set up a flourishing radio repair shop.

The conditions surrounding the invention of the Z4 were astonishing—every morning, the inventors had to clean up damage and debris from bombings of the night before. One morning, Schreyer decided he needed, as a conductor, a piece of copper-rich bronze. His two assistants decided to find some—and they did so by wandering the bombed-out streets of Berlin looking for a piece of dead streetcar cable. They managed to cut off and steal a fifty-centimeter piece without getting shot for looting. Since the computer was still not considered a government priority, Schreyer had to get a contract for the development of a dud-bomb-detecting instrument in order to have access to other materials. Once he attained first-class status through that, though, his personnel could order almost anything, and one thing they ordered was "a bottle of radioactive material" for painting on the inner surfaces of the diodes they were making. They also painted the faces of their old watches. The watches were soon stolen by invading Russian troops.

One by one, Zuse's inventions, wherever they were around Berlin— the Z1, Z2, and Z3—were destroyed in the bombing, but work on Z4 continued; it was being built in a basement. And the use of unorthodox personnel continued—Zuse's first programmer was blind. Watching

Charles Babbage, 1791–1871, inventor of the Difference Engine and Analytical Engine, analog computing devices. (*Photograph courtesy of the Charles Babbage Institute, University of Minnesota, Minneapolis*)

A section of Babbage's Difference Engine, showing rods and gears. (*Science Museum/SSPL*)

Vannevar Bush with his Differential Analyzer, 1931. (*Courtesy MIT Museum*)

John Vincent Atanasoff, around the time he completed his PhD at the University of Wisconsin. (*Iowa State University Library/ Special Collections Department*)

Atanasoff in the 1930s, teaching at Iowa State College. (*Iowa State University Library/ Special Collections Department*)

The physics building at Iowa State College. Atanasoff and Clifford Berry built the ABC in a corner of the basement. (*Iowa State University Library/Special Collections Department*)

Clifford Berry, 1918–1963, standing with the ABC in 1942.
(Iowa State University Library/Special Collections Department)

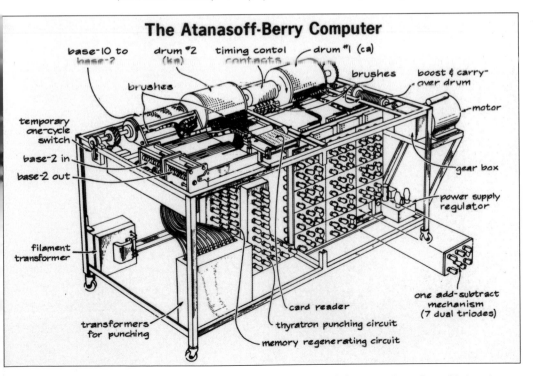

The Atanasoff-Berry Computer

base-10 to base-2   drum #2 (km)   timing contol contacts   drum #1 (ca)

brushes

brushes   boost & carry-over drum

motor

temporary one-cycle switch

base-2 in

base-2 out

gear box

power supply regulator

filament transformer

one add-subtract mechanism (7 dual triodes)

transformers for punching

card reader

thyratron punching circuit

memory regenerating circuit

An undated schematic of the ABC, prepared for a campus exhibition at Iowa State University.
(Iowa State University Library/Special Collections Department)

The ABC in May 1942. (*Iowa State University Library/Special Collections Department*)

One of the ABC's two electrostatic memory drums, the only surviving part of the original machine. (*Courtesy of U.S. Department of Energy's Ames Laboratory*)

Konrad Zuse's Z1 computer, built in his parents' Berlin apartment c. 1936.
(*Courtesy of Horst Zuse*)

Konrad Zuse, 1910–1995. (*Courtesy of Horst Zuse*)

Alan Turing, 1912–1954, upon his election as a Fellow of the Royal Society in 1951. (© *National Portrait Gallery, London*)

Bletchley Park staff at work on deciphering codes, Hut 6.
(*Bletchley Park Trust Archive*)

A Lorenz SZ42 *Schlüsselzusatz* cipher machine on display at Bletchley Park. (*Bletchley Park Trust Archive*)

Thomas Flowers, 1905–1998. (*Bletchley Park Trust Archive*)

Colossus at work in 1943; note paper tape. (*Science Museum/SSPL*)

Aiken's Mark I analog device in use, 1944.

(*Courtesy of the Computer History Museum*)

John Mauchly, 1907–1980 (*left*), and J. Presper Eckert, Jr., 1919–1995 (*right*), with Major General G. L. Barnes, 1944. (*University of Pennsylvania Archives*)

ENIAC in 1946—Eckert stands front left, while Mauchly is by the column.
(*University of Pennsylvania Archives*)

John von Neumann with EDVAC in 1952; note Williams tubes along the bottom of the machine. (*Alan Richards. photographer. From the Shelby White and Leon Levy Archives Center, Institute for Advanced Study, Princeton, NJ, USA*)

him work led Zuse to realize that Braille was a type of computer alphabet. Subsequently, he happily employed blind or sight-impaired programmers.

While he was working on the Z4 and trying out designs for the prototype electronic computer mentioned above, Zuse understood that there was a price to pay. He writes, "Our prototype did not have the slightest practical value." He could not quite solve the old Turing problem—how to mediate between the desirable simplicity of operation and the huge (or even infinite) number of operations required to solve a problem. But throughout the war, Zuse and his workers and programmers pursued their objectives. Reminiscing after fifty years, he writes:

> Today when I look back to these days, it seems unbelievable,
> even to me, that we kept working while the bombs continued to
> fall on Berlin. We spent a great deal of the night in an air-raid
> shelter. All around us, bombs fell and houses burned. More than
> once after a heavy attack, we thought it was finally over, that
> nothing would work anymore. We had no water, no electricity,
> and no telephones, and there was hardly any serviceable means
> of transportation. But each time, after a few hours, almost every-
> thing was working again. And somewhere, all of the employees
> found ways to pull through.

After Germany surrendered, Zuse heard that Albert Speer had suggested to Hitler that the development of the computer might aid in the war effort. "Hitler is said to have replied that he didn't need any computing machine, he had the courage of his soldiers."

But toward the end of 1944, after D-Day, when conditions of every sort were getting desperate in Germany, Konrad Zuse's savior showed up in the person of a mysterious man named "Dr. Funk." Dr. Funk was a physicist who had been drafted into the army and was looking for a way to avoid service. Zuse had no illusions—he told Dr. Funk he had nothing for him and sent him to Henschel to ask around for a position. Three days later, Dr. Funk returned with an exemption from military service. His powers only increased from there, Zuse suggests, by means of well-executed forgery. He did seem to know his way around—toward the end of the war, he managed to get Zuse, his assistants, and the machine safely away from Berlin and the encroaching Soviet army. But the evacuation was not without suspense:

> The stairway was too narrow for the large relay cabinets; the only way to get them [out] was with the freight elevator. And once again at the wrong moment, the obligatory air raid alarm sounded. The power went out, and we found out just how helpless modern man is without electricity. The elevator had no hand crank, and the only way we could operate the winch was by hand, with indescribable difficulty. Millimeter by millimeter, we raised the device from the cellar to the ground floor. Then the Z4 was on its way for fourteen days on a heavily bombed route between Berlin and Göttingen. It had hardly been unloaded when the freight depot was hit.

Berlin was about 210 miles from Göttingen—John von Neumann and his friends at the University of Berlin had been accustomed to traveling back and forth between the two universities in the 1920s, taking about three hours each way. And Dr. Funk had divined the way to save the machine, as well—for its travels, he christened it, not the Z4, but the V-4 (for *Versuchmodell,* or "Experimental Model" 4). He allowed those in charge of transportation and evacuation to believe it was a *"Vergeltungswaffen"* 4, or an advanced version of the V-2 rocket.

In Göttingen, Zuse and his assistants assembled and demonstrated the machine—it still worked—but they were then ordered to take it to "one of the underground ordnance factories," tunnels where thousands of concentration camp prison workers manufactured weapons and ammunition in appalling conditions. Surprised, shocked, and frightened by what he saw there,[1] Zuse managed yet another evacuation, this time to Bavaria. Dr. Funk procured for the journey a Wehrmacht truck and one thousand gallons of diesel fuel.

"For fourteen days we fled along the front, past burning neighborhoods and over bombed-out streets. We usually drove at night; during the day we found makeshift shelter with the farmers." When they got to their destination, they discovered Wernher von Braun and his team (the designers of the real V-2 rocket). They ended up at the same temporary quarters as von Braun—possibly the most prominent scientist in Germany—thanks to Dr. Funk: "Dr. Funk had free run of the place, and even after we left Berlin, he obtained papers firsthand, whenever it was necessary. How he was able to find us a place in Oberjoch [on the Austrian border] remains a mystery to me to this day." Zuse did talk to von Braun once—they were close in age and had attended the Technical University of Berlin at about the same time. Zuse was not especially impressed, because he did not get the sense that von Braun foresaw much use for computers in future rocket travel. Von Braun said nothing of his plans to "go over to the Americans. We soon felt it better to keep away from them and to look for our own quarters." Some years later, though, upon reading von Braun's memoirs, he saw that von Braun had understood their perilous situation better than he had at the end of the war—an SS man told von Braun that storm troopers had been billeted among the scientists with orders to shoot them "to keep you from falling into the hands of the enemy." Major General Walter Dornberger, who was in charge of von Braun and the V-2 rocket, managed, with the help of several shots of cognac, to elicit the plan from the commander of the SS, and then to persuade him to abandon it ("And when the Allied troops have learned that you carried out a bloodbath, you will be hanged immediately!").

---

1. One reason that Zuse's autobiography is interesting is that it gives Americans a perspective on life in Nazi Germany that we rarely get. Zuse seems perennially surprised by the power of the Nazis and the events he lives through. My interpretation is that this is a feature of his dedication to and focus on his machine—that thinking about it and building it simply occupied his mind almost completely and drove almost every other consideration, including mortality, out of his consciousness.

Although the war was ending and the French were gaining control, surrendering was a complicated business—first the Zuse cohort used their truck to move the Z4 to the village of Hinterstein, Austria, some 125 miles farther east, where they hid the machine in a cellar. Dr. Funk then tried to make contact with the Americans nearby but was arrested, though he was soon released. In Hinterstein, they encountered a local eccentric, an Indian soothsayer who had a way of knowing, or seeming to know, about everything that was going on, including atom bombs and vast caches of food. He was interrogated by occupying French authorities several times; information he gave them came to nothing, so that when he told them that "a large computing machine—which he [the soothsayer] had invented—was hidden in the village," the French authorities didn't bother to investigate. Subsequently, a local Englishwoman, a duchess who had lived in the village for a long time, did report to British authorities that there was a V-4 rocket in the village. When the British investigated and found only the Z4 computer, "they left, disappointed." Not long afterward, Dr. Funk, Zuse's mysterious savior, disappeared, too.

Zuse, his wife (he had married one of his employees in January), and his machine stayed in Hinterstein, living as best they could on limited means—they foraged for firewood and food, often eating nettles, spinach, wild mushrooms, and snails. He also managed to sell small paintings of local alpine chamois in a souvenir shop owned by his landlord. For his own pleasure, returning to his love of art, he made intricate woodcuts of the scenery. The scene was more pastoral than Zuse was used to, which led him to think in new ways—he turned his attention to software rather than hardware, spending the next two years on a theory of computer programming that he called "Plankakul," or "plan calculus," an "algorithmic computer language" that led him to think about the nature of computer logic. He writes, "This environment did anything but nurture the concept of mechanizing thought processes . . . the Allgau's flower-strewn surroundings and—not to be forgotten—the childish laughter of my first son were not exactly conducive to analysing the world into yes/no values." Like Alan Turing, and at around the same time, Zuse began to think about the nature of the mind, the nature of human free will, and even the nature of the universe. He wrote a paper, uncompleted, that he called "Freedom and Causality in the Light of the Computing Machine."

In 1946, Zuse moved the Z4 to a stable, where he, his wife, and their two children also rented a room. But the machine wasn't doing anything—"although we could have taken over fat content analysis for the local alpine dairy." And once again, there were no supplies for working on the computer—"We joked that the Americans had forgotten only one thing—their soldiers carelessly threw away tin cans. But we really did collect and use such garbage." In 1947, Zuse and his friends, still living in the Austrian Alps, now in the village of Hopferau, with the Z4 in the stable, began to make contact with the outside world when the trains resumed service (though the trains were so crowded and dangerous that "we were happy just to arrive home safe from our travels").

Zuse and another friend named Stücken decided to found an engineering firm. Every single item they might need to continue work on the computer was hard to attain, but, he writes, "our courage resulted not least from the fact that we felt we had nothing to lose." His old friend Helmut Schreyer had a different idea—he had met a South American businessman who wanted him to pursue his computer ideas in Brazil, and Schreyer tried to talk Zuse into joining him. Years later, Zuse was glad he had declined—when Zuse managed to visit him in Brazil, Schreyer was working three jobs, and the suitcase of computer parts that he had managed to salvage after the war had been stolen on the train between Hopferau and the town of Erlangen.

But Zuse's courage did not extend to believing that his machine had much of a future, and later he deeply regretted that he didn't bother to file patents on what he had invented. Part of the problem was formulating his insights into patentable ideas—he and a friend who was later to become a patent attorney believed that his thoughts about mathematical and logical relationships would not get through a system that was more geared to devices. He had filed patents in 1937 and 1941. His 1937 patent was granted, but it took so long that it was worthless by the time he got it. His 1941 patent was denied in 1967, with the reason that "the innovation and progressiveness of the object concerned in the main application are not doubted. Yet a patent cannot be granted due to insufficient inventive merit."

In 1949, Zuse got lucky. One day "an elegant car from Switzerland" drove up, and a man from the Swiss national technical institute in Zurich got out and asked around about a computer he had heard was to be found in the village. The man, a Professor Stiefel, had recently returned from the United States, where he had been shown all sorts of computers "in beautiful cabinets with chromework." Zuse took him to the stable and turned on the machine. Professor Stiefel presented a problem, a differential equation, and the Z4 solved it. Stiefel then leased the Z4, which stayed in the stable, and Zuse received a small monthly payment for its use.

At the end of the war and right afterward, it was clear that technological advances during the war left research questions related to the war that needed to be answered, but research personnel were quickly return-ing to civilian life; indeed, Iowa State asked Atanasoff to come back as head of the physics department. For him, though, projects for the navy took precedence over teaching, and Lura and the children were no lon-ger in Ames. While the foremost of Atanasoff's projects was the plan to build the navy computer, he had not been relieved of his duties in the Acoustics Division. Atanasoff had no choice but to attempt, by work-ing even harder, to run both the Acoustics Division and the Computer Division at the same time. In the Acoustics Division, he had two main projects, the first which was to travel to Bikini Atoll, the scene of atomic tests in the summer of 1946. The immediate purpose was to test the effects of atomic blasts on the junked hulls of ninety-five surplus ships. The assignment for the Acoustics Division was to measure sound waves set off by the tests, with an eye to future detection of atomic tests by other nations. At Bikini Atoll, Atanasoff was put in his usual position of making do, scrounging, repairing, and do-it-yourself, but the tests were both successful and interesting—the column of water discharged by the second, underwater atomic blast rose a mile into the atmosphere and "launched" the aircraft carrier *Saratoga* (which displaced more than 38,000 tons) almost half a mile. Atanasoff's acoustic results set a standard for subsequent detection of atomic explosions. It was when he returned from Bikini that Atanasoff was informed that the navy had dropped the computer project. One result of the navy dropping the project was that the "need to know" request Atanasoff had submitted to the navy in order to find out the workings of ENIAC became moot. He would not find out this information until years later.

However, the Acoustics Division at the NOL had another big project. Helgoland Island, about sixty miles north of Bremerhaven, west of Jutland, had served as a German ammunition dump, and the British had decided to blow it up. The navy wanted to take acoustical readings on the shock wave that would be produced, a kind of man-made earthquake. Atanasoff was put in charge of the project. The detonation was to take place in mid-April 1947. Atanasoff had eight weeks to prepare. He subsequently learned through the grapevine that several other scientists had been approached to oversee the project and had refused, thinking that the lead time was too short. He was even advised by a colleague not to accept the assignment, but he did so and accomplished what was asked in his standard way—by noting what was wrong with the preliminary plan, resurrecting old ideas for a seismograph he himself had once designed, then modifying existing equipment to measure seismic waves and sonic waves, no matter how large they might prove to be.

In the meantime, the postwar declassification of ENIAC had other ramifications—when ENIAC's security was lifted in 1946, the scientific and technological world reacted with oohs and ahs. Tommy Flowers realized that he had invented and made use of a more advanced machine, but he was in no position to protest: Colossus would never be on his résumé. He writes:

With no administrative or executive powers, I had to convince others, and they would not be convinced. I was one-eyed in the kingdom of the blind. The one thing I lacked [for pursuing a computer project] was prestige, which knowledge of Colossus would have amply provided. Personal rivalries also played their part. These were exacerbated, and some were even provoked, by what was considered pretentiousness on my part. Little or none of that would have been possible had Colossus been known.

One person who, of course, knew all about Colossus was Alan Turing. The end of the war meant that Turing had several options available to him. In June 1945, he received an Order of the British Empire for his war work, and then he accepted a position at the National Physical Laboratory with the goal of developing a general-purpose computing machine. The NPL was about thirteen miles southwest of central London, in Teddington. The primary work of the NPL was akin to what was then being done in the National Bureau of Standards (now the National Institute of Standards and Technology) in the United States—it established systems of measurement and standards of quality that would then form the basis for the systematic manufacture and production of goods. The British government had realized in the course of the war that the problem of calculation that had frustrated Atanasoff, Turing, and almost every other physicist before the war was going to be a limiting factor in postwar consumer society, and so a new mathematics division of the NPL was begun and a Cambridge man named J. R. Womersley was put in charge of solving the problems of calculation. The head of the whole laboratory was Charles Galton Darwin, grandson of Charles Darwin and son of astronomer George Darwin.

In spring 1945, right around the time that the order was going out for the ten Colossus machines to be destroyed, Womersley went to the United States and was shown ENIAC (before, in fact, it was unveiled to the general public). When Womersley got back to the UK, he was eager to build a UK version. Since, unlike Mauchly and Eckert, he happened to be quite familiar with "On Computable Numbers" and had even toyed with designing a mechanical version of a Turing machine before the war (his partner, like Mauchly and Eckert's original partner, was in the horse-racing pari-mutuel totalizer business), he offered Turing £800 per year—£200 more than he had received at Bletchley Park—to come to the NPL. Turing began work on October 1, 1945, and he was ready with plenty of ideas. Many of his new colleagues at the NPL had also been recruited from the war effort, though from the Admiralty Computing Service, not from Bletchley Park. They were doing calculations on analog desktop calculators.

Turing did not reciprocate Womersley's respect or get along with him; he was openly contemptuous of Womersley's shaky grasp of mathematical principles and had no appreciation of the political skills that had allowed Womersley to extract the financing for his section from the increasingly parsimonious British government. In spite of the difficulties, though, Turing understood that this was his opportunity to realize the theory behind "On Computable Numbers" in electricity and hardware, and, indeed, the theory that had been realized in Colossus. He set about doing so, writing a report that laid out his theory and design of a computer called "Proposed Electronic Calculator."

The basic feature of his design was a large memory and the ability to program it (that is, to supply the computer with a set of instructions that the computer could always consult—the program would always contain an instruction for the next step, just as the "computer" in "On Computable Numbers" would always know whether to add or not to add the next number on the infinite tape), so human input would be minimized. And the large memory was to be very fast (no doubt Colossus had shown him how fast a computer could operate).

Turing had a copy of von Neumann's "First Draft" (who did not?), and he considered his own ideas to contrast decidedly with von Neumann's, especially in that he expected to construct his memory not like a paper tape, as in Colossus, which would be long and sequential, presenting the problem to the computer of "finding" an instruction somewhere on the tape, but more like wallpaper on a wall, allowing the computer to quickly scan for instructions. The former is called "serial access memory," the latter, "random access memory." The shift from one to the other is, according to computer scientist John Gustafson, "almost as big a deal as going from decimal to binary calculation." Turing's proposal, in terms of both theory and engineering, was quite specific. According to Jack Copeland, he "supplied detailed circuit design, full specifications of hardware units, specimen programs in machine code, and even an estimate of the cost of building the machine." It seems likely, comparing this production with his prewar efforts at computer design, that he had learned as much from Tommy Flowers (and the other engineers he had known in the war) as Flowers had learned from him.

When Womersley and Turing made their proposal in March 1946, the meeting went well enough that Darwin granted them £10,000 ($400,000 in 2010 funds) to try out a small prototype, but not so well that they got enough money to build the machine that Turing really wanted to build. Certainly, the same problem obtained with the ACE (as it was called, standing for "Automatic Computing Engine") as obtained with Tommy Flowers's efforts in the same direction—so few knew what had been done at Dollis Hill or at Bletchley Park during the war that no one was prepared to give Turing the respect or the benefit of the doubt that his experience warranted. Darwin, who knew more than most, did request the Post Office to allow Flowers to help with the computer, but with the ACE, Turing was in much the same position that Atanasoff had been in in 1940 with the Iowa State College Research Corporation—his ideas were so advanced that he had to prove they were worth something to people who did not really understand them. Womersley was his advocate and had some political skills, but Turing himself had none—he needed to be able to refer those who controlled the money to his wartime résumé to convince them, but he was forbidden to do so.

He also had a rival for funding—Maurice V. Wilkes, at Cambridge. Wilkes was almost exactly Turing's age and he had also gone to Cambridge (St. John's College, in mathematics). He had also joined the war effort, but in radar development rather than code breaking. In 1945, when Turing was heading to the NPL, Wilkes was returning to Cambridge, to the Mathematical Laboratory. Wilkes also read the "First

Draft" when it was published, and he was inspired by it to get to Philadelphia and attend the last two weeks of the Moore School Lectures. He traveled around the United States and investigated as many computer projects as he could before returning to England. Unlike Turing, his goal was not to innovate—it was to supply the university with a working computer as quickly as possible. He visited the NPL at the end of November and wrote to Womersley in December. Womersley apparently either did not understand Turing's ideas or did not understand Turing, because he passed the letter to him, who wrote back rather sharply: "The code he suggests is . . . very contrary to the line of development here, and much more in the American tradition of solving one's difficulties by means of much equipment rather than thought . . . I favor a model with a control [that is, a CPU] of negligible size which can be expanded if desired." Turing thought that if the hardware was fast enough and the program detailed and complex enough, roomfuls of processor units could be avoided. However, such a machine would have had difficulties of its own, according to John Gustafson, who maintains,

> It is clear that what he had in mind building was something very like the theoretical model in his Computability paper, the model we now call a Turing machine. It worked on one bit at a time, but used a huge amount of memory to do anything of consequence. Since he had proved that anything that was computable could be theoretically computed on such a simple device, why not build one? The CPU would only have required a handful of vacuum tubes. But such a machine is horrendously difficult to program, and even at electronic speeds, it would have been painfully slow for many simple things like floating-point arithmetic.[2]

One of Turing's difficulties (or Womersley's, as his director) was that he didn't mind talking to the press (either the general press or jour-

---

2. A Turing machine has been constructed. It can be seen on YouTube: http://www.youtube.com/watch?v=E3keLeMwfHY.

nals of particular groups, such as the Institution of Radio Engineers), but when he did talk, he raised hopes that did not seem realistically capable of fulfillment, and he was often met with skepticism. And he himself met with skepticism, owing to his odd manner and excessively casual (or, you might say, sloppy) mode of dress, which hadn't changed much since his older brother had despaired of getting him into his sailor suit with his shoes on the proper feet in 1916. When Turing himself gave a few lectures on the proposed NPL computer, Wilkes attended only one. He felt that Turing's ideas were irrelevant, because they "were widely at variance with what the mainstream of computer development was going to be." Womersley sent Turing to the United States to attend a computing symposium in January 1947, and then to visit Princeton and have a look at the project von Neumann had begun there as an academic alternative to the EDVAC. The trip did not change Turing's mind about his own computer, but momentum was carrying the project away from his ideas. Delays were mounting along with the disagreements. In the meantime, Wilkes, who didn't have to apply for funding, put his computer together very quickly. In February 1946, Turing had requested that Tommy Flowers, at Dollis Hill, build the prototype of the computer he was designing. Flowers promised the machine by August, but postwar repairs and improvements to the telephone system superseded the project, and by February 1947 the ACE was going nowhere because Turing could not persuade Womersley to commit himself to Turing's ideas—for example, an engineering department was set up, but made no progress. Possibly, Womersley was the sort of administrator who thinks contradictory ideas constitute a backup plan, but in the end they constituted no plan at all because what had come to be called "von Neumann architecture"— the principles of computer design set out in the "First Draft"—were simply taking over by coming to seem tried and tested.[3] Turing quit. In the autumn of 1947, he returned to Cambridge.

---

3. One computer that conformed to Turing's ideas was built by two engineers from Tommy Flowers's Colossus engineering team. It was called MOSAIC and was used during the cold war to calculate aircraft and anti-aircraft trajectories.

Chapter Eight

B y the time Atanasoff was home from Bikini Atoll and finished with
his aborted computer project for the navy, John Mauchly and Pres
Eckert were deep into their own patent conflicts with the University
of Pennsylvania. Originally, Penn had shown little or no interest in
Mauchly's project. As of late 1944, they had accorded Mauchly and
Eckert patent rights if something were to come out of ENIAC—the
university itself retained only a license to build and use a computer
of their own. In late 1945, though, the university was rethinking this
policy, and then, in 1946, the army lifted security restrictions on the
machine. Penn informed Mauchly and Eckert that, having been constructed with public funds, ENIAC and its parts could not produce
private patents. Mauchly and Eckert had put together their patent
application in the fall. When ENIAC was unveiled, Herman Goldstine claimed in the publicity material to be one of the three inventors,
along with Mauchly and Eckert. He also put his name on the patent
application, but Mauchly and Eckert removed it. Goldstine was not
pleased.

Plans for EDVAC, the computer that would replace ENIAC, were
even more contentious. In 1941, Mauchly had mentioned in his October
letter to Atanasoff that the inventor of the earlier Moore School analyzer,

Irven Travis, had left to join the navy. Travis returned in 1946, and he was determined that the university would not relinquish any rights to any future machines. He stated point blank that "all people who wish to continue as employees of the university must turn over their patents to the university." In an interview in 1977, Travis said, "Well, the record is clear. I'm the one who precipitated the blowup." Travis felt that the fact that the research was being done under the sponsorship of the military and the university meant that individual researchers did not have property rights in the research. He also felt that the ENIAC patents as they were eventually submitted did not give sufficient credit to other members of the research team, especially Arthur Burks—whom Travis considered "brilliant." In his interview with Nancy Stern, for the Charles Babbage Institute of the University of Minnesota, he also suggested that the president of Penn, an English professor, had given in to coercion on the part of Mauchly and Eckert, who had threatened not to complete ENIAC if they did not gain patent rights to the machine. The patent dispute quickly escalated, driven, according to Scott McCartney, on the part of Travis and other Moore School engineers by the feeling that Mauchly was an outsider (having not gotten his degrees at the Moore School), while Eckert was volatile and difficult to get along with (by this time nearly twenty-seven years old and having earned only a bachelor's degree). Travis later said that there were researchers at the Moore School who were doing patentable research on their own and profiting from it and that there was no difficulty with that. The problem had entirely to do with research done on university time and funded by public money. Travis may also have been influenced by the design of ENIAC, which, according to Alice and Arthur Burks in their 1988 history of the Atanasoff computer, owed a great deal to his own modification of the Bush Analyzer. But Mauchly and Eckert felt that Travis's position was unprecedented at Penn—other faculty members had gotten patents in the past. The university would not yield, and it issued an ultimatum: if Mauchly and Eckert did not give up their claims to patents on EDVAC, they could no longer be employed by the university. Mauchly and Eckert quit that day. One result was that what with the patent brouhaha and von Neumann's 1945 publication of the principles behind the projected EDVAC, other inventors managed to get ahead of Penn, and when EDVAC was finally completed, it was no longer a first.

Von Neumann, now deeply interested in computers, invited Eckert, Burks, and Goldstine to go to Princeton and join the team at the Institute for Advanced Study, but he did not invite Mauchly (no doubt reflecting the general sense that Mauchly was something of "a space case"). Eckert declined the invitation, saying, according to McCartney, that expeditious and inexpensive production of computers, leading to widespread use, would be more beneficial than "perfect[ing] them in more detail for a long while in universities." Goldstine and Burks went with von Neumann.

Thomas J. Watson, Sr., builder of Aiken's Mark I, who had furnished the punch-card system for ENIAC, offered Mauchly and Eckert a lab and financing, though he was not convinced that computers were the wave of the future. Mauchly balked—he thought they had been overcharged for the punch-card machines. It was clear to both Mauchly and Eckert that they worked well together and should stick together. Later, Mauchly's second wife remarked, "Mauchly was a dreamer. Without Eckert he would never have built a computer. But we often said that without Mauchly, Eckert wouldn't have thought of it." In general, Mauchly never seems to have inspired confidence, wherever he went and whatever the circumstances.

Mauchly and Eckert were tempted to start their own company, and in the late spring of 1946, only a few months after the unveiling of ENIAC, they did. From the beginning, there were uncertainties and conflicts. The main difficulty was that they did not have much money. Pres Eckert's developer father cosigned a loan for $25,000, but ENIAC had cost $400,000 to build. Investors were skeptical: Howard Aiken, to whom everyone seems to have turned for advice, thought that computers would always be specialty items—sales might run to five or six machines around the nation. Mauchly and Eckert cast about for government contracts and came up with a prospect—a contract with the National Bureau of Standards on behalf of the Census Bureau. Though George Stibitz, of Bell Labs, suggested a more conservative approach—giving Mauchly and Eckert an exploratory grant—the Bureau of Standards was enthusiastic and agreed to award the "Electronic Control Company" $270,000 (about $3.25 million in 2010 dollars), which would be paid out over two years.

In July and August 1946, the Office of Naval Research sponsored forty-eight lectures at the Moore School on the subject "The Theory and Techniques for the Design of Digital Computers." Mauchly and Eckert had already signed contracts to give their lectures (eight[1] and eleven, respectively) before leaving Penn, so they had to take time from their new company to participate. Three other lectures were delivered by Arthur W. Burks. The course was taking place while Atanasoff was at Bikini Atoll, and his naval computer project was terminated shortly after he got back. Clearly, the navy felt that his efforts would be redundant. It also seems clear that von Neumann (who was scheduled to give a lecture, though no record of the lecture exists) and Goldstine continued to use their influence to nudge computer theory and building techniques into the public domain, and that their efforts continued to bear fruit.

When the lecture series was finished, Mauchly and his wife, Mary, went to the Jersey shore for a vacation. They arrived late on the evening of September 8 and immediately went for a late-night dip. The surf was more treacherous than they had expected, and Mary seems to have been caught in a riptide. She could not save herself and he could not save her. Her body washed up on shore two hours later. Their son, who had accompanied John to Ames in 1941, was now eleven, and their daughter was now seven.

But the new corporation had to move forward. Mauchly and Eckert signed their contract with the Bureau of Standards at the end of September and wrote up a business plan. They got two other contracts—one from the Air Controller's Office and another from the Army

---

1. McCartney says six.

Map Service. Even so, the patents remained a contentious issue, in part, according to filmmaker Kirwan Cox, because "Mauchly was assigned the patent work, and he did it, but he did it slowly, which was a problem." Cox also points out that the reason that EDVAC was an advance in ENIAC was that its inventors (including von Neumann) "seemed to realize they could get further by going back to ABC concepts. EDVAC was closer to the ABC than to ENIAC. ENIAC was a hybrid machine—partially ABC, partially Bush analyzer, and partially ganged calculators. As they were building it, the inventors realized that they could improve it—and did so by going back to ABC, to a binary counting system and regenerative memory." According to John Gustafson, they also copied the use of capacitors arranged on a rotating drum.

In England, another attempt was being made to build on what had been learned through Colossus without acknowledging that Colossus had ever existed. The third important figure in the Bletchley Park computer story was Max Newman, Alan Turing's old professor from Cambridge, from whom he had taken a course in the foundations of mathematics in 1935. It was as a result of Newman's explications of Hilbert's questions that Turing had begun to think of the search for mathematical truth as a question of "provability" and even as a "mechanical process" (Newman's words), thereby conceiving his "On Computable Numbers" paper of 1936.

Max Newman was the only son of Herman Neumann, who had been born in 1864 in Bromberg, Germany (now Bydgoszcz, Poland), a town that passed back and forth between Poland and Prussia from 1346 until the end of the Second World War. Originally a fishing town, and then a trading town, Bromberg/Bydgoszcz came to have a large Jewish population. Like Max von Neumann of Pecs, Hungary, and Ivan Atanasov of Boyadzhik, Bulgaria, Herman Neumann emigrated to the west, in 1879, not to New York or to Budapest, but to London. There he trained as a bookkeeper, and, like John Atanasoff, at thirty-two he married a schoolteacher, twenty-six-year-old Sarah

Pike. Max Neumann was born in 1897. Young Max, like young John Vincent Atanasoff, was publicly educated. World War I brought pain and disruption to the Neumann family—Herman was interned at the beginning, then released, but the experience was so grueling that he and Sarah changed the spelling of their name to "Newman." Nevertheless, Herman returned to Germany after the war and was still there, separated from his family, when he died in 1926. In the meantime, Max attained a scholarship to St. John's College, Cambridge, in 1915, and though his studies were interrupted by the war (he served as an army paymaster and a schoolmaster), he returned to Cambridge in 1919 and graduated as a mathematician in 1921. He became a fellow of St. John's in 1923, specializing in topology, which was a more or less unexplored field in England at the time.

It was Newman who had introduced Turing to the *Entscheidungsproblem*, and it was to Newman that Turing gave the first draft of his paper in the spring of 1936. Newman, who had been interested in mathematical machines since working on his own dissertation in 1921, instantly recognized the brilliance of Turing's ideas and, more important, understood them, and it was Newman who helped get Turing's paper into the *Proceedings of the London Mathematical Society*. Newman was well connected in the mathematical world and in the literary world, too—he was married to writer Lyn Irvine, whose first book was published by Leonard and Virginia Woolf's Hogarth Press in 1931.

Newman and Lyn followed Turing to Princeton in 1937, and at the Institute for Advanced Study Newman worked on a proof for the Poincaré Conjecture ("Every simply connected, closed 3-manifold is homeomorphic to the 3-sphere").[2] When he thought he had it, he gave

---

2. From the Clay Mathematics Institute website: "If we stretch a rubber band around the surface of an apple, then we can shrink it down to a point by moving it slowly, without tearing it and without allowing it to leave the surface. On the other hand, if we imagine that the same rubber band has somehow been stretched in the appropriate direction around a doughnut, then there is no way of shrinking it to a point without breaking either the rubber band or the doughnut. We say the surface of the apple is 'simply connected,' but that the surface of the doughnut is not. Poincaré, almost a hundred years ago, knew that a two dimensional sphere is essentially characterized by this property of simple connectivity, and asked the corresponding question for the three

a five-hour lecture about it to the assembled mathematicians, and no listener found a flaw. Unfortunately, it was Newman himself who found the flaw, shortly after returning to England. The conjecture, one of the most famous in theoretical mathematics, was proposed in 1904 and not proven until a hundred years later (by Grigori Perelman, a reclusive Russian mathematician—his proof was accepted in 2006, and he won a million dollars for it from the Clay Mathematics Institute). But even though Newman's Poincaré proof failed, he was awarded a fellowship to the Royal Society in 1939.

At the beginning of the war, Max Newman was forty-two, and he and Lyn had two sons. That he felt that he had to send his wife and his half-Jewish children to the United States in 1940 is an index of how uncertain the outcome of the war with Germany seemed at the time. Newman continued at Cambridge and then tried for another fellowship to Princeton, in order to join his family, but finally, in August 1942, he followed many of his friends from Cambridge to Bletchley Park. He was asked to choose between work on Enigma and work on Tunny, and he chose Tunny. Soon after he got there, one of the young mathematicians, William Tutte, came up with an insight into how the Tunny code functioned. Newman began to consider how the repetitive and time-consuming parts of the decoding could be done by machines, and he was put in charge of what came to be known as "the New-manry." The first machine they came up with was the Heath Robinson, which the members of the Newmanry improved and tinkered with for many months until it was succeeded by Colossus. Newman, like Turing, came to know Tommy Flowers quite well. It eventually became Newman's job to oversee the Colossus and coordinate how it worked to break Tunny codes.

As soon as the war was over, Newman accepted a position at the University of Manchester, and in 1946 he got a university grant of £35,000 for computer development. He then went back to Princeton for a year,

dimensional sphere (the set of points in four dimensional space at unit distance from the origin). This question turned out to be extraordinarily difficult, and mathematicians have been struggling with it ever since."

and there met up with von Neumann, who, as we've seen, was full of his own computer ideas. Newman, privy to the "First Draft" report, very quickly adopted several of von Neumann's ideas for the Manchester computer. The chief engineers on the project, who came from the Telecommunications Research Establishment (TRE), were F. C. Williams and Thomas Kilburn, whose experience was in radar and electrical circuit design rather than code breaking—they didn't even know that Colossus had existed.

F. C. Williams was not at first impressed with the computer lab in Manchester: "It was one room in a Victorian building whose architectural features might best be described as 'late lavatorial.' The walls were of brown-glazed brick and the door was labelled 'Magnetism Room.'" Williams was ready to go, though—he brought with him an idea he had already been working on at the TRE, using a cathode ray tube as a storage device. What he then invented was called a Williams tube. The stored program was a "pattern of dots" on the face of the tube. Williams tubes were installed in the first Manchester computer, known as the Manchester Baby, as the repository of the computer's random access memory.

By that September, Turing had given up on the project at the NPL and was back at Cambridge. There, he wrote two papers, played chess, went for walks, and attended a wide variety of lectures. He gave a lecture in January 1948 entitled "The Problems of Robots" to the Moral Sciences Club, an association under the auspices of the philosophy department at Cambridge that for many years had offered a venue for the philosophical jousting of thinkers such as Hegel, Wittgenstein, and Karl Popper. At the end of his two Cambridge terms, he wrote a paper entitled "Intelligent Machinery," in which he at first likened the human brain to a machine "which can be organized by suitable training" and went on to define and give examples of machines that did various forms of work (a bulldozer, a telephone, ENIAC) and to propose an as yet uninvented machine that could do work and could also develop or, you might say, learn—his model was the cryptanalysis work done by Colossus, though of course he could not mention it.

In early 1948, Max Newman invited Turing to Manchester to work on the computer project there. Since Williams and Kilburn knew nothing about computers and nothing about Colossus, Newman and Turing had to communicate to them what a computer might do and how it might work without describing what they had accomplished at Bletchley Park. But the two engineers were too far along in the project to allow for much input from the two mathematicians—Newman and Turing were interested in theory, but the engineers were more intent upon producing a workable memory system. As with ENIAC and Colossus, time pressures were pushing the project forward in a way that didn't allow for what Williams and Kilburn considered to be untested ideas, though the pressure this time came not from war, but from the fact that the British government already had a contract with a local weapons and electronics manufacturer to produce the machines once the prototype was built. And Tommy Flowers was having difficulties, too: even though he had invented Colossus, he could not get a computer job, and even though he had done a successful experiment with electronic telephone exchanges in 1939, he made no headway on that front, either.

In the spring of 1949, Atanasoff was invited by General Jacob Devers to leave the Naval Ordnance Lab and move to Fort Monroe, Virginia, as chief scientist for the Army Field Forces. Devers was a West Point contemporary of George Patton who, as an army administrator between the two world wars, had upgraded and reconceived the Field Artillery, then, as an administrator in London, had organized and trained many D-day divisions. His own Sixth Army Group had landed at Marseilles, and according to David P. Colley in the *New York Times:*

The Sixth Army Group reached the Rhine at Strasbourg,
France, on Nov. 24 . . . His force, made up of the United States

Seventh and French First Armies, 350,000 men, had landed Aug. 15 near Marseilles—an invasion largely overlooked by history but regarded at the time as "the second D-Day"—and advanced through southern France to Strasbourg. No other Allied army had yet reached the Rhine, not even hard-charging George Patton's.

Atanasoff was eager to work with Devers, but the general, now sixty-two, retired at the end of September that year. Atanasoff's new boss was General Mark Clark, who had run the Italian campaign. Clark had a reputation for being difficult and egocentric. One history relates that during the war, he had a rule that "every [press] release was to mention Clark at least three times on the front page and at least once on all other pages—and the General also demanded that photographs be taken of him only from his left side." Clark killed several of Atanasoff's projects, and in 1950 Atanasoff returned to the navy to run a program overseeing the development of artillery detonators. Also in 1949, Atanasoff and Lura were divorced, and Atanasoff married Alice Crosby, from Webster City, Iowa, whom he had met through her job in the publications department at the Naval Ordnance Lab.

By mid-1950, Atanasoff felt that his career with the military had reached a dead end, and he was disheartened, too, by the idea that all of his enterprise and inventiveness had gone into making weapons.

In the summer of 1949, Turing was interviewed by a newspaper in relation to a dispute between two other men about machine intelligence and the possibility of a machine having a sensibility. The two men were Norbert Wiener, who had just published *Cybernetics*, and a neurosurgeon, Geoffrey Jefferson, who gave a speech that attempted to debunk any ideas that a machine could have emotions or self-consciousness and could, therefore, be said to think in a human way (Jefferson was a pioneer of the frontal lobotomy). When Turing was interviewed by the *Times* (London), he declared that "the university [of Manchester] was really interested in the investigation of the possibilities of machines for their own sake." This was an inflammatory statement on a sensitive topic, especially in light of the scarcity of government funding for research projects. Max Newman had to write to the *Times* and reassure readers that the Manchester computer then being developed was intended to have practical applications and was, therefore, both worth building and not intended to usurp human beings.

But Turing was not deflected by the outcry. For the next year, he discussed and pondered the question of thinking—how, indeed, could a machine be said to be "thinking"? How could a human interacting with a machine without knowing it detect whether he was interacting with a machine or with another human? The result was a paper, published in October 1950, entitled "Computing Machinery and Intelligence." Turing proposed a thought experiment, a situation in which an investigator would question a man (A) and a woman (B) in order to determine which was the man and which was the woman. The man would be told to obstruct the investigator, and the woman would be instructed to help the investigator. They would supply their answers in written form. Once the reader has considered this situation, he is then asked to consider the same situation, but the man has been replaced by a machine. In this situation, Turing asks, will the investigator be able to solve the puzzle correctly more or less often if A is a machine or a man? In other words, Turing proposed, if a machine can imitate a man answering questions well enough so that there is no difference in the ability of the investigator to pass a given test, then the machine may be said to be thinking. Turing extrapolated from this game to a future date when computers would have sufficient memory storage so as to be able to appear to make decisions and best guesses—at that point, he thought, what they would be doing would be called thinking. More important than answering the question of whether machines might think, though, was the posing of the question. The job of science, Turing felt, was to conjecture, to not be shy about being "heretical."

It was Max Newman who was deflected—for him, the media brouhaha was the beginning of his retreat from computers. According to his son, William Newman, he soon went back to mathematics and focused on his old love, topology. In later years, Max ascribed this withdrawal to the dominance of the engineers, but in addition to that and the public outcry, his son also suspected "that his decision was influenced by his opposition to using the Manchester computer in the development of nuclear weapons." Given his connections to von Neumann, his suspicions were certainly well grounded because von Neumann, of course, was even more involved in the development of the hydrogen bomb than he had been in the development of the atom bomb. He firmly believed that the West had to stay ahead of the Soviet Union, remarking that "with the Russians, it is not a question of whether, but when." According to Norman Macrae, he felt that "all those sitting around the Soviet decision-making tables should know that in the first few minutes of a nuclear war, a bomb would arrive where they were and personally kill all of them."

Chapter Nine

Ｂy the spring of 1947, Mauchly and Eckert had not yet filed the ENIAC patents, which their original agreement with the University of Pennsylvania had given them rights to. That April, they met with von Neumann, Goldstine, Dean Prender of the Moore School, and Irven Travis, the man who had first declared the new, more restrictive patent policy. Ostensibly, the meeting was to discuss potential EDVAC patents; von Neumann brought a lawyer with him. It was at this meeting that the university and Mauchly and Eckert learned for the first time that von Neumann, according to Scott McCartney, "had met with the Pentagon legal department about the patent situation, and had filed an Army War Patent Form himself" on the basis of the "First Draft" document Goldstine had typed up in June 1945. The fact that hundreds of people had read the document constituted publication, as far as the army was concerned, and so the ideas in the document could not be patented. McCartney maintains that this argument on the part of the army was a surprise to von Neumann and Goldstine as well as to Mauchly and Eckert, but, given von Neumann's connections and his habit of being "five blocks" ahead of the competition, it seems unlikely that his lawyer would not have informed him of this possibility before the meeting. The meeting served to spur Mauchly and Eckert's own patenting efforts, and they filed their paperwork at the end of June 1947. According to McCartney, "The application was broad and unfocused and it attempted to make more than one hundred claims covering the computing waterfront." Crucially for the future of computing, Eckert and Mauchly assigned the patent rights they claimed not to themselves, personally, but to their company, in order to lure potential investors and contracts.

Mauchly's job was to manage the company and to find financing and contracts. Eckert's was to oversee the building of their first machine, now dubbed UNIVAC (for UNIVersal Automatic Computer). By December 1947, the company had thirty-six employees, including several engineers and other technicians who had followed Mauchly and Eckert (or had been lured by them) out of the Moore School. Another was Grace Murray Hopper, who had worked for Aiken at MIT and later developed COBOL, the first data processing language that worked like English. Company culture was energetic and exciting—Eckert was an inventive dynamo who showed up late every morning, sometimes six or seven days a week, and worked until late in the evening. But without Goldstine's discipline, Eckert's ideas were not focused on building his machine in a progressive and productive manner—he tinkered with every part and redid everyone's designs. And he did not care for disagreement. McCartney characterizes the engineering side of the company as a "dictatorship," but it was a chaotic dictatorship, which turned out to be a bad form of organization, since the contracts Mauchly was procuring were fixed-price contracts, as if the products were ready, although they were only in development. Even though working on UNIVAC was exciting, cost overruns meant that contracts could not be fulfilled in a timely manner, and new projects had to be added in order to pay for old projects. Eventually, UNIVAC cost $900,000 to develop, though the contracts were worth only $270,000. Eckert and Mauchly were incapable of being frugal, and nothing in their experience at the Moore School had trained them to attempt such a thing. They were accustomed to both the stimulation and the chaos that large teams of inventors generated, but having always been administered, they did not themselves know how to administer. The number of employees crept upward, and at one point engineers were encouraged to purchase stock in the company for $5,000 just to keep the company afloat.

In the meantime, von Neumann took Goldstine and Arthur Burks to Princeton to work on a computer for the Institute for Advanced Study (though Burks left within a few months for a teaching job at the University of Michigan). In the book *Colossus* by Jack Copeland, photograph 50 is a picture of John von Neumann, standing beside the Princeton IAS computer. The picture is undated, but the IAS computer began to operate in the summer of 1951 and was officially operational on June 10, 1952. Along the bottom of the wall of hardware runs a row of shiny metal cylinders, their ends pointing upward at about a forty-five-degree angle (fifteen are visible in the photo). These cylinders are Williams tubes, and they constituted the memory of the IAS computer.

At this point, von Neumann had been organizing his computer project for at least seven years. Back in the summer of 1946, when Atanasoff was told that the navy computer project was off, he was not told why, but part of the reason was that in late 1945, the very well connected John von Neumann had entertained letters of interest from the University of Chicago and MIT, with further feelers from Harvard and Columbia. Von Neumann was drawn to Princeton even though, as the letter from Norbert Wiener of MIT (soon to get in trouble with Dr. Jefferson) predicted, the problem that would plague the development of the IAS computer was that at "the Princestitute [the Institute for Advanced Studies] . . . you are going to run into a situation where you will need a lab at your fingertips, and labs don't grow in ivory towers." Von Neumann got something that he considered more important from the Institute for Advance Study—$100,000 for development (equivalent to $1 million today), with another $200,000 readily available. Even $300,000 would not be enough, though, so von Neumann approached both the army and the navy. Something that von Neumann understood (and that, of course, Atanasoff had also understood) was the computing difficulties of solving nonlinear partial differential equations. But if Atanasoff, writing his dissertation on the dielectric constant of helium in 1930, was forced to grapple with the vast tedium of his equations, von Neumann, overseeing the mathematical side of the Manhattan Project, understood the difficulty even more sharply because he had a greater experience with what the military wanted to do with such equations. Though the equations he had worked out for the detonation of Fat Man and Little Boy were done to the best of the Manhattan Project's mathematical ability, they did not prove as predictive as the army and air force had hoped they would. And von Neumann was also interested in the applicability of such equations to weather patterns and forecasting.

And so, in late 1945 and into 1946, von Neumann wooed both the army and the navy—to the navy, he promised analysis of explosions in water, weather prediction, and even weather control. According to Norman Macrae, von Neumann did not hesitate to threaten the navy with the idea of Josef Stalin using computer-driven weather control to launch a new ice age in North America (though there was no reason to believe that the Soviets were developing a computer and nothing of the sort has since come to light). The army and the navy both kicked in funds for von Neumann's computer, and the navy ended Atanasoff's computer project. To his credit, though, von Neumann understood that the army and the navy had to agree to the same terms in their contracts, so that the project would not be subject to cost cutting by one branch or the other, and he also insisted that the intellectual property that might come out of the project would neither be made top secret nor be patented, thereby ensuring that other projects could also emerge from the IAS project. He seems to have understood all along the implications of the fact that he would be building upon ENIAC, upon the "First Draft," and upon EDVAC, that he would be recruiting to Princeton at least Goldstine and Burks, and that he would make use of his connections with Manchester through Max Newman, and through him to F. C. Williams and Thomas Kilburn. It is quite possible that he understood the relationship between Atanasoff's ideas and what he intended to do, but there is no evidence for it one way or another, other than the fact that he did have conversations with Atanasoff at the NOL.

At Princeton, von Neumann, Goldstine, and, to some extent, Arthur

Burks wrote the papers that codified and described the ideas about computer memory that von Neumann had introduced in the "First Draft." According to Macrae, von Neumann described the ideas, Goldstine and Burks wrote them up, and von Neumann then rewrote them. The final draft was up to Goldstine, but it carried von Neumann's name.

Von Neumann wanted Eckert as his engineer for the Princeton project. Eckert turned him down, according to McCartney, because he remained loyal to Mauchly and, according to Macrae, because he wanted to patent his inventions and profit from them. But Eckert and von Neumann also had a history of conflict, which might have played a part in Eckert's decision. Von Neumann did not approach Atanasoff, although it's hard to avoid the thought that his conversation with Atanasoff at the NOL constituted something of a job interview. Atanasoff found von Neumann congenial—but then, so did almost everyone else. At any rate, the team von Neumann set up did not include Atanasoff. Kirwan Cox maintains that Atanasoff was known at Iowa State for being abrupt and hard to get along with—he had a disconcerting habit of turning away in the middle of conversations: "People thought he was walking away in anger, but he was just finished with the conversation in his own mind. He was tough on people." It may be that von Neumann recognized that Atanasoff was not a team player and that in any project Atanasoff might be involved in, he would insist on calling the shots.

The memory system Eckert was developing was, in the eyes of John von Neumann, one of UNIVAC's main drawbacks. This system, called a mercury delay line, owed something to Eckert's radar experience. The UNIVAC mercury delay line required an array of horizontal cylinders filled with liquid mercury through which electrical impulses could travel rather slowly. The memory worked by recycling the electrical impulses through the mercury over and over, using quartz transducers.[1] Mercury delay line memories had an advantage in that the acoustic conductivity of quartz and mercury were about the same, but

---

1. A computer engineer in England suggested using a delay line with the cylinders filled with gin.

they also had serious drawbacks—the architecture of each cylinder was very particular and they were easy to damage. The word "unwieldy" doesn't even begin to describe a mercury delay line memory—for UNIVAC, the memory required its own room, in which stood seven memory units, each composed of eighteen columns of mercury. This room could store 15,120 bits of memory (equivalent to 1,890 bytes, or not quite 2 kilobytes, although bytes and bits of memory were not standardized at the time—in the UNIVAC I, a byte was 7 bits, not 8). Added to that was the weight and the toxicity of mercury, which in itself limited the general usefulness of the UNIVAC, as well as its potential commercial appeal. And the UNIVAC was a decimal machine, making it even more unwieldy.

When von Neumann, Goldstine, and Burks began on the IAS computer, von Neumann asked RCA (nearby in Philadelphia) to develop a tube that could be used for memory storage. They did, calling their product the Selectron, but the tubes took too long to develop—they were expensive and complicated—so by the end of 1948 von Neumann had decided to adopt Williams tubes.

Another issue von Neumann and his team addressed was that of translation. Just as Atanasoff had realized in 1939 that not every mathematician was comfortable with base-two numbers, and so the results put out by the ABC were automatically translated into decimal numbers, von Neumann realized that the more powerful and useful a computer might become, the more essential a translating mechanism for input and output would be. And von Neumann wanted his computer to do more than solve math problems—he also wanted it to be able to use language (like Colossus, which could decipher a code more easily than it could perform a large multiplication problem—and we will never know whether von Neumann's friends on the Colossus project ever chatted with him about what they had done). Unable to get Eckert, von Neumann hired an engineer named Julian Bigelow to put together the IAS computer, thinking that the project would take ten people about three years.

But von Neumann could not work with Bigelow, who, he felt,

tended to go down blind alleys, trying things without a good sense ahead of time of how those ideas would work. And Norbert Wiener turned out to be correct about the lack of receptivity at the IAS toward the computer project. It was housed in a boiler room and then an outbuilding, and even then there were complaints about it from the other scholars. Work that was farmed out went to corporations that didn't know what was really wanted. Von Neumann himself was an ideas man, not a technology man (though when his wife declared that he could not handle a screwdriver, she added that he was good at fixing zippers). Adding to these difficulties, after January 1950, once Truman gave the go-ahead, von Neumann was hard at work on the hydrogen bomb, work that accelerated through 1950, when Edward Teller's first ideas were proven wrong, and into 1951, when Teller and Stanislaw Ulam came up with an idea that worked. Through both these phases of H-bomb development, the IAS computer did produce necessary calculations, especially after James Pomerene was installed to replace Bigelow. One can only wonder how the construction of the computer would have gone if John Vincent Atanasoff had been allowed to bring his exceptional improvisational talents to it—but perhaps from their conversations, von Neumann understood that in addition to being difficult to work with, Atanasoff had an even greater claim to the computer concepts von Neumann wanted to utilize than Mauchly and Eckert did, and, having experienced what he considered to be Mauchly and Eckert's greed, he did not want to risk that possibility again.

In 1948, a member of Mauchly and Eckert's business team, George Eltgroth, a patent attorney, was approached by a racetrack owner about using computers to break the monopoly of the American Totalizer Company over bookmaking at American racetracks. Eltgroth saw his chance and went to American Totalizer itself. He found a willing partner in Henry Straus, vice president of the tote company—Straus oversaw the investment of $550,000 into UNIVAC—a $62,000 loan and $488,000 for 40 percent of the company stock. But Mauchly's payroll continued to expand—by 1949, there were 134 employees—while the contracts kept contracting. At one time, Mauchly had orders for six UNIVACs, but he had received only $150,000 apiece for the machines, and UNIVAC was still not completed. And then, in November 1949, Henry Straus was killed in a plane crash, and American Totalizer asked for their investment back—now worth $432,000. Eckert and Mauchly then approached IBM. Thomas J. Watson, Sr., later said that he wasn't impressed by Mauchly, but it also turned out that, according to IBM lawyers, antitrust laws forbade IBM from acquiring UNIVAC.

In early 1950, Mauchly and Eckert's company was denied security clearance and therefore banned from accepting top-secret military contracts—a significant portion of those available to private industry. The reasons for the denial of clearance were a mix of anti-Communist paranoia (a member of the engineering team had supported Henry Wallace; Mauchly himself had signed a petition in 1946 supporting civilian control of nuclear energy) and general suspicion—army intelligence asked the FBI to investigate the drowning of Mary Mauchly, which it did, exonerating Mauchly. A few weeks after the denial of security clearance, Remington Rand bought the Eckert-Mauchly Computer Corporation. They paid off the debt to American Totalizer and gave Eckert and Mauchly $100,000 for the remaining 60 percent of the stock, which included the ENIAC patents. The two principals also got a guaranteed $18,000 per year salary and 5 percent of the yearly profits for eight years, should any profits accrue. Thirteen months later, UNIVAC was finally working.

The first UNIVAC, which had been assembled on the second floor of the Eckert-Mauchly building, an old knitting factory, weighed 29,000 pounds and covered 380 square feet of floor space. It used 5,200 vacuum tubes (less than a third of the number in ENIAC) and consumed 125 kilowatts of electricity (as much as 1,250 100-watt lightbulbs, about 16 percent less than ENIAC). The mercury delay line memory was made up of large horizontal cylinders containing liquid mercury that circulated acoustic vibrations representing stored instructions and other data. The external memory, or ROM, was stored on either magnetic tape or punch cards.

Some difficulties with the manufacture of the first UNIVAC arose almost at once—the Eckert-Mauchly building was not air-conditioned and could get so hot in a Philadelphia summer that tar from the roof would melt onto the computer through the ceiling. In fact, no thought had been given to the computer's environment—holes were cut in the walls for summer ventilation that then made the vast room impossible to heat in the winter. And, a serious drawback for a commercial venture, the machine could not be delivered—it was too complex and delicate to be quickly disassembled. At any rate, Mauchly (and Remington Rand) wanted to use the first one for demonstrations only in order to gain more contracts.

But eventually, forty-six UNIVAC I computers were manufactured, sold, and delivered to such companies as Metropolitan Life Insurance, Westinghouse, and U.S. Steel, as well as to government agencies: the Army Map Service (one of the original contracts), the Pentagon, and the Census Bureau (though this one stayed at company headquarters and was operated there). Although Mauchly had charged only $159,000 for the computer in the first contracts, the price eventually rose by almost a factor of 10. UNIVAC I gave way to UNIVAC II in 1958.

In 1951, like Mauchly and Eckert, Atanasoff decided to go into private enterprise, but unlike them, he first mastered the basic principles of accounting (which took him three days) and of business law (about a month). He wrote his own articles of incorporation and lured some of his fellow researchers away from the NOL. The plan was to offer testing services, especially to the military—the cold war meant that there were lots of military contracts, and they were lucrative. He set up his offices in Frederick, Maryland, which he chose after studying the weather patterns in the Washington, D.C., area and deciding that, should there be an atomic attack, Frederick would be outside of the radiation plume, and therefore somewhat safer than his first location of choice, Rockville. In Frederick, he had his corporate headquarters built and equipped with what he considered to be the best supplies for protecting and cleaning the building in the event of an attack—a neoprene-coated roof, sheets of plywood to protect the windows, and boxes of Tide detergent for spraying on the building.

With his usual confidence and frugality, Atanasoff used his own savings as capital for his business, along with investments of those who would be working with him. According to Tammara Burton, the company, which operated on military contracts, was always solvent and never had to borrow money. Atanasoff now focused on his company and deliberately ignored what was going on in the world of computers. The testing Atanasoff's company performed ranged from determining how a projectile might approach and strike an airplane in flight to figuring out how best to drop leaflets on a populated area as a form of psychological warfare (the army gave him this contract during the Korean War). Though the company was successful, entrepreneurial life was taxing in some ways—Atanasoff later recalled, "I have a great deal of affection for the men who are associated with me and we generally understood each other pretty well, but nevertheless they regarded me as a kind of a harsh director, always attempting to advance the work at all times of the day and night . . . I found this discipline severe."

In February 1951 the first Ferranti-manufactured Mark I, the computer developed at the University of Manchester, was delivered to the new university computer lab. According to Andrew Hodges (and this is important for the development of the computer as we know it), "In many ways, [because of Turing's lack of interest in the project], the Computing Laboratory remained as secret as Hut 8," restricting the public relations potential, and therefore sales, of the Manchester computer. EDVAC and UNIVAC dominated the news.

In March of the same year, Alan Turing was elected to the Royal Society, but then, in January 1952, Turing met a young man named

Arnold Murray. Turing was now almost forty, Murray was nineteen. Turing cultivated the acquaintance, and Murray bragged about it to a friend. The unfortunate result was that the friend broke into Turing's house outside of Manchester and stole some of Turing's possessions. Murray managed to get some of the things back from the friend, but by this time, Turing had already reported the burglary. His report alerted the police, who, upon uncovering an illegal homosexual relationship between Turing and Murray, arrested Alan Turing under the draconian Labouchere Amendment to the Criminal Law Amendment Act 1885 (Section 11), which stated that "any male person who, in public or private, commits any act of gross indecency with another male person shall be guilty of a misdemeanour, and being convicted thereof shall be liable at the discretion of the court to be imprisoned for any term not exceeding two years, with or without hard labour," the same law that had been used to prosecute Oscar Wilde.

In his usual unashamed fashion, Turing detailed the nature of his relationship to Murray (he had never been ashamed of his homosexuality, nor had he ever shown caution in expressing himself on any subject). In early April 1952, Turing was convicted of "gross indecency" and given a choice between a year in prison and a year of drug therapy designed to inhibit his sexual desires—a course of estrogen shots (chemical castration). Although such a conviction meant, in the cold war atmosphere of the 1950s, that Turing could no longer work for the British government. His friends felt that he was unrepentant about what had happened—under security surveillance (which he knew about), Turing went to Norway, where he had heard that there were venues for all-male dancing. The letters he wrote to his friends were often bemused and, apparently, lighthearted, though not uniformly so. In a 2009 article in the *Daily Mail* discussing what sort of posthumous honors Turing might receive for his intelligence work during World War II, Geoffrey Wansell points out that the estrogen "transformed his body. The man who had run a marathon in 2 hours and 46 minutes— when the world record was 2 hours and 25 minutes—was reduced to a shadow of his former self. 'They've given me breasts,' he was reported to have said to a friend, describing the shameful process as 'horrible' and 'humiliating.'"

Through 1952 and 1953, Turing engaged in more travel and more work on his theories of brain as machine/machine as brain. And then, on June 8, 1954, Alan Turing was found by his housekeeper, dead of cyanide poisoning in his house in Manchester, a half-eaten apple by his bedside (he customarily ate an apple before going to bed). There was no suicide note.

Turing's mother never believed that he had committed suicide—she thought that he had died accidentally, as a result of a careless chemistry experiment. Others pointed out that as a convicted homosexual who liked to travel abroad and make contact with young men, he was seen by the British security services as not only a risk, but a growing risk, since the cold war was escalating quickly. Turing was highly knowledgeable about Colossus and all sorts of other state secrets, and now he was a convicted but unrepentant homosexual who was associated with King's College, which, along with Trinity College, was considered to be a hotbed of Soviet spies (Guy Burgess and Donald Maclean, who had defected to the Soviet Union in 1951, had been at Trinity College in the thirties and were also homosexuals). Some people continue even in 2010 to feel that he was assassinated, with a "suicide" staged by British security. Or perhaps they had simply invited him to commit suicide. Friends remembered Turing wondering aloud about methods for committing suicide—they thought at the time that he was merely engaging in one of his frequent thought experiments. Others have suggested that, thanks to his gross indecency conviction and to his unorthodox ideas, Turing was at the end of his career and knew it. In any event, he died in obscurity, thirty years before either his role in World War II cryptanalysis or his role in the invention of the computer would emerge.

Chapter Ten

By the early 1950s, three computers had made their way into the marketplace.

In England, a second Ferranti Mark 1 was ordered for the Atomic Energy Research Establishment, near Oxford, to be delivered in 1952. But after the Labour government headed by Clement Atlee was thrown out in October 1951, the new Tory government, headed by Winston Churchill, canceled all government contracts worth more than a hundred thousand pounds, and so the second Ferranti machine was never completed. Work on the computer was halted, and it was later bought for very little by the University of Toronto. However, seven other Ferranti computers (of a slightly different design) were sold, one to Shell Labs in Amsterdam. But it was not only expense that killed the development of computers in England, it was also vigilant secrecy. According to Kirwan Cox, the Canadian filmmaker, because Churchill had found himself quoted in *Mein Kampf* about how England had won the First World War, he "became paranoid about information that had enabled the British victory getting out again." Presumably, the enemy to be wary of was now the Soviet Union.

There was much more money and much more self-promotion in the United States. In March 1951 UNIVAC became available, and in 1952 the IBM 701 was unveiled at the end of April. The 701 was an offshoot of von Neumann's IAS computer. Like the IAS, it used Williams tubes for memory (72 in one version, 144 in another). It was intended for use as a scientific calculator (and had been known while in development as the "Defense Calculator"). The 701 was joined by the 702, the 650, and the 705. The 701 and the 650 were designed for business use; IBM seemed destined to consolidate a share of what was turning out to be an actual market, but then, in the November presidential election between Dwight D. Eisenhower and Adlai Stevenson, the UNIVAC scored a big public relations victory when it predicted the outcome for CBS based on early returns. The PR coup might have been designed by an advertising agency—at first the UNIVAC's predictions looked so out of whack that network operators fiddled with them in order to avoid embarrassment, but then the network had to admit even greater embarrassment—the original unfiddled predictions turned out to be very close to the actual results of the election. When CBS revealed what had happened on the air, UNIVAC became the face of the computer in the 1950s public imagination, and the result for Remington Rand was more sales, this time lucrative ones, to companies rather than to the government.

IBM had two commercial advantages, though: one was the punch-card system that many offices already had in place, and the other was the business model, which focused upon leasing and service rather than outright sales. It looked as though IBM was to dominate the business market and foil von Neumann's plan for the computer to be based upon common intellectual property rather than proprietary patents.

But von Neumann's dissemination of the ideas behind ENIAC meant that there were people working on designing and building computers all over the United States—challenges to the original ENIAC patents by Control Data, Honeywell, Burroughs, General Electric, RCA, and National Cash Register began almost immediately, and they meant that the ENIAC patents (which made more than a hundred proprietary claims) were slow to be awarded to Remington Rand, who had obtained them when they bought out Mauchly and Eckert.

In October 1953, Pres Eckert published an article on computer memory in the *Journal of the Institute of Radio Engineers* in which he knowledgeably described the structure and the function of the ABC's memory system and also expressed admiration for its frugality: "There may have been similar systems prior to Atanasoff's, but none was as inexpensive to construct." Eckert's article served to motivate the patent department at IBM, which, like the smaller companies, had come to believe that Eckert and Mauchly's ENIAC patents might be broken. Clifford Berry learned that IBM was looking for information about "capacitor drum storage devices," or, as Atanasoff had called his invention, "regenerative memory." Berry's work on the ABC was known at Consolidated Engineering, his place of business in Pasadena, and what the IBM representative learned from a lawyer in the patent office at Berry's company was the subject of an IBM in-house memorandum of September 30, 1953—Consolidated Engineering planned to visit Iowa State and look into Berry's claims. IBM decided to collaborate on this investigation. The Consolidated Engineering patent attorney also informed IBM that "he had heard rumors that Burroughs, National Cash, and IBM were planning, as part of a team, to form a patent pool, particularly with a view of fighting the Eckert-Mauchly patents." Kirwan Cox believes that the sequence of events was slightly different— Berry saw Eckert's article, read the patent, and told his employer that the patent was based on the prior art of the ABC. Consolidated Engineering was already doing business with IBM, and so contacted IBM about the apparent patent infringement. The younger Thomas J. Watson, much more interested in computers than his father had been, was eager to circumvent the ENIAC patents. In April 1954, a representative from IBM interviewed Clifford Berry in California. On June 14, when he visited Atanasoff in Frederick, Maryland, the IBM representative, a man named A. J. Etienne, even said, "If you will help us, we will break the Mauchly-Eckert computer patent; it was derived from you."

According to Burton, Atanasoff was floored by this declaration—he had believed Mauchly when he told him at the Naval Ordnance Lab eleven years earlier that the new computer he and Eckert were developing was different from the ABC and "better" than the ABC. But Etienne seemed to know what he was talking about. He said that the particular patent that IBM wanted to challenge was the patent for the memory system—that is, the rotating drum with the rows of capacitors that were regenerated by vacuum tubes. This patent had been finally issued to Remington Rand in the previous year, 1953; possibly IBM knew that Atanasoff had invented this memory system, so this was the patent that they chose to challenge. Etienne asked Atanasoff for all of the relevant paperwork concerning the ABC, but thirteen years, a war, a divorce, and several moves had intervened, and Atanasoff was unable to find what he needed immediately. On June 21, Etienne sent him a copy of Eckert and Mauchly's patent and Atanasoff wrote back, promising to get him as much of the paperwork as he could. But he never heard from Etienne again, and as far as he knew, the patent challenge was dropped. When Atanasoff read through Eckert and Mauchly's patent, he saw that it was based on his ideas, but he assumed the case was dropped because the IBM lawyers had decided that breaking the patent was not feasible.

It was not that IBM had decided that breaking the patent was not feasible; rather, they had decided to make a secret deal with Remington Rand. The deal was to be beneficial for both parties—UNIVAC mostly used an awkward and unfamiliar magnetic tape system for external storage of data; most offices in the market for a computer already had lots of data punched onto IBM cards, and the IBM 650 used these cards. It was not as powerful a computer as UNIVAC, but because of the punch-card storage system, it was a successful entry into the business computer market. But IBM was sued under antitrust laws for using leasing agreements and proprietary punch-card systems to monopolize the office machine market. The solution seemed to be that IBM would sign a consent decree with Remington Rand. The two companies sued each other for patent access. In the meantime, in 1955, Sperry, originally a company specializing in aviation and navigation products (such as gyroscopes, but also the ball turret gun mounted underneath the B-17 during the war), bought Remington Rand.

About two years after Etienne's contact with Atanasoff, IBM entered into a private agreement with Sperry Rand, agreeing to pay $10 million over eight years in exchange for access to the ENIAC patents. Once the agreement had been signed, IBM and Sperry aggressively pursued what they considered patent violations by other companies.

However, IBM and Sperry Rand were busy looking around for other computer ideas. One man whom Konrad Zuse had impressed with the Z4, Helmut Goeze, had married an American woman and moved to the United States. Goeze not only knew that the Z4 could calculate, he knew the amazing tale of its journey from Berlin to Austria at the end of the war. As Zuse writes, "Now in the United States, Goeze wanted to lend his support to this world-important something." Somehow, Goeze contacted Thomas J. Watson, Sr., who in turn contacted Hollerith Germany, an IBM subsidiary.[1] Representatives from Hollerith Germany visited Zuse and the Z4, but they wanted neither the machine nor Zuse's services—they wanted his intellectual property rights. Over the course of the next year, Zuse negotiated with the company, and as it happened he did make a nice sum of money, in part because the negotiations took so long, and in part because the sum negotiated was in reichsmarks—by the time he cashed the check, reichsmarks had become deutschemarks, which were worth twice as much as reichsmarks. But Hollerith Germany would not hire Zuse for any kind of research—it seems clear in retrospect that throughout the fifties, IBM's main interest was in cornering the computer market. Zuse did get a research grant from Remington Rand, but it was for a technology that Zuse felt was already superseded—mechanical switching. Zuse thought that he got the grant simply because Remington Rand "still did not completely trust their own [ENIAC-based] electronics, so they wanted to have more than one egg in their basket, just in case."

---

1. For more information about this connection, see Edwin Black's *IBM and the Holocaust: The Strategic Alliance Between Nazi Germany and America's Most Powerful Corporation* (New York: Crown, 2001).

John von Neumann was busy, too, but not on the computer. Once the cold war arms race was well under way, he devoted more and more of his time to advising the United States government, and he gained more and more influence. He may have decided that he had done what he could for computers and that, as Max Newman felt, they were now in the hands of the engineers. And then, in the summer of 1955, he suffered a spontaneous shoulder fracture. That August, he learned that he had a tumor on his left clavicle, probably a metastasis from undiagnosed pancreatic cancer. There was some suspicion that his illness was the result of radiation exposure during his time in A-bomb labs. He was not yet fifty-two. By November 1956 he was in a wheelchair, and by January 1957 he was in and out of the hospital with brain cancer (the Atomic Energy Commission posted a security guard by the door to his hospital room for fear that he would reveal atomic secrets when he was "screaming in horror"). But he continued to advise the government from his deathbed and died on February 8, not quite three years after Turing.

In early 1959, an IBM official sent an inquiry to Sperry, asking to see the copy of Clifford Berry's master's thesis, "Design of Electrical Data Recording and Reading Mechanisms," which Sperry had obtained in 1953 and in which Berry described the ABC's regenerative memory. This alerted Sperry, and a Sperry vice president, R. H. Sorensen, began to poke around—he called Iowa State to inquire about the ABC. According to Kirwan Cox, Sperry also hired Howard Aiken to go to Iowa State and look into the matter—he would have, of course, discovered that the ABC had been dismantled. Sorensen took Atanasoff to lunch at the exclusive and elegant Cosmos Club in Washington, D.C. After the lunch, Sorensen sent an in-house memo that conceded that the patents Sperry had inherited from Mauchly and Eckert did overlap with technology already realized in the ABC, but as a result of his meeting with Atanasoff, he doubted that Atanasoff would pursue any legal action—Atanasoff had tried to interest Sorensen in another idea he had for a calculating machine that would have some character-istics of a desktop calculator and some characteristics of a punch-card electronic tabulator. Sorensen politely put him off. Atanasoff was not as gullible as Sorensen thought, however, because after the lunch, he obtained copies of the patents in question, and he saw that they did replicate work that he had done on the ABC. He then went back to his own ordnance business, but not without stowing his new information in a safe place.

Atanasoff's Ordnance Engineering Corporation had prospered. In 1956, it was bought for a healthy sum by Aerojet General Corporation, a California company specializing in rocket propulsion technology. Atanasoff took half the proceeds in cash and half in stock—subsequently, the stock split so many times that Atanasoff became a wealthy man. For a few years, Atanasoff worked as vice president and head of the East Coast division, and then, in 1960, he was offered the chance to head the space division, which he turned down. Corporate life did not suit him in several ways—later he said, "I did not want to spend the rest of my life selling and it looked as if the principal effort of the Vice-president of Aerojet was to sell." Now with plenty of money after a life of frugality, he decided to retire. He was fifty-eight. He immediately embarked upon several projects—he purchased two hundred acres in Maryland and began to design and build an innovative house of a more-than-modern design that incorporated just the sort of unorthodox ideas that a man like Atanasoff would want in his dream house—not only energy-efficient cooling and heating systems and a functional layout, but also tilt-up panel construction and an eight-hundred-pound front door that rotated on brass bearings. He continued to involve himself in the lives of his grandchildren, which could be, according to Burton, less than com-fortable for them. She writes, "Retirement mellowed Atanasoff very little, and he remained intense and challenging to others. One reporter described him as 'creative and cantankerous,' while his daughter Joanne postulated that 'conflict was his favorite pastime' . . . He enjoyed test-ing people and was fond of drawing friends and family into intense dis-cussions—or arguments—as a means by which to grade their mental acuity . . . he kept tabs on his grandchildren's schoolwork and carved out time during visits to test us on pertinent material."

By 1960, Turing and von Neumann were dead, Arthur Burks was teaching philosophy at the University of Michigan, Max Newman had returned to topology, and Mauchly and Eckert had failed at owning and running their own computer business (though Mauchly had run the UNIVAC division at Sperry until 1959, then started his own consulting firm). Mauchly had received an honorary doctorate from the University of Pennsylvania, the Scott Medal from the Franklin Institute, and other Philadelphia-based awards. Eckert was still with Sperry Rand (he stayed with Sperry, and then Unisys, until 1989). Neither Mauchly nor Eckert had profited directly from the ENIAC patent, but they did get credit (and they did seek that credit) for inventing the computer. Eckert, in particular, was vocal about the inaccuracy of the phrase "von Neumann architecture"—he thought it should be called "Eckert architecture." But the vagaries of patent law and the delay in awarding the Eckert and Mauchly patents seemed to be working for Sperry. If the patent had been awarded in 1947, it would have run out by 1964, before computers became big business. However, in 1960, the patent was still being challenged. It would not be finally awarded until 1964. At that point, it looked as though it would run into the eighties.

Zuse finally got to visit the United States and see what computers had been and were being built there, when he and his partner, Harro Stucken, accompanied their mechanical punch calculator test model to Sperry Rand headquarters in Norwalk, Connecticut. Although Zuse understood that the future of computers was electronic, he had contrived a method of doing mathematical operations on punch cards that allowed as many as ten cards to operate simultaneously. It was a mechanical calculator, but it was fast and cleverly conceived, and even though it was never put into mass production, it provided Zuse with funding for his company. Among those they got to visit were General Leslie Groves, who had run the Manhattan Project, and Howard

Aiken, who was still advocating using decimal numbers for computers. Zuse writes, "At Harvard they were still completely convinced that the computer was an American invention." Some years later, Aiken wrote to Zuse, acknowledging the foresight of his earlier ideas. They were also taken to see the Whirlwind at MIT and were most impressed by its size.[2] But Zuse's business connections were Swiss more than American, and eventually the Z4, after years in a barn in the Austrian Alps, and thanks to the man in the elegant automobile, was sent to Zurich, "the sixth transport we put it through." When the day came to demonstrate it, the Z4 started sparking and then went dead during an afternoon test run. Zuse and his partners did not panic, though—they discovered that the problem had to do with a newly installed transformer and fixed it: "We had exactly a half an hour to correct the error and replace the burned out lines. We did it, aired out the faint burning smell, and at four o'clock our illustrious guests witnessed a perfect demonstration." Eventually, Zuse came to have his "fondest memories" of his years in Zurich. He admired his colleagues, and his computer continued to operate so reliably that it could be left on, unattended, overnight. He writes, "Many a night, I walked through the lonely streets of Zurich, on my way to check on the Z4. It was a strange feeling, entering the deserted ETH[3] and hearing, already by the time I reached the first floor, that, on the top floor, the Z4 was still running perfectly. In those days you could tell from the rhythm of the punched tape reader."

In 1962, Richard Kohler Richards, who had a doctorate in electrical engineering, had worked at IBM, and had written several books on computers including *Arithmetic Operations in Digital Computers* and

---

2. The Whirlwind was another offspring of ENIAC. A man named Perry Crawford was working at MIT, trying to create computerized flight simulators for the navy. They were using analog ideas before Crawford saw ENIAC in 1945. Subsequently, the U.S. Air Force based the SAGE early warning system on the Whirlwind.
3. Eidgenössische Technische Hochschule Zürich.

Digital Computer Components and Circuits, decided to return to Ames, where he had been an undergraduate at Iowa State, and write a book about the history of the computer. His neighbor turned out to be a man named Harry Burrell, who remembered writing a press release about the Atanasoff-Berry Computer around the time that the *Des Moines Tribune* ran a brief article, with a picture, about the machine (January 15, 1941). The article stated, "An electrical computing machine said here to operate more like the human brain than any other such machine known to exist is being built by Dr. John V. Atanasoff, Iowa State College Physics Professor. The machine contains more than 300 vacuum tubes and will be used to compute complicated algebraic equations. Dr. Atanasoff said it will occupy about as much space as a large office desk. The instrument will be entirely electrical and will be used in research experiments." But there was no record of or paperwork concerning the machine in either the library or the engineering publications office. It was then that Richards visited Sam Legvold, who had returned to the physics department at Iowa State after the war and had worked with Atanasoff on his defense department project in the basement of the physics building, right next to the ABC, and later with him at the NOL.

Legvold remembered the ABC quite well, and not only that, he had a drum from the computer that he had salvaged from the 1948 wreckage. He also remembered talking with Berry about the computer, though not with Atanasoff—with Atanasoff, he had only discussed the defense project they were working on. Legvold was not the only physics professor who remembered the ABC, but no one remembered how it worked (if they had ever known) or the principles behind it. In February 1963, Richards wrote to Atanasoff to inquire about the machine, but Atanasoff was too busy with his retirement projects to give him much help. Once again he was moving house—this time building the house—and once again, perhaps, the paperwork didn't seem worth finding. Atanasoff always invested himself fully in his project of the minute, and in addition, none of his contacts with IBM or Sperry about the ABC had ever come to anything. He suggested that

Richards contact Clifford Berry, who was younger and might remember the ABC in more detail.

In March, Richards wrote to Berry. Berry was now in his early forties, still married to Atanasoff's former secretary, and gainfully employed in the research and development department at Consolidated Engineering Corporation (later to become a part of Bell and Howell and then DuPont). Consolidated Engineering specialized in developing mass spectrometers. In 1945, Berry had invented his own small computer for the purpose of sorting through the large amount of data produced by the mass spectrometer. Berry had invented many other things— eventually, he owned almost thirty patents in addition to the patent for his small computer. Richards also wrote to the UNIVAC division at Sperry, looking for John Mauchly's address.

Berry replied ten days later. He remembered the ABC perfectly well. He directed Richards to his master's thesis in the Iowa State library and also told him about the report for the Iowa State College Research Corporation and the patent applications that had been written but never filed. He added, "An interesting sidelight is that in 1940 or 1941 we had a visit from Dr. John Mauchly who spent a week learning all of the details of our computer and the philosophy of its design. He was the only person outside of the Research Corporation and the patent counsel who was given this opportunity, and he may still have notes of what he learned from us." Berry then went on to give a concise description of the ABC. He wrote:

> I am not sure what Dr. Atanasoff told you about the machine so I will describe it briefly. The machine was designed specifically to solve sets of linear simultaneous algebraic equations up to 30 x 30. All internal operations were carried on in binary arithmetic; the size of the numbers handled was up to 50 binary places (about 15 decimal places). Initial input of data was by means of standard IBM cards, with five 15-place numbers per card; the machine translated the numbers to binary numbers. The machine's "memory" consisted of two rotating drums filled

with small capacitors. The polarity of the charge on a given capacitor represented the binary digit standing in that position. A "clock" frequency of 60 cycles per second was used, the mechanical parts of the machine being driven with a synchronous motor. Storage of intermediate results was by means of a special binary card punch, with which 30 binary numbers, each 50 digits long, could be punched on one card. The mathematical method employed to solve sets of equations was that of systematic elimination of coefficients through linear combinations of pairs of equations.

He included six pictures as well as copies of the news stories about the ABC. For the next few months, Richards and Berry conducted a detailed correspondence about the ABC. Berry, still in the computer business, was amazed to discover that the record of the ABC at Iowa State was so thin, and also that Atanasoff himself had not kept up with what was going on in computers sufficiently to maintain the record of his own contributions. The correspondence supplied Richards with enough detailed information to establish apparent links between the ABC and ENIAC.

Mauchly did not respond to Richards's first letter and then did not return his calls. But Richards was persistent. When he finally reached Mauchly in the late summer, Mauchly was not happy to hear from him. He derided the ABC, but he did admit to staying in Ames for several days, looking at the computer, and discussing it with Atanasoff. Richards later wrote in his book *Electronic Digital Systems*, "The Atanasoff Berry computer . . . does . . . appear to predate every other electronic digital system by a matter of years."

In the meantime, Berry decided to take another job, this time in Huntington, New York, on the North Shore of Long Island, at the Vacuum-Electronics Corporation. He left Pasadena in early October and went to Long Island, stopping at a conference for a week on the way. He rented a room, intending to look for a house (he found two), buy a new car, and prepare the way for his family to move east. The company agreed to his request to bring Jean Berry east to New York so that she could choose between the two houses. Berry called Jean every night, and he seemed to her to be excited about both his new job and their new life. But on October 30, before she was due to leave for New York (on November 6), she received a phone call from the Huntington police—Clifford Berry had been found in his rented room, dead, with a plastic bag over his head. The cause of death was listed as "probable suicide."

Jean Berry discovered when she went east that the police were not sure of what had happened—they maintained a sealed-off crime scene in the room where the death occurred for three weeks. Atanasoff was suspicious enough to drive from Maryland to Long Island and talk to the landlord, who declared that he himself had easily removed the plastic bag from Berry's face. Jean Berry and Atanasoff eventually became convinced that Berry had not committed suicide, though Scott McCartney raises doubts about Berry's mental condition in his defense of Eckert and Mauchly, by stating that he had been in two car accidents, which "left him in substantial pain," and that "he was intoxicated at the time of his death." In fact, when Jean Berry first told Atanasoff about Clifford Berry's death, she did not mention suicide at all, but said she thought that it might be related to head injuries suffered in a car accident in 1956 that had resulted in occasional seizures. But Jean Berry later wrote, "When I told a physician what I knew, he said that Cliff could not have possibly killed himself—he was murdered: 'It's like trying to hold your breath; you can't.'" She believed to the end of her life that he had indeed been murdered (though there is no public record of who she thought was responsible). Others shared her belief. Kirwan Cox, the Canadian filmmaker who has researched Atanasoff and Berry and done numerous interviews, maintains that whether Berry was or wasn't murdered, the unarguable result of Berry's death was its "huge impact on Atanasoff. Prior to Berry's death, Atanasoff had not wanted to discuss the ABC, because he was too upset about the destruction of the ABC. But Atanasoff believed Berry was murdered, and that he would not have died if Atanasoff had not hired him to work on the machine.

[The] death of Berry changed his attitude to the patent lawsuits, and he became quite energetic in pursuing the patent conflict."

When R. K. Richards's book *Electronic Digital Systems* was published three years later, in 1966, some of the first people to read it were patent lawyers at several computer companies. One of these was a man named Allen Kirkpatrick, who had been hired by Control Data Corporation (the home of Seymour Cray, who was later to found Cray Research) to defend CDC against a case of patent infringement brought by Sperry Rand. CDC was being sued along with Honeywell, and they had decided to collaborate on their defense. Richards's book was sizable and respectable, given his earlier work. It was Richards who coined the term "Atanasoff-Berry Computer," and in the book's preface, he stated point-blank, "The ancestry of all electronic digital systems appears to be traceable to a computer which will be called the Atanasoff-Berry Computer." Since in spite of the lingering patent controversies ENIAC was famous for being the world's first computer, it proved something of a shock to the computer world when Richards stated, "There was, however, one interesting link between the machine and later work. One of the few people to study the [ABC] in detail was Dr. John Mauchly . . . According to oral reports from Dr. Atanasoff and Dr. Mauchly, the two met at an American Association for the Advancement of Science Meeting. As a result of conversations at this meeting, Dr. Mauchly made a visit to ISU in 1941 for the specific purpose of studying the computer. As mentioned later, Dr. Mauchly is given credit for subsequently initiating the ENIAC project."

Control Data Corporation may have had a special desire to break the Eckert-Mauchly patents because they had firsthand knowledge of them. CDC had originally been a company called Engineering Research Associates and had grown out of a World War II U.S. Navy code-breaking operation. Just after the war, ERA continued to build code-breaking machines designed around rotating drums and paper tape readers (there is no evidence that the ERA inventors knew about Colossus), and they did successfully break several Soviet codes, but when in 1949 the Soviets changed the code that had been broken the previous year (shades of what had happened with Enigma in 1942), the machine they had devised stopped being useful. ERA at first decided to go into scientific computers, but then there was a conflict-of-interest scandal on the military procurement side, and the company went broke and was sold to Remington Rand. In the mid-fifties, when Remington Rand was bought by Sperry, the ERA computer group was consolidated into the UNIVAC division. The original ERA group grew restive at UNIVAC and left to form Control Data. They did well—by 1964, the Control Data CDC 6600 supercomputer had successfully challenged the comparable IBM computer, especially in terms of processing speed (three times faster than the IBM). CDC was hard at work on the next version; the stakes were high, and Sperry Rand, IBM, and Control Data knew it.

Honeywell was a much older company, owing its existence to the 1885 invention of a thermostat for coal furnaces. By the 1960s, Honeywell's technological products had ranged away from heating and plumbing inventions into all sorts of other fields, including the autopilot mechanism for aircraft, which was invented during the war, the ubiquitous round wall-mounted thermostat, and many sorts of gyroscopes. Honeywell got into the computer business by joining with Raytheon to form Datamatic and then buying out Raytheon (Raytheon was the company founded in 1922 by Vannevar Bush, inventor of the Bush Analyzer).

CDC and Honeywell were beginning the suit at a disadvantage— Bell Labs, where George Stibitz had invented his K-for-Kitchen calculator in 1937, had already tried suing Sperry and lost. The judge said that Bell had not produced evidence of "prior public use" of the ideas incorporated into ENIAC. The lawyer assigned to the Honeywell/CDC case knew this because he had worked at the law firm that pursued the Bell Labs case. Before Richards's revelations, the CDC/ Honeywell defense focused on the competing claims of engineers and scientists who had worked with Mauchly and Eckert on ENIAC— plenty of them felt that in their broad patent, Mauchly and Eckert claimed ideas that other people had come up with. Because of this,

Honeywell and CDC hoped that Sperry might be willing to negotiate, but they couldn't count on such an eventuality, and even while proposing a settlement, they began working on a different approach.

Honeywell and CDC had several pieces of luck—one of these was that the general counsel of the patent division at Honeywell was an Iowa State College graduate in electrical engineering, and a classmate of R. K. Richards. Allen Kirkpatrick and his assistant, Kevin Joyce, were also electrical engineering graduates who had gone on to law school. When they read what Richards wrote about the ABC, they understood it, and when they visited Atanasoff, always prickly and impatient with the ignorant, they could talk to him and convince him that they understood what he was saying. Perhaps their greatest piece of luck, though, was that when Atanasoff at last took the time to rummage through all of the old boxes he had been moving over the twenty years since leaving the house on Woodland Street in Ames, he found everything he had kept, and everything they needed.

The most important member of the legal team was a young lawyer named Charles Call, who in 1966 was twenty-eight years old and had already worked on six successful patents for Bell Labs. Call was familiar with vacuum tubes and ham radios. He understood the Richards book, and he was able to understand two other documents that he obtained from Iowa State—Clifford Berry's master's thesis and Atanasoff's thirty-five-page description of the ABC, written in August 1940. By the time he read the Atanasoff documents, he had done considerable work on the case already, and, as Clark Mollenhoff points out, "Studying Atanasoff's memorandum against the background of his months of study of the ENIAC, EDVAC, and UNIVAC patents, Charles Call became convinced that Atanasoff's concepts at the time of Mauchly's visit were far ahead of his time. Also, they went beyond ENIAC and included many of the most important concepts of such second-generation . . . computers as EDVAC." As Kirwan Cox notes, in contradiction to Mauchly's remarks to Atanasoff during his visits to the Naval Ordnance Lab, progress toward the modern computer involved adhering more closely to the ABC model, not moving away from it.

But Call knew that Honeywell and CDC were still at a disadvantage — as good as the documentation looked, it would be difficult to establish to the satisfaction of a judge that Atanasoff's claim to prior art (something publically known or published about an invention that challenges that invention's claim to novelty or "nonobviousness") was more important than leaving things as they were. And Atanasoff himself was now in his mid-sixties — though he looked healthy, with Berry dead, he was the only source for detailed technical information. To safeguard this aspect, Call videotaped Atanasoff's depositions (a first, according to Tammara Burton) and photographed every page of his documentation. It was only after reading through these copies that Call began to feel confidence in the Honeywell/CDC case.

There were in fact two cases — the Honeywell case concerned the ENIAC patents, which covered more than a hundred ideas (after Mauchly and Eckert lost possession of the EDVAC ideas in 1947, they had decided to claim as much ground as possible). The CDC case covered only one patent, patent 827, concerning what Atanasoff had called "regenerative memory" — this was the same patent IBM had proposed challenging in 1954. The Honeywell case had a rather dramatic beginning — on May 26, 1967, as soon as the Sperry lawyers signaled the company's unwillingness to settle, a runner from the Minneapolis law firm hurried to the courthouse to file the case. He arrived there fifteen minutes before his counterpart in Washington, D.C., arrived at his local courthouse. This, plus a subsequent finding by Judge John Sirica, in Washington, that the case would take up too much time in the crowded District of Columbia schedule, meant that the case was to be tried in Minneapolis. The less dramatic CDC case was to be tried in Baltimore.

Sperry Rand, in the meantime, wasn't focusing only on CDC and Honeywell — the company was also suing General Electric for patent infringement. One of the attorneys for General Electric turned out to be George Eltgroth, who had helped Eckert and Mauchly file the original patents and connect with American Totalizer (another of the GE attorneys was an electrical engineer who had helped Berry build the ABC while at Iowa State). Eltgroth had never heard of Atanasoff, Berry, or Mauchly's trip to Ames in 1941. This meant that if a connection could be proven, and Mauchly had knowingly withheld that information, he would have failed to comply with full-disclosure rules for patents. In this context, Eckert's October 1953 remarks about the ABC in the *Journal of the Institute of Radio Engineers* that had originally alerted IBM to a potential patent problem were also significant. Eltgroth heard about Atanasoff in a meeting devoted to GE defense. He exclaimed, "If I had known, I could have protected them!" Why Mauchly had acted as he did, and indeed how his mind worked, subsequently became a matter of considerable interest and deepening mystery.

Another piece of luck for Honeywell and Control Data was that on the very day when Call finished reading over his copies of Atanasoff's documents, including Mauchly's enthusiastic letters to Atanasoff after seeing the ABC, he happened to go to a panel on computer science chaired by a man named Isaac Auerbach, who had, in 1960, established the International Federation for Information Processing Societies. Mauchly was to be on the panel and was listed in the program as the "inventor of the first automatic electronic digital computer." Auerbach, who had worked on ENIAC and had been employed at Sperry UNIVAC, had also read Richards's book. He asked Mauchly to comment on Richards's assertions about the Atanasoff-Berry Computer. Mauchly admitted that he had gone to Ames to see the computer and that he had talked to Atanasoff about it. Then he gave Call a foretaste of his future testimony—the computer hadn't worked, he hadn't learned anything from Atanasoff, he hadn't spent much time with the machine. Since Call had Atanasoff's letters and documents, all of which corroborated an entirely different story, Call knew that such a defense would hurt Sperry's case, whatever Mauchly's motives. Whether he remembered what had really happened and was banking on Atanasoff not retaining the documents, or whether he actually had no memory of his response to the ABC, he would be seriously compromised either way.

Chapter Eleven

Before the death of Clifford Berry, Atanasoff had been reluctant to involve himself in the patent dispute between Sperry Rand on one side and Honeywell and Control Data on the other because the only thing in it for him was recognition, and that was uncertain because as far as the courts were concerned, it meant returning to a question that had already been decided in favor of Sperry Rand and it meant abrogating patents that had long been in dispute and then issued by the U.S. Patent Office. The case therefore involved at least an implicit challenge to the patenting process itself. For that reason, Honeywell and CDC had a small advantage in the fact that the case would be tried in Minneapolis rather than in Washington, D.C. But all the lawyers for Honeywell and CDC knew it was an uphill fight, and Atanasoff did too, because he had studied patent law with his usual energy in the course of his business ventures.

Once he was engaged, Atanasoff took his customary pedagogical position and tested the lawyers to see if he could count on them to understand the ideas behind the ABC. But there was more to it—it was as if he could only participate wholeheartedly if he could thoroughly understand a process and a system. He had to learn everything he could about it in order to get it into his mind and go forward—just as he had taught himself to drive the family Ford at age twelve by learning everything he could about how the automobile worked and how to fix it if something went wrong. And so he used the lawyers to learn what he needed to know. Probably they privately considered the old man a pest.

Atanasoff made a list of witnesses to be interviewed and deposed. On the list were those whom he remembered as having been around during the construction of the machine and during Mauchly's visit to Ames—notably absent, and profoundly missed, of course, was Clifford Berry. Prominent on the list was Robert Mather, a professor at Berkeley who had worked on the computer with Berry as an undergraduate at Iowa State. But Mather, who had not been around for Mauchly's visit, told Call and Kirkpatrick, "I just wasn't sophisticated enough to particularly notice who [people who visited the machine] were." He also said, "You see, Cliff did most of . . . the more complicated things, the more routine things were turned over to me. I was soldering the wires to brushes and the terminal board to the binary-to-decimal converter." An interesting addendum to this quotation from Mollenhoff's book is the observation by John Gustafson that "I'm not sure we could have reconstructed the ABC without Mather's input. He was proud of the fine job he had done of wiring the machine neatly, and it was one reason he took those sharp black-and-white photos of the computer. I'm not sure we have a single photo of the original ABC that was not taken by Mather."

A more productive interview was conducted with Sam Legvold. Though he had never talked to Atanasoff about the computer, he had been very good friends with Clifford Berry. He also had both a strong interest in the ABC and an excellent memory. A new graduate student in the fall of 1939, Legvold remembered the pre-ABC prototype in considerable detail—he had seen it operate, and he also remembered many things Berry had told him about how it worked and how it was constructed. He remembered, too, visits by experts—a representative from the Rockefeller Foundation and a man from MIT and the NDRC. He also remembered Mauchly, and in some detail.

Legvold, about twenty-two at the time of Mauchly's visit, remembered going to lunch with the thirty-three-year-old Ursinus professor and finding him "a rather delightful fellow, pretty bright and stimulating." He remembered him "being in there with his shirtsleeves rolled up, pitching in to help do some things on the computer as we sat and talked about it." In the course of his own work, Legvold passed through the computer room quite frequently. He remembered that Mauchly had been around for three days — "more than just a drop-in-for-an-afternoon-kind of thing." He also remembered that Mauchly had taken "a sharp interest" in the ABC; the discussions among Berry, Atanasoff, and Mauchly had been "free and open," and he had seemed to understand the principles behind the machine.

Once Charles Call (who was representing Honeywell) had finished with Legvold, it was time for Allen Kirkpatrick, who was representing Control Data, to interview Mauchly. Kirkpatrick was canny and unrevealing in his questioning, and Mauchly, though under oath, seemed naive, or guileless, in his answers. (Scott McCartney says his memory was bad because he was in poor health.) He acknowledged that he had written to Atanasoff in the six months after his visit to Ames, and that his letters had been enthusiastic. He acknowledged that he had asked Atanasoff about building "an Atanasoff calculator" at the Moore School, but he became confused (or "flustered" as Mollenhoff says) when asked to explain the questions in his letter a little more clearly (neither his memory nor his records were as good as those of Atanasoff and his associates). When shown the October letter, he said, "The center portion of this letter indicates that I was probing whether there would be any objection to using some of his [Atanasoff's] ideas. This is not quite as strong as saying that I had a strong desire to, but at that point, on September 30, 1941, I think the letter makes it clear that I was still seeking a good way of implementing an electronic calculator, and this is the same interest which I displayed with respect to many other ideas with respect to computation, such as those which I saw at the World's Fair in 1939."

Kirkpatrick asked Mauchly questions designed to get him to elaborate on his replies, which he did, without challenging him or giving away the fact that the Honeywell and CDC lawyers had plenty of documentation that contradicted Mauchly's testimony almost completely. In the meantime, Charles Call took a deposition from Lura Atanasoff in Boulder, where she was now living. Even though the lawyers had been somewhat nervous about how her divorce would influence how she would report events in Ames, she was clear, concise, and in complete agreement with Atanasoff's version of Mauchly's visit.

The lawyers for Honeywell and CDC were exceptionally thorough, and they had plenty of information to work with. The lawyers for Sperry Rand were less fortunate. One day in mid-November 1967, Atanasoff answered the phone. John Mauchly was on the other end of the line. He said that he would like to see Atanasoff and proposed that he come to Atanasoff's Maryland farm with one of the Sperry lawyers, to discuss the case. Atanasoff was suspicious enough by this time to ask his wife, Alice, to listen in on the extension and take notes. Atanasoff did not immediately agree to the meeting—he called the Honeywell/CDC lawyers and reported Mauchly's proposal. Once Atanasoff indicated that he would not reveal what he knew about the case, or what the Honeywell/CDC strategy was, it was decided that a meeting might be informative. It was.

When he called again to set up an appointment for bringing the Sperry lawyer, a man named Lawrence B. Dodds, to Maryland, Mauchly and Atanasoff chatted rather cordially. Mauchly explained to Atanasoff that Dodds was representing Sperry Rand in a case against Control Data and Honeywell, thus revealing to Atanasoff that neither he nor Dodds knew of Atanasoff's central position in the case Honeywell and Control Data were preparing. Mauchly's attitude indicated that he had no idea that Atanasoff might be his antagonist in the patent dispute. His immediate reason for calling Atanasoff was that he had been subpoenaed in the patent dispute and had discovered old letters to Atanasoff that he had forgotten in the course of twenty-six years. He had also given a deposition. By this time, Atanasoff had read Mauchly's deposition, but he didn't reveal this, just suggested that he would try to get hold of it. In his deposition, Mauchly told Atanasoff, he had said a few things that might make Atanasoff "mad," for example "that when you got into administrative work you lost interest in computers." Atanasoff said, "Maybe I did seem to." Mauchly was surprised that Jean Berry appeared on the list of witnesses, but not Clifford Berry. Then Mauchly speculated that Berry had died recently, since he had seen Berry's letter to R. K. Richards describing the ABC and stating that only Mauchly had seen the ABC "in full." Hadn't Caldwell seen it? suggested Mauchly, referring to Samuel Caldwell of MIT, who had been asked to make an evaluation of the ABC for grant purposes. Atanasoff told him that no, Caldwell had never had the same detailed access that Mauchly had had. Mauchly then complained about Allen Kirkpatrick, the lawyer who had deposed him, who, he thought, "had practically accused me of plagiarizing everything I've done."

Mauchly arrived for his visit on the morning of December 16, 1967. Dodds appeared an hour later. Mauchly's manner revealed that he still did not understand Atanasoff's position in the case, and Atanasoff remained reticent. When Dodds arrived, Atanasoff was straightforward about what information he would give the Sperry lawyer—he would speak generally, but not specifically, about his deposition, and his position on Mauchly's visit would be clear. "Dr. Mauchly came to Ames on approximately June 15, 1941. He spent considerable time with the machine; he understood it fully, and in substantially every detail. If you don't like it, that is just too bad, because those were the facts."

Mauchly observed, "You are taking a very positive posture which I cannot take. Your memory is better than mine."

Gradually in the course of their conversation, it seemed to dawn on Dodds and Mauchly that Atanasoff was not as uninformed about the case as they had thought he was. Finally there was a revealing exchange:

Mauchly: "Do you contend that I read the book?" (meaning the thirty-five-page description of the ABC)

Atanasoff (after hemming and hawing): "However, the answer is yes, and you also asked me if you could take a copy home with you. I denied the request, and so you did not take the copy away."

Dodds: "Will you treat us as well as our opponents?"

Atanasoff: "I do not see why I should place you and your opponents on the same footing. It is obviously to your advantage to prove that there was no development of a computing machine at Ames, Iowa. Your opponents contend the contrary and my interests must lie in that direction."

Dodds then asked if anyone else "now alive" had read the manuscript and Atanasoff pointed out that it had gone to various agencies in hopes of funding. Then Atanasoff remarked that he had read the 827 patent that summer—"The 827 patent almost exactly described my own apparatus and its specifications." Then Mauchly had to be shown the 827 patent (which Atanasoff had a copy of), since he did not remember which one it was. Dodds and Atanasoff sparred a bit about the language of the 827 patent, Dodds saying that the patent didn't mention "regenerative memory" and Atanasoff pointing out that what was described— "interaction of logic circuits in the computing elements"—was his idea. Dodds acknowledged that this was so. Mauchly kept quiet.

Alice served lunch. As they got up to go to the table, Atanasoff remarked that the Honeywell/CDC lawyer had encouraged him to find every document and potential witness and remember every detail. Mauchly replied, "Our lawyers don't want me to remember anything."

Sometime later, Atanasoff could not help exclaiming, "Mr. Dodds, in the face of the facts, how do you expect to win this case?"

Dodds, irritated, replied, "You don't know anything about how federal judges are likely to act. They may decide the question upon their own impulse instead of fact, law, or reason." Mauchly and Dodds, it seems, could not help revealing themselves to Atanasoff. Atanasoff, on the other hand, did not reveal that Mauchly and Dodds's assumption that there had been no witnesses to Mauchly's work on the computer was wrong. Throughout the interview, Mauchly retained his strange presumption that he and Atanasoff were on the same side. Once Dodds left, Mauchly even remarked that Sperry was paying him a healthy consulting fee for his work on the case and suggested that Atanasoff might try to get the same sort of arrangement, and then he reiterated what he had said before, that the Sperry lawyers had advised him to remember his Ames trip as vaguely as possible. Throughout the rest of the afternoon (Mauchly was not inclined to depart), Mauchly continued to reveal details of the case, things he had seen, bits of advice he had received, royalties he had gotten for the patents, how he had gotten them, what he had done with the money. He showed a friendly interest in Atanasoff's own career (and evident prosperity), and Atanasoff was left with the feeling "that Dr. Mauchly was genuinely pleased to find that he had not entirely deprived me of living substance."

Atanasoff did not at all share Mauchly's casual attitude toward the suit—like Jean Berry, he had become convinced that there had been foul play in Clifford Berry's death, and he even persuaded the Honeywell/CDC lawyers to send a lawyer along with him back up to New York to look into the case. As usual, Atanasoff devoted himself to finding out everything he could, to thinking it through, and to persuading those in charge to see things his way. He did, in fact, talk to the detective in charge of investigating the case into reopening it—he did not think the levels of alcohol and medicines in Berry's blood (they were low) and the way that he had died (quietly, his arms at his sides) added up to a realistic case for suffocation by plastic bag. He was convincing enough for the immediate investigator, but not enough for his superior, and the case was not reopened. Atanasoff remained uncertain, at least publicly, about the cause of Berry's death—in subsequent interviews, it was clear that he could see both sides of the issue. Jean Berry was always certain that her husband had been murdered—he was the person who had the clearest information both about what the ABC was and how it worked, and how much time Mauchly had spent with the machine, what he had done, and what Berry himself had told him.

Each of the Honeywell/CDC witnesses had something different to offer: Sam Legvold had seen Mauchly around the computer in the basement of the physics building; Lura Atanasoff had seen him in her home, with the copy of the description of the ABC in his hands, and pens, and bond paper, with his light on late into the night; R. K. Richards had Berry's clearly stated correspondence on the issues under question. And then, Atanasoff offered to have several technicians in his Maryland machine shop take the thirty-five-page written description of the machine and build a complete demonstration model. Alice Atanasoff went shopping for the exact outmoded parts that they would need (though the proper 1940-vintage vacuum tubes were hard to find). It was agreed that Atanasoff himself would neither oversee the construction nor participate, just to demonstrate that the description was enough of a blueprint. When it was built, in the summer of 1968, it worked beautifully and did everything Atanasoff said it would. Atanasoff himself was so pleased with it that he built another one for himself.

Data gathering and record gathering continued through 1968, with the Honeywell lawyers and the CDC lawyers seeking out every document and witness. The Sperry lawyers were not as industrious, and neither was Mauchly—when he appeared for discovery in October 1968, he had only a few papers with him, all, he said, that he could come up with. The Honeywell/CDC lawyers had to remind him that he was legally bound to search out everything that he could find. They questioned him for three days, most particularly about three separate issues—what were the precise concepts he had thought up on his own before his December 1940 discussion with Atanasoff at the annual meeting of the American Association for the Advancement of Science, what had he done and learned in his June trip to Ames, and what had he intended to say in his correspondence with Atanasoff after his visit. Mauchly could hardly remember anything, and he remarked over and over that he had a bad memory. The lawyers could not tell whether he actually could not remember anything or whether he was following instructions from Sperry lawyers. He repeated that he had not used any of Atanasoff's ideas and that the ABC was "an incomplete machine" and "would not do" what it was intended to do. At least that much he remembered. He did not seem to realize that he was contradicting himself.

Atanasoff's deposition, which began eleven days after Mauchly was finished, was the exact opposite of Mauchly's in many ways—he had plenty of evidence that he had thought about and tried out various concepts before and after his revelation of December 1937, including grant proposals. He also had a clear memory of his own thinking, and of events surrounding Mauchly's visit (a memory that was corroborated by his witnesses). He was so organized that the lawyers could suggest only very small ways to shape his testimony to make it more forceful or more clear—he had an excellent grasp not only of what he had done with the ABC, but also of what he was doing in the case.

When Mauchly returned for a second session of questioning in April 1968, he brought a large stash of documents that he had managed to uncover. Unfortunately, they had the effect of supporting Atanasoff's contentions, not his own—whether or not Mauchly now remembered that the ABC worked, he had written enthusiastically to friends in 1941 that the computer could "perform all kinds of mathematical feats." Charles Call read the documents while another lawyer deposed Mauchly. Call then told the other lawyer what he found in the documents, and, using this information, the other lawyer challenged Mauchly's testimony. Mauchly thereupon modified his testimony. As his own biographer remarks, "He made a huge mistake by obfuscating the facts of his Iowa visit." In *ENIAC*, McCartney tries to make a case for Mauchly having had ideas about a computing device before he went to Ames—according to a colleague, he invented a "little computing device . . . [that] used neon tubes as trigger circuits. And he'd done some simple arithmetic work on the desk setup, using those triggers." But this is a defense of Mauchly that Mauchly did not make for himself, possibly because, according to Mollenhoff, his device was a single neon tube mounted on the lid of a Quaker Oats box that turned on and off.

In some ways, John Mauchly remains the most mysterious and contradictory figure of all of our computer innovators. There is no evidence that he was coldly calculating in any sense of the word. His efforts in every direction seem to have been expansive, impulsive, and inclusive rather than cool and directed. When J. Presper Eckert's second wife remarked that Mauchly could not have put together ENIAC without Eckert, but that Eckert would not have thought of it without Mauchly, she was portraying Mauchly as a certain type of genius— a disorganized dreamer full of inspiration that comes from nowhere. However, everyone, including those who knew him through Atanasoff, remarked on his sociable nature and his aptitude for conversation, and so the evidence is that his ideas did come from somewhere—from others, if only in embryonic form. This, too, accords with certain theories of creativity (most particularly those delineated by Malcolm Gladwell in *Outliers*)—that "genius" is a social phenomenon, that ideas grow out of human intercourse, that certain communities produce a wealth of talent because of certain mores of interaction. One such habit, Kati Marton would say, was the way Jews in Budapest of the 1920s loved to linger in cafés, smoking and talking—perhaps the world in which John von Neumann came to believe that some ideas should not be possessed and patented by individuals. Mauchly was a connector extraordinaire—every story about him attests to that; in each description of him, even when he begins by asserting something (for example that he remembers nothing of a particular event) he soon comes round to remembering it much in the way his interlocutor does. As Atanasoff discovered in December 1940, Mauchly was by nature an enthusiast, and in 1941, when his colleagues at Iowa State were skeptical of his computer, the very person Atanasoff needed to support his own confidence in his machine was an enthusiast who seemed at least somewhat knowledgeable.

Atanasoff seems not at all like Mauchly—he was well organized and well directed above all things. As a "problem finder," he had a special talent for formulating specific questions that required solution—as at Bikini Atoll, for example—and then using available materials to come up with the best available solution, if not necessarily the ideal one. But like Mauchly, his talents thrived on social interaction—as he taught his students, he learned from them; as he directed their work, he came up with ideas for his own. His quest for the computer grew out of his understanding of a general need belonging to his community of mathematicians, physicists, and engineers. He was stimulated by everything from the slide rule he got from his father as a boy to methods of house construction he employed in retirement. What had already been discovered and invented served Atanasoff as a springboard to other things. At the same time, he was good at progressing from level to level—at learning from Charles Babbage's unfortunate experience not to try to invent the universal machine before you have gotten the specific one to work. Atanasoff was Mauchly and Eckert rolled into one—he had grand mathematical ideas and he had specific engineering ideas. He understood what both kinds meant and he understood how the two fit together. And then he was blessed with a perfectly congenial partner, Clifford Berry, whose building process was smooth, thoughtful, and efficient. Like Atanasoff, it did not occur to Berry to try a zillion things at once or to drop one project and begin another before the first was completed.

Sperry had one advantage at the trial, the considerable one of the reluctance of courts to overturn patents already granted. But Honeywell and CDC had one, too—Mauchly was required to prove a negative, to prove that he had not been influenced by the time he had spent in Ames, and to prove that he was neither lying about his memories nor simply failing to remember things that he had thought and done. McCartney maintains that the case "boiled down to one scientist's words against the other," but in fact many of the words the Honeywell and CDC lawyers were using against Mauchly were his own. And the Honeywell lawyers went about their case in an Atanasoffish way—exhaustively. They put all their documents together in electronic legal files, which gave them excellent organization and ready access. They seemed to realize, as the Sperry lawyers did not, just how useful computers could be.

The Honeywell and CDC lawyers also understood that they had to supply expert witnesses for the trial who could explain to the judge, Earl R. Larson, what the issues at stake were—how computers worked, how the ideas in the ABC were linked to ENIAC. Larson had an excellent reputation as a scrupulous judge whose opinions were rarely appealed and even more rarely overturned. He intended to preserve this reputation in what he soon came to understand was one of the most important intellectual property cases of the twentieth century. He knew that he had plenty to learn and that he had to take the time to learn it. The Honeywell/CDC lawyers hired Isaac Auerbach Associates (the same Isaac Auerbach who had asked Mauchly at the panel Call witnessed about his visit to Iowa State), and Auerbach supplied him with three computer experts who had worked on both ENIAC and EDVAC. The witnesses had several jobs: corroborating and explaining Atanasoff's testimony to the judge; informing the judge of the relevant history of the computer; reading and explaining the thirty-five-page report on the ABC; corroborating that the model newly constructed from the old plans was as it was said to be; and ultimately tracing connections from ABC to ENIAC and EDVAC.

The trial in Minneapolis began on June 1, 1971.

The question of whether the ABC had existed and the question of whether Mauchly pirated Atanasoff's ideas for ENIAC were separate though related. What Mauchly and Eckert had fallen prey to with von Neumann and Goldstine's 101-page publication of the ideas that led to EDVAC was a question of prior art—in typing up and sending out under von Neumann's name the ideas underlying EDVAC, Goldstine established them as prior art to any claims that Mauchly and Eckert might make to the same ideas (von Neumann's biographer, Norman Macrae, sees this as von Neumann's intentional attempt to preempt the patenting of the ideas underlying the computer). If Atanasoff's thirty-five-page description of the ABC had had the same sort of distribution as von Neumann's paper (at least two hundred copies), then it would have stood as prior art. But Atanasoff had made only five copies on the assumption that because Iowa State was planning to patent the machine, it was dangerous to make more copies.

Much of the case, especially Atanasoff's testimony, revolved around the question of what ideas he had come up with and how he had come up with them. Because of this, the first part of his testimony was autobiographical—Attorney Henry Halladay questioned him about his childhood and his education in a detailed manner intended to delineate the steps by which he came to a set of concepts so unusual and innovative that other geniuses had not been able to come up with them, including Mauchly. Atanasoff obliged—yes, his fascination with his father's slide rule had driven all other, more common passions like baseball out of his mind; yes, he had read his father's books on engineering and his mother's books on algebra, not because he was required to, but because he enjoyed them. His education at the University of Florida and the University of Wisconsin and Iowa State showed that he was a more-than-exemplary student (and chimed nicely with Judge Larson's own career at another land-grant university, the University of Minnesota).

Atanasoff was not the first to testify—Sam Legvold and others set the stage, so when Halladay brought Atanasoff's testimony around to the subject of his years at Iowa State, it was easy to see that his teaching career in the thirties, and the evidence of not only his own work, but also the work of his students (one piece of evidence was the titles of papers his students had written under his tutelage) showed that he had thought through computing ideas for a long time and in more than one way. This history prepared the way for Atanasoff's clearly remembered and detailed recollection of that night in the Rock Island tavern in December 1937.

Halladay pressed him on two ideas, regenerative memory and logic circuits. Of the first he said, "I'm thinking about the condensers for memory units, and about the fact that the condensers would regenerate their own state so their state would not change with time. If they were in a plus state, for instance, they would stay in a plus state; or if they were in the negative state, they would stay in the negative state. They would not blink off to zero. Or if you used two positive charges, they would retain their individual identity and would not leak across to one another."

Concerning logic circuits, Atanasoff was honest about the fact that he did not perfectly visualize how the logic circuits would work. He imagined a black box, with input from two memory units—"the box would then yield the correct results on output terminals." Although he did not envision the contents of the box specifically, he did understand that "since I was going to use condensers, why then I supposed the innards would be electrical in character, and I was well aware that the electrical entities which would be as suitable for such a purpose were vacuum tubes." He explained that "condenser" was an archaic term for "capacitor." Atanasoff then described how for the next fifteen months, he worked out these two ideas on paper: the idea for the regenerative memory was fairly simple; what was to be in the black box was much more difficult, but he worked that out for both a binary number system and a decimal number system. When he compared the two, it was evident that the decimal system would be too unwieldy. He declared that he had clarified his ideas by March 24, 1939, when he submitted his two-page grant application, asking for funds. Although the letter was short, it was detailed, describing the three sorts of problems Atanasoff expected his calculator to be able to solve (electrical circuit analysis, approximate solution of differential equations, and multiple correlation). His machine would be able to solve these sorts of problems for many more variables than was then practical with mechanical calculators. The letter also described previous efforts he had made to solve these sorts of problems using already invented methods. He asked for and was granted $650 (some $7,800 in 2010 funds). All of his papers were in order and were presented to the court.

On the second day of testimony, more papers were presented. In fact, so many papers were presented—letters, notes, papers, diagrams, drawings—that Atanasoff began to weary of the tedium of court procedure, which meant putting descriptions of every piece of evidence introduced into the record. He was pleased, however, with the *Des Moines Tribune* article from January 15, 1941 (see page 164). The importance of the article for the case was clear—the ABC was not a piece of junk that barely functioned, as Mauchly had gotten in the habit of saying.

The next item on the agenda was Atanasoff's version of Mauchly's visit. He was equally detailed. Mauchly had arrived on Friday evening. Over the weekend, they had visited the computer several times and talked about it constantly—with only one small break, during which they spoke of Mauchly's interest in meteorology. Mauchly had carried around the green-covered thirty-five-page description of the computer. Atanasoff had seen him reading it, and he and Atanasoff had discussed some of the things in the booklet that Mauchly wanted to understand. Atanasoff had explained the binary number system to Mauchly, though he was unsure how clearly the Philadelphian had grasped it. To Atanasoff, Mauchly had seemed eager to understand the ABC:

"He seemed to follow in detail our explanations and expressed joy at the results, at the fact that these vacuum tubes would actually compute. He was shown addition and subtraction and multiplication and he was also shown the process of punching cards but we only had one unit in operation during his visit and we weren't prepared to punch all of the thirty 'Abaci' simultaneously and no effort was made to fill the entire machine. He was shown the operation of converting base-ten cards to base-two numbers on the system, then the rest of the controls which we planned for the machine to make it operable in regard to solutions of simultaneous linear equations . . . We discussed logic elements in considerable length with Dr. Mauchly." Halladay also introduced as evidence a letter Mauchly had written to a friend on June 28, 1941, only a few days after returning to Philadelphia. The third paragraph included the following: "Immediately after commencement here, I went out to Iowa State University to see the computing device which a friend of mine is constructing there. His machine, now nearing completion, is electronic in operation, and will solve within a very few minutes any system of linear equations involving no more than thirty variables. It can be adapted to do the job of the Bush Differential Analyzer more rapidly than the Bush machine does, and it costs a lot less." The Sperry lawyer tried to get this letter excluded on the grounds that it was hearsay, but the judge allowed it.

Even though the court procedures were tedious, Atanasoff's answers were so detailed and self-reinforcing, since he rarely contradicted himself or seemed confused, that when the Sperry lawyer cross-examined, both on technical issues and concerning his relations with John Mauchly, he succeeded only in bolstering Honeywell's case by giving Atanasoff the opportunity of adding more to the record. At one point, the lawyer asserted that Atanasoff had referred to Eckert as "a high-powered electronics expert." Atanasoff coolly denied this and said that he had no knowledge of Eckert's skills. The lawyer asked him why he hadn't progressed with the naval computer when he was at the NOL. Ignorant of von Neumann's funding machinations, Atanasoff replied that he had been short of both personnel and time—the navy had promised to relieve him of his ordnance responsibilities but had failed to do so. His reply made perfect sense.

When Atanasoff was finished testifying—seven days of direct examination and three days of cross-examination—he had made the best case he could that Mauchly had not only visited the ABC, but he had given every evidence of understanding the principles underlying Atanasoff's theory of computing, as well as how he had realized these ideas in a piece of machinery.

One of the star witnesses for Honeywell, who testified at the end of August, was Edward Teller. His job was not to say where he thought Mauchly had gotten his ideas, but to help Honeywell's prior-use case against the ENIAC patents. According to Teller, the scientists at Los Alamos, thanks to the von Neumann connection, had made use of

ENIAC for calculations concerning the feasibility of the hydrogen bomb in late 1945 and early 1946. The calculations were not especially accurate, but accurate enough to show Teller where he was in error and to suggest which direction he might go in when development of the H-bomb was resumed in 1949. The use of ENIAC for these calculations, and their significance as prior use, had not been employed in the previous trial that resulted in Sperry being awarded its patent. Its significance was in the fact that Mauchly and Eckert had not bothered to write up their patent application until August 1947, two and a half years after the machine was employed for the H-bomb calculations. It was a similar argument to the one that had been made about the EDVAC patents after the dissemination of von Neumann's 101-page "First Draft." Prior use was the second string to Honeywell's bow.

John Mauchly did not testify until November 1971. The Sperry lawyers had already discovered that Mauchly's depositions were easily challenged: such assertions as the one that he had spent only an hour and a half with the computer, or that he had not seen it running, or that he had not seen it with the cover off were so easily disproved that Mauchly's story had changed from deposition to deposition. The Honeywell lawyers knew how to press him because he had already given them plenty of ammunition.

However, the Sperry lawyers did what they could to establish Mauchly's credentials—like Atanasoff, he told his life story. Like Atanasoff, he outlined what he had done before ENIAC that might have pointed to his computer ideas. Then Halladay cross-examined him. Judge Larson had prohibited witnesses from hearing the testimony of earlier witnesses, so Mauchly did not know what Legvold, Atanasoff, Lura Atanasoff, and others had said about his visit (though he had read their depositions). Throughout his testimony, he persisted in denigrating the ABC and forgetting what was in the thirty-five-page description of the machine. Then Halladay began to cross-examine him, and Mauchly's inability to remember fairly elementary aspects of his earlier inventions (such as whether his Harmonic Analyzer was mechanical or electronic) worked against him. He could not come up with any drawings or ideas he had made prior to meeting Atanasoff. He could call no witnesses who remembered talking to him about such devices, and he could not point to having invented a digital device—his Harmonic Analyzer was analog. He talked about having discussed electronic computing in his classes at Ursinus but could recall no student who could attest to these discussions. The only papers or notes he had about electronic computing were dated after he met Atanasoff in December 1940 or after he had been to Ames.

One of the most striking pieces of evidence that Halladay introduced was a paper Mauchly had written in August 1941, two months after seeing the ABC, in which Mauchly had stated "computing machines may be conveniently classified as either analog or impulse types," appending a footnote that read, "I am indebted to Dr J. V. Atanasoff of Iowa State College for the classification and terminology here explained."

At one point, Halladay showed Mauchly the thirty-five-page report, which the Ames people remembered him studying. Mauchly said that he had not read it very carefully, because he was not interested in the machine it described. Halladay pushed him, and he became resentful but finally admitted, in a roundabout way, that Atanasoff had told him that he could not take it back to Philadelphia, and so he must have asked to do so. Throughout the cross-examination, Mauchly quibbled and resisted, but Halladay did eventually establish several points—that after the twenty- to thirty-minute December meeting in Philadelphia, Mauchly had understood that Atanasoff was building a calculator based on different principles from the Bush Analyzer and that if he came to Ames, he could see it and Atanasoff would tell him about it. Concerning the June visit, Halladay established that Mauchly had been there for five days, that he had discussed the computer for many hours with both Atanasoff and Berry, that he had seen the ABC operate and read the report, that he had expressed enthusiasm for and understanding of the ABC and Atanasoff's ideas after returning to Philadelphia, and that he had asked Atanasoff if he could use some of his ideas in a calculator of his own. It was also established that after he got back to Philadelphia, he had changed his career path and enrolled in the summer course in computing theory, where he met Eckert.

In Mauchly's defense, Scott McCartney reports that at the time of the trial, Mauchly was suffering from an illness that damaged his memory. I think we can also infer that Mauchly looked back at the ABC through the lens of ENIAC. There is no disagreement that ENIAC was a more complex and powerful computer than the ABC, and that it also owed some of its design and construction to the Bush Analyzer at the Moore School that had been designed by Irven Travis before he left for the navy. ENIAC was intended to perform a war-related function and had to be put together as quickly as possible, which was why EDVAC was designed—to finally realize the most advanced computing concepts without the pressures of speed or limited funding. There is also no disagreement that J. Presper Eckert and the others who worked on ENIAC contributed to the development of a sophisticated machine that was in some ways advanced (and in some ways not) compared to the ABC. What the Honeywell lawyers endeavored to show was a "sine qua non" or "without which not"—that without Atanasoff, Berry, and the ABC, Mauchly could not himself have come up with the ideas that led to ENIAC. Nothing Mauchly could or could not remember proved that he could have, whereas all of the Honeywell/CDC evidence showed that Atanasoff had done so.

Mauchly might have had better luck in another country. Because he had to file his patent applications in the United States, he had to deal with a "first-to-invent" system (as opposed to a "first-to-file" system). In the U.S. system, invention is seen as both conception and "reduction to practice"—that is, more or less, making something. In order to get a patent, an inventor can't just think something up, and he also can't just make something—he must do both. Once the invention is made (or put into practice), however, the date of the invention is considered to be the date of conception rather than the date of filing. As a result, a patent application filed later can supersede one filed earlier if the inventor can prove both conception and diligence. It was pretty clear from the testimony that Atanasoff had been diligent in conceiving the computer and in "reducing it to practice." But the United States is the only country that uses such a standard. In any other country in the world, Atanasoff would have entirely lost his chance to claim the ideas behind the computer when Iowa State and Richard Trexler failed to file his application, and Mauchly would have been awarded the patent.

In this regard, it is also important to note that Mauchly could have avoided patent problems if he had been more careful, as GE lawyer George Eltgroth understood. If he and his lawyers had submitted material acknowledging and documenting what he had learned from Atanasoff in June 1941, as they were required to do, the patent examiner would have considered his claims in light of that material and determined if Atanasoff's machine (and his thirty-five-page report) qualified as prior art. The fact that he did not do so left him open to having the patent abrogated for what is called inequitable conduct. But Mauchly and Eckert, possibly hyperaware of the commercial possibilities of the computer (for which McCartney, a writer for the *Wall Street Journal*, specially praises them) were loath to give any credit to others — when they filed their patent, it covered more than a hundred different concepts, even though they were part of a large group working on the machine and Mauchly was also consulting Atanasoff from time to time on technical details of the ABC. It may be that when von Neumann was himself chatting up Atanasoff at the NOL, in late 1945, he was not only getting the benefit of Atanasoff's ideas, he was also coming to understand that the computer as it existed in 1945 could not be owned by one or two men and was figuring out how to make sure that it would not be. It may also be that it was von Neumann's insufficient credit to Mauchly and Eckert in his "First Draft" that put them in a possessive frame of mind when they were writing up their own application.

At any rate, the Sperry Rand defense of having Mauchly forget as much as possible was the best the Sperry lawyers could come up with. It was certainly one that was congenial to Mauchly, however well it was or was not designed to work, and he stuck to it. Another irony of the case, which Charles Call communicated to Kirwan Cox, was that if Sperry had offered to share the patents for the same fee as they asked from IBM ($10 million), Honeywell would not have gone to court; but Sperry asked for $250 million before the publication of R. K. Richards's book, and then $20 million afterward. Twenty million dollars was still too high for Honeywell, and so they went to court.

The challenge to Sperry Rand's patents was lengthy and involved. According to Clark Mollenhoff, it "consumed over 135 days or parts of days." A total of seventy-seven witnesses had given oral testimony, and an additional eighty witnesses were presented through deposition transcripts. Honeywell had introduced 25,686 exhibits to be marked by the court; and lawyers for Sperry Rand and its subsidiary, Illinois Scientific Development (ISD), had directed the court's attention to another 6,968 exhibits . . . The highly complicated trial transcripts stretched to over 20,667 pages." Honeywell's brief, filed in September 1972, was five hundred pages long. The key claim in the brief was not that Atanasoff had invented ENIAC, but "that there is no difference between what Mauchly learned from Atanasoff in June 1941, and what Eckert and Mauchly were later to claim to have invented alone." The Honeywell brief went on to point out that even if the ABC had not worked, under U.S. patent law "one cannot claim a conception derived from another as his 'original' invention, even though he may have built the first device based upon that conception." The Sperry brief, filed in August, rested its case on the fact that Sperry had already been awarded the ENIAC patents and that Atanasoff had not invented ENIAC, and that Mauchly had done a few electronic projects before meeting Atanasoff.

In April 1973, Judge Larson sent copies of his proposed decision to both the Sperry lawyers and the Honeywell lawyers, asking for their responses. It was clear from the proposed decision that Larson was leaning toward abrogating the Sperry patents, but also that he was giving the Sperry lawyers one last chance to make their case. They could not make it. In October, Larson decided in favor of Honeywell, in no uncertain terms. He stated, "Between 1937 and 1942, Atanasoff, then a professor of physics and mathematics at Iowa State College, Ames, Iowa, developed and built an automatic electronic digital computer for solving large systems of simultaneous linear equations." He then went on to describe the steps by which Atanasoff solidified this claim—for example, it was enough that the breadboard prototype worked and was the subject of further funding. The ABC did not have to work perfectly at the time of Mauchly's visit in order to have established that Atanasoff's ideas were valid, that they were his ideas, and that he communicated them to Mauchly sufficiently so that Mauchly could build on them. Larson stated that "as a result of this visit, the discussions of Mauchly with Atanasoff and Berry, the demonstrations, and the review of the manuscript, Mauchly derived from ABC 'the invention of the automatic electronic digital computer' claimed in the ENIAC patent."

Larson also addressed the issue of who had invented ENIAC. He found that "work on the ENIAC was a group or team effort and that inventive contributions were made by Sharpless, Burks, Shaw, and others," but that since these people had not asserted their claims in a proper manner, Honeywell could not use these claims to abrogate the patents.

On the same day that Judge Larson gave his decision, Archibald Cox was fired as special Watergate prosecutor, and Larson's decision was lost in the news shuffle of Watergate. But in spite of the wishes of those involved, the decision was in fact a technical matter, of interest to computer geeks and corporate lawyers, not the public at large. Computers themselves were still seen as room-sized, specialized pieces of machinery, not accessible to the average person. The importance of Judge Larson's decision would not really be clear until the computer companies had acted on it. The result was as John von Neumann had suspected—once the ideas became common property, innovation blossomed, and the computer revolution took hold.

Chapter Twelve

S perry Rand, John Mauchly, and J. Presper Eckert did not go down easily. They took advantage of the limited dissemination of the Minneapolis decision to continue claiming credit for inventing the computer. Possibly they did not understand the details of patent law that destroyed their claim—from the beginning, they seem not to have seen themselves as team members or as the beneficiaries of social networks engaged in a common purpose, but rather as stars and owners who stood to gain fame and fortune. When they claimed ownership of more than a hundred ideas in their 1947 patent application, or when they failed to acknowledge Atanasoff in that same application, they were setting themselves up for an eventual failure that might have been avoided with smarter legal counsel, more scrupulous honesty, or, just possibly, better recordkeeping.

For years, Sperry Rand and Mauchly and Eckert fought a rearguard action to retain the PR rights to the invention, if not the legal rights. One patent lawyer, Sheldon L. Epstein, of Wilmette, Illinois, recalls how difficult it was to get any mention of Atanasoff or the Larson decision into a Smithsonian exhibition on the history of the computer: "In the 1980s, the Smithsonian Institution started work on an exhibit to commemorate the invention of the computer. Because it lacked funds to proceed on its own, the Smithsonian solicited and received computer industry funding. One of the more prominent contributors was Sperry Rand. The Smithsonian Institution took the position that contributions from Sperry Rand and other supporters of Mauchly and Eckert would not influence the content of its exhibit. Nevertheless, the exhibit as originally conceived did not contain any reference to Atanasoff's inventions or to Judge Larson's opinion. Instead the Smithsonian Institution credited Eckert and Mauchly with invention of the electronic computer. Atanasoff's supporters strenuously objected and had some limited success in getting a very small portion of the exhibit allocated to Atanasoff's inventions. That same problem was to reappear a few years later when PBS produced a program—financed by many of the same contributors—on the invention of computers."

In 1999, *Wall Street Journal* writer Scott McCartney took up the cudgels again, this time in the interests of private enterprise. In *ENIAC*, McCartney maintains that it was Mauchly and Eckert who started their own company, and Mauchly and Eckert who foresaw the computer revolution as we know it. The idea of individual access to inexpensive and powerful machines that would be used for all sorts of things was unimaginable to people like John von Neumann, who thought that computers would be large tools for government agencies, academia, and giant corporations, but limited in their usefulness for the average person. Even though Mauchly and Eckert actually showed no aptitude for private enterprise, McCartney views von Neumann as the real thief, with his attempts to spread the principles behind the computer to anyone who might be interested and thereby spark greater and more powerful inventions. For McCartney, Atanasoff and his claims are just an annoyance to be dispatched with assertions that the judge didn't know what he was doing and Sperry's lawyers didn't either. But Sperry never appealed the decision, and so they must have accepted it. One especially interesting response to McCartney's book demonstrates the resentment that lingered for a long time. At Amazon.com, in the reviews of *ENIAC*, JBartik writes:

Scott struggles hard on the Atanasoff saga. Atanasoff never claimed he invented the computer and nobody ever heard of him until Honeywell dug him up to keep from paying royalties on the ENIAC patent. Much is made of John Mauchly's memory of his association with Atanasoff as recorded at different times. John suffered from a disease called Hereditary Hemoragic Talengetasin (HHT) [sic] which causes lesions to be formed in the brain and holes in the lungs. One of the interviews was taken shortly after he had had an episode and had been very ill in the hospital. It is no wonder he couldn't remember incidents then that he could remember when he was in better health.

"JBartik" turns out to be Jean Bartik, whom McCartney acknowledges at the end of his book: "Jean Bartik was a fountain of information and a burst of energy who spurred me on several times during research and writing." She is pictured in one of the famous photos of ENIAC (identified as Betty Jean Jennings). McCartney also declares that he owes a great deal to Mauchly's wife, Kathleen Mauchly Antonelli (a good friend of Bartik's) and to Eckert's wife, Judy. It is clear from these acknowledgments that what happened to ENIAC and EDVAC gave rise to bitter feelings on both sides of the patent issues. In the 1980s, Alice and Arthur Burks wrote a book supporting Atanasoff and demonstrating the links between the ABC and ENIAC—Arthur, of course, worked on ENIAC and the IAS computer. Alice worked on ENIAC with Jean Bartik. In 2003, Alice Burks returned to the fray with *Who Invented the Computer?* The customer reviews on Amazon.com give a sample of the passions raised on either side by the dispute of the ENIAC patents.

But Atanasoff was not without his own advocates and promoters. While the trial preparation was going on, in 1970, Isaac Auerbach happened to meet a Bulgarian mathematician named Blagovest Sendov at a conference in London and to mention Atanasoff. Sendov was immediately interested and did some of his own checking into the case.

He also wrote to Atanasoff, requesting information about his father, Ivan. Iva Purdy Atanasoff, then visiting John and Alice, put together her memories, and Sendov used this information to find Atanasoff's relatives in Bulgaria. Atanasoff was invited to return for a visit, and, while there in November 1970, he was awarded the Order of Cyril and Methodius, First Class, for inventing the computer. He was also shown around the city of Sofia and taken to Boyadzhik and the Yambol district, where his father was still remembered.

When the Larson decision was handed down, Atanasoff was just seventy. He was still enormously active on his Maryland farm, busy with his wife, Alice, his three children, and his grandchildren. How busy is apparent from Tammara Burton's reprint of a letter written by Atanasoff's mother Iva (now almost a hundred) after she moved to the farm in the mid-1980s: "Vincent . . . wants me to walk to the gate [about 850 yards] every day even when it is below freezing. Then I have this bell which rings every hour for me to get up and walk around." Iva comes to rather enjoy her freezing exercise, though one day when there is blowing snow, she persuades Alice to intercede with her son. As for Atanasoff himself, she reports, "One fourth of the time he spends lecturing me about the great necessity of eating less, drinking more, and walking more. The other three-fourths . . . he spends in the machine shop. All we can hear is screech screech scrunch. I asked him what he was making and he said a boat. I supposed a small pleasure boat but wondered because he does not care for fishing. But he said it would be about as big as a house."

Atanasoff's real passion late in his life became language and alphabets. He viewed the Bulgarian version of the Cyrillic alphabet, with thirty-two letters until 1945 and thirty thereafter, as superior to the English alphabet, and when interested groups wanted him to talk about the invention of the computer, he wanted to steer the conversation toward the benefits of reinventing the alphabet (the reader may view this as an eerie evocation of Alan Turing and the purpose of Colossus). He told a Bulgarian newspaper in 1985, "I hear them; I hear the voices and the hearts of the people who pronounce them . . . I want each letter or each symbol to carry more meanings, to support with full power the alphabet."

Atanasoff gained more and more recognition for the invention of the computer as the twentieth century progressed (in spite of his omission from the MIT website). He was celebrated at Iowa State in 1974, and he was the subject of a meticulous biography that focused on the relationship between the ABC and ENIAC by Arthur Burks and Alice Rowe Burks, who had worked on ENIAC, in 1989, called *The First Electronic Computer: The Atanasoff Story*, as well as a biography called *Atanasoff: Forgotten Father of the Computer*, by Clark Mollenhoff, a writer for the *Des Moines Register*, in 1988. The Burkses, according to Tammara Burton, had been unaware of the ABC until they wrote an article for *The Annals of the History of Computing* about ENIAC. They read the transcripts from the trial and wrote, "Atanasoff's principles for electronic computation played a crucial role in the circuitry of ENIAC and all its successors." But the Burkses' book was published by the University of Michigan Press and the Mollenhoff book was published by Iowa State University Press. Burton's own excellent book, which contains more personal information about Atanasoff, was published in 2006 by the All Bulgarian Foundation and the Center for Research on the Bulgarians.

In 1990, Atanasoff went to the White House and received from George H. W. Bush the 1990 Medal of Technology "for his invention of the electronic digital computer and for contributions toward the development of a technically trained U.S. workforce." He was also nominated for the Nobel Prize in Physics three times during the 1980s, but, according to Burton, since his thirty-five-page paper describing the ABC and other papers concerning the theoretical and technical aspects of the ABC were never published, he was not eligible. Atanasoff died on June 15, 1995.

Many of the questions that McCartney and Bartik attempt to dismiss in *ENIAC* concerning the ABC were addressed in the 1990s, when a team of computer engineers and graduate students led by John Gustafson rebuilt the ABC, replicating as closely as possible the tools, materials, and construction methods that Atanasoff and Berry had used in the late 1930s. The building of the replica was informative in several ways, according to Gustafson. For one, "The ABC replica took three years to build, the same as it took Atanasoff and Berry. It was hard to get the parts, and a lot of the necessary skill sets don't exist anymore, such as putting together gear trains and synchronous electric motors. We needed people who were good old-fashioned electronics engineers. The replica cost about $600,000, about the same adjusted for inflation, as it cost when Atanasoff and Berry built it." And, contradicting a frequent assertion by ENIAC partisans, it did work. Gustafson says, "One of the reasons I built the replica was to see if it worked, and yes, it did work, but not on full size problems (ones with 29 variables)— it could do five equations and five unknowns. Beyond five, it would get messed up in the 'scratch result,' that is, writing down the output. [Atanasoff] had to invent a way of storing the intermediate results, and he invented electric arcs zapping holes into paper cards. You could sort of read it back, and it made a mistake in about 1 out of 100,000 holes, which seems like a lot, but in a binary system is not, really." Gustafson estimates that it would have taken him and his group two years to solve the scratch result (or charring) problem, the same amount of time it probably would have taken Atanasoff and Berry, because it was not only the nature of the card stock that was the difficulty, it was the size and capacity of the card stock—"The computer worked well up to five equations and five variables, but it was another step of difficulty to go from five to six—part of the difficulty rose from the setup of the IBM card, and part was owing to the setup of the switches. The theory of the computer was in terms of groups of five."

If we survey the history of the invention of the computer, the path by which the instrument on which I am typing came to exist, then we have to say that it was a peculiar and tortured path. Absolutely pivotal to the existence of the computer was the Second World War. From Atanasoff's point of view, without the Second World War, he would have been in Ames to make sure that his patent application was filed and, possibly, to make sure that the lawyer, Richard Trexler, understood it; he would have found the proper card stock for charring his results; his machine would not have been dismantled and hauled away. From Zuse's point of view, his machines would not have been bombed into smithereens; he would have filed his patents and secured proper component parts; he would have, perhaps, more easily benefited from the insights and aid of Helmut Schreyer, who might not have left Germany for South America; he would not have had to evacuate Z4 in the mountains where he was stranded for years; he would have had access to computer experts in other nations. From Tommy Flowers's point of view, he might have taken his vacuum-tube idea and used it to invent a computer, but he also might not have met Alan Turing or Max Newman; the computer he invented would not have been Colossus, but on the other hand, he would not have had to invent it and then destroy it within two years, never referring to it again for decades. From Turing's point of view, he might have had plenty of good ideas about how the mind works and what a computer would be like, but he would not have met Tommy Flowers and the other engineers who understood how to make something. From John Mauchly's point of view, he would not have had access to Herman Goldstine or the team of physicists, engineers, and operators that gathered together in Philadelphia to solve the problem of those firing tables, and the money they had access to. From John von Neumann's point of view, he would not have had his Los Alamos experience, which showed him both what a computer was needed for and how successful (but destructive) collaboration could be, and he would not have met Herman Goldstine on a train platform—von Neumann was not the man to invent the computer, but he was the man to understand its history and its potential. Indeed, von Neumann might never have left Germany. And instead of joining the army, Goldstine might have whiled away many quiet academic years teaching.

The computer I am typing on came to me in a certain way. The seed was planted and its shoot was cultivated by John Vincent Atanasoff and Clifford Berry, but because Iowa State was a land-grant college, it was far from the mainstream. Because the administration at Iowa State did not understand the significance of the machine in the basement of the physics building, John Mauchly was as essential to my computer as Atanasoff was—it was Mauchly who transplanted the shoot from the basement nursery to the luxurious greenhouse of the Moore School. It was Mauchly who in spite of his later testimony was enthusiastic, did know enough to see what Atanasoff had done, was interested enough to pursue it. Other than Clifford Berry and a handful of graduate students, no one else was. Without Mauchly, Atanasoff would have been in the same position as Konrad Zuse and Tommy Flowers—his machine just a rumor or a distant memory.

John Vincent Atanasoff was a lucky man in many ways. He lived to see his hard work and enterprising intelligence vindicated. He spent a long life trying many things and, because of his energy, organizational skills, and persistence, mastering everything he tried. Perhaps Atanasoff would have said that he succeeded in doing something very rare, which is doing what he wanted to do in the way he wanted to do it and discovering that the way he wanted to do it was, indeed, the best way. Kirwan Cox points out that what happened to the ABC also had much to do with Atanasoff's personality: "Mauchly was the only person to be shown the computer in such detail. Why? Atanasoff had a tendency to focus on something, and then he did it and moved on. Mauchly encountered him just at the moment he was most enthusiastic." Cox calls him the "lone inventor" type, who explores and invents and then exhausts his interest in a given idea. Money and fame are secondary to passionate curiosity.

The question remains: would the computer as we know it have been invented without Atanasoff? I do not think ENIAC would have been;

therefore, the computers that grew out of ENIAC and John von Neumann's thoughts about ENIAC might not have been invented. When Konrad Zuse found himself in the mountains at the Austrian border and pondered his future testing the fat content of milk at the local dairies, he heard from IBM—they were interested in his ideas—but they might not have been had they not felt the prick of computer development in the United States. It does not seem as though Howard Aiken's decimal Mark I–IV computers and those similar to it were likely to evolve very quickly into the small, powerful, and handy machines we have; the inventors devoted to analog machines did not believe in electronic machines even when they saw them work. It does not seem likely, therefore, that they would have switched to electronic machines on their own. Tommy Flowers, Max Newman, and Alan Turing knew what electronics could do—it is possible that the computer industry could have blossomed in England rather than the United States, but even aside from the problem of British security concerns after the war (as far in philosophy from von Neumann's practice of encouraging and even forcing the sharing of information as it is possible to be), Colossus operated on different principles from the American computers designed originally to solve mathematical problems. On the other hand, if the ABC had not been invented, the need to solve very complex mathematical problems, especially those, at first, relating to the invention of the H-bomb, would have pressed mathematicians into some sort of calculating solution. The need was there. It would have been met at some point. But the ABC was invented, and as Kirwan Cox puts it, "The ideas [about computers] Atanasoff had were things that have continued to this day—the machine has been completely surpassed, but the concepts he had have not been surpassed."

For those of us who aren't mathematicians, inventors, physicists, or engineers, the history of the invention of the computer is a fascinating look at both human history and human character. There was no inventor of the computer who was not a vivid personality, and no two are alike. It is Alan Turing who has captured the imagination of the culture, perhaps because of his brilliant mind and his tragic death, but Konrad Zuse is at least as idiosyncratic, and his life was even more dramatic. Like Atanasoff, he lived until 1995, long enough to be remembered, and vindicated, too. The most poignant figure, in some ways, may be Tommy Flowers, who remains largely unsung. But perhaps our most problematic character is John von Neumann. Scott McCartney considers him a thief, Norman Macrae and Kati Marton consider him a visionary. Everyone considers him a genius. As for me, von Neumann is the man whose memoirs I would have liked to read, the man at the center of everything, the man of Budapest and the man of Washington, D.C. I would like to know who he thought had invented the computer.

Acknowledgments

Thank you to the Sloan Foundation for funding this project. The invention of the computer is a wonderful story, and an important one.

Thank you to William Silag, for telling me this story the first time, in 1984, and for writing an article about Atanasoff in the *Palimpsest*, the Iowa history magazine, that year (and for plenty else, besides).

Thank you to John Gustafson, for much help in understanding all the issues, and for his contributions to the manuscript.

Thanks to Kirwan Cox, documentary teacher/writer/researcher, who discussed information from the interviews and other research he has done for a television documentary on John Atanasoff and the ABC, which is being produced by Eyesteelfilm, Montreal, for History Television in Canada.

Thank you to Robert Armstead, for editing and information.

All mistakes are mine.

Appendices

John Gustafson, PhD

Appendix A | Linear Solvers

The problem that motivated John Atanasoff to build an electronic computer was one that had challenged mathematicians for many centuries. In about 300 BC, a Babylonian clay tablet gives this example of how a system of two equations can arise:

> There are two fields whose total area is 1,800 square yards. One produces grain at the rate of 2/3 of a bushel per square yard while the other produces grain at the rate of 1/2 a bushel per square yard. If the total yield is 1,100 bushels, what is the size of each field?*

Translated into equations, with x and y for the areas of each field, this word problem says that

$$x + y = 1,800 \text{ square yards}$$
$$2/3x + 1/2y = 1,100 \text{ bushels}$$

The Chinese also studied such problems, and in the *Jiuzhang Suanshu*, or *Nine Chapters on the Mathematical Art*, they provided examples of systems involving up to six equations in six unknown quantities as early as 200 BC.

---

* Units of area have been translated into English units, for readability.

Even though such problems could be posed very easily, the effort to solve them seemed extraordinary and out of proportion to the simplicity of the statement of the problem. At the risk of reminding the reader of some of the more tedious moments spent in middle school algebra class, the way to solve the above system of two equations is to scale one equation so that the number multiplying x or y in one equation matches that of the other equation, and then subtract the equations to eliminate that variable. If we multiply both sides of the first equation by 2/3, for example, the two equations line up nicely:

$$2/3x + 2/3y = 1,200$$
$$2/3x + 1/2y = 1,100$$

and we can subtract the second equation from the first to get a system that involves only y:

$$1/6y = 100$$

This is called "forward elimination," where you eliminate one variable at a time from the system. After that, you "backsolve"; in the example above, y must be 600, and we can use the first equation $x + y = 1,800$ to conclude that $x = 1,200$.

What stymied human calculators was that the work to eliminate every variable grew as the cube of the number of equations. In the two-by-two example above, all one had to do was scale the first equation and subtract it from the second. But in a six-by-six problem (the largest one attempted in the Chinese tome), the first equation would have to be scaled for each of the other equations to eliminate that first unknown variable, and that task requires the performing of arithmetic on the entire six-by-six problem description (thirty-six numbers). That leaves a problem with five equations in five unknowns, so one has to repeat the elimination task, until all that is left is a simple equation in one unknown quantity. The "forward elimination" to get to a simple problem of one equation in one unknown is like a pyramid of arithmetic work. For a system of n equations, the base of the pyramid of work is n by n, working up to a tip that is 1 by 1, and the volume of that pyramid (the total amount of work) is proportional to the cube of n. (The backsolving task is still tedious, but only grows as the square of n.)

In the 1700s, to solve even ten equations in ten unknowns was considered a nearly insurmountable task. It requires more than three thousand multiplications and subtractions, and each arithmetic operation usually must be done with at least ten decimals of precision to avoid rounding errors that would make the result unacceptably inaccurate. The German mathematician Karl Friedrich Gauss needed to solve a system of six equations in the early 1800s when he was trying to plot the course of an observable asteroid, Pallas, and spent years grinding away at the numbers using a method almost identical to that explained by the Chinese two millennia earlier; that method now bears the name Gaussian elimination.

By 1836, Charles Babbage had conceived his mechanical (steam-powered) Analytical Engine, and in pitching his plan for it to the funding agencies of his era, he led with the idea that it could be used to solve systems of equations:

> In the absence of a special engine for the purpose, the solution of large sets of simultaneous equations is a most laborious task, and a very expensive process indeed, when it has to be paid for, in the cases in which the result is imperatively needed.

When a physical problem demanded a logarithm, or a cosine, or for a physical quantity like energy to be calculated, it might have required a few dozen calculations per input quantity, and human calculators knew it was tedious work but not intractable. Solving systems of equations was regarded as intractable, since the work grew as the cube of the number of unknown quantities. Whether one used an abacus, a slide rule, or a desktop calculator like those made by Monroe or Marchand in the twentieth century, it was simply a matter of patience and a bit of skill to bull through the problems that arise with a single unknown variable. But to solve systems of n equations in n unknowns was, and is, the standard by which computational speed is measured.

The speed of computers at solving systems of linear equations has been tracked and publicized since the 1970s. The Top 500 list of computers in the world, analogous to the lists business magazines maintain of the Top 500 companies in the world, is based on this time-honored problem: how fast can the system solve n equations in n unknowns? In 2010, the computers at the top of the list solve problems that have more than a million unknown quantities, and they solve them at speeds exceeding a quadrillion operations per second. Compared to the Atanasoff computer of 1940, they are astronomically faster, yet they use the same procedure and the same precision for what remains the fundamental test of any computer more than seven decades later.

Appendix B | Binary Arithmetic

People accustomed to working with numbers using the usual decimal (base ten) arithmetic notation tend to forget that the basis for that notation is biological and not mathematical: we have ten fingers (digits) to count with. From our earliest years, we are taught the Arabic system of writing the symbols 1, 2, 3, 4, 5, 6, 7, 8, 9 for the quantities one to nine, and that numbers larger than that require more than one symbol. By recording how many tens there are in a number, then how many hundreds, and so on, every whole number is expressed in a unique way. And because Arabic is written from right to left, the tens and hundreds and thousands position are added to the *left* as numbers get progressively larger, not to the right. This is "base ten" or "decimal" arithmetic because it uses powers of ten. When one reads the number 7,239, say, it immediately conveys the quantity $(7 \times 1000) + (2 \times 100) + (3 \times 10) + 9$.

We also commonly use clock arithmetic, which uses base sixty. The number of seconds goes up to 59 and then requires a new symbol, 1:00, to indicate 1 minute, 0 seconds. In other words, we work up to 59:59 and then one more second causes us to write it as 1:00:00 — 1 hour, no minutes, no seconds. There are many ways to represent numbers other than decimal notation.

The decimal system is convenient for counting on fingers, but it creates the inconvenience of having to memorize large tables for addition and multiplication. With rote memorization and many hours of practice, children learn to recite combinations like $7 \times 8 = 56$ without working through the derivation that 7 groups of 8 is the same number as 5 groups of 10 plus 6.

For automatic computation, it is certainly possible to build machines that work with decimal numbers. The older-style mechanical odometer on a car worked by rotating a wheel numbered 0 to 9, and at the point where the wheel rolls over to 0, a peg advances a similar wheel to the left by one digit to indicate another group of ten has accumulated. That's the "carry," and all computing mechanisms require a way to make sure that when an operation produces a number too large to store in one place, the overflow is carried to the next higher place in the notational system. More complex mechanisms allow counting down as well as counting up, which can be repeated for addition and subtraction, and addition and subtraction can be repeated for multiplication and division. Each string on a Chinese abacus holds beads in positions to represent the numbers 0 to 9, where the operator manually manages propagating the carry from ones place to tens place to hundreds place, and so on.

Binary arithmetic uses the number 2 instead of the number 10 as its base. It thus requires only two symbols, 0 and 1, to record numbers. It takes more symbols to record numbers, as can be seen simply by looking at the rather bulky-looking binary equivalent of the numbers 0 to 10:

Decimal	Binary
0	0
1	1
2	10
3	11
4	100
5	101
6	110
7	111
8	1000
9	1001
10	1010

However, the binary system has at least one major advantage over the decimal system: the arithmetic tables are extremely small and simple. For addition, there are only four entries:

$$0 + 0 = 0$$
$$0 + 1 = 1$$
$$1 + 0 = 1$$
$$1 + 1 = 10$$

(where "10" is binary for the number 2, not decimal for ten).

For multiplication they are even simpler, since there is no need for a carry; the table looks the same as it does in decimal:

$$0 \times 0 = 0$$
$$0 \times 1 = 0$$
$$1 \times 0 = 0$$
$$1 \times 1 = 1$$

The information theorist Claude Shannon was the first to shorten the phrase "binary digit" to "bit," which was a play on words because it also was the smallest bit of information that could be represented: yes or no, on or off, one or zero, true or false.

Making automatic devices that have two states is much simpler than making devices that have ten states. The two states could be a wire in an electric circuit being at one of two voltages, or a mechanical lever being in one of two positions, for example. The design problem for building an automatic multiplier changes from having to somehow mimic the entire ten-by-ten table one learned in grade school, to this:

If both inputs are 1, then the answer is 1. Otherwise, the answer is 0.

If the automatic computing device is mechanical, like the first Zuse computers, then this rule means something like letting a pin slip through two holes only if both are lined up on the right. If the device is electronic, like the Atanasoff-Berry Computer, then this rule means building a circuit that allows current to flow only if both switches in series are closed.

The early decimal machines, like the ENIAC and the Harvard Mark I, still used on-off states in their circuits but bundled them into subcircuits that represented the decimal digits 0 to 9. They were essentially electrical versions of the earlier mechanical calculators that used wheels to count in decimal. Both ENIAC and the Mark I were the size of a room, largely because of the inherent inefficiency of decimal representation, whereas the Zuse and Atanasoff designs were the size of a desk. It was not because the larger machines held more data; the ENIAC needed 18,000 vacuum tubes to compute with a maximum of twenty ten-decimal-digit numbers. The Atanasoff-Berry Computer needed only 600 vacuum tubes, yet it computed with a maximum of thirty fifteen-decimal-digit numbers — 50 percent more numbers, each with 50 percent greater precision.

Because very few people can look at a representation like 0001110001000111 and grasp its numerical value, all computers that use binary arithmetic also provide a way of accepting human-readable decimal representations as input and converting their answers to decimal output. That conversion is a small price to pay for an overwhelming simplification of the design of the computing device, so computers that use decimal arithmetic internally have disappeared from the computing landscape in favor of the binary arithmetic approach used by Atanasoff and Zuse.

Appendix C | Electronic Switches

In a biological organism, a neuron might cause a muscle to contract or convey a sensation, but a neuron can also trigger other neurons. A brain is a collection of neurons, interconnected so the firing of one can cause or suppress the firing of many others. That capability is what permits organisms to exhibit such complex and intelligent behavior. For any artificial device to rival the computing abilities found in nature, it must similarly have control elements that trigger other control elements.

The control elements of early electronic computing progressed from relays to vacuum tubes (or valves, the British term) to transistors. Such devices, sometimes called "switching elements," mimic the behavior of neurons in that they are switches that can control many other switches.

When something closes a switch to complete a circuit, the current that flows can operate another switch, either to open it or close it. The small amount of current needed to operate a switching element can result in a lot more current either flowing or not flowing, so a switching element can operate several other switching elements, not just one. That is why switching elements are often referred to as "amplifiers": the power they control is larger than the power it takes to operate them. Switching elements let electronic devices perform binary arithmetic (see appendix B) because their on-off state can represent the binary digits 0 and 1.

Imagine a waterfall with a gate at the top that can dam up the flow of water. When the gate is open, water spills down with much more energy than that needed to operate the gate. That flow of water could operate mechanisms that open or close other gates of other waterfalls, creating quite a complicated series of events. If, say, water not flowing represents the binary digit 0 and water flowing represents a 1, then a set of waterfalls could represent numbers in binary. Changing the gates performs operations on those numbers. What electrical devices do is similar, but with a flow of electrons instead of a flow of water.

An everyday example of switches in combination is what electricians call a double throw switch. Most homes have at least one room with two entry points and separate wall switches by each entry that can operate the overhead light. Perhaps you have had the experience of entering a dark room at one door when someone else enters another door, and you both hit the wall switches at the same time, which keeps the room dark. The pair of wall switches performs the logical operation that computer scientists call an "exclusive OR," because the light turns on if one or the other switch flips, but not when both flip.

An example of the logical "AND" operation is an appliance plugged into a power strip that has a switch. You have to flip on the power strip switch AND the appliance switch for the appliance to work. Switches, properly coupled, can represent logical operations, and logical operations in turn can mimic arithmetic operations on binary digits.

Suppose we want to build a circuit that takes two binary inputs a and b, which can be 0 or 1, and produces their sum c in binary. If we allow two digits in the result, the addition table looks like this:

213

$$a + b = c:$$
$$0 + 0 = 00$$
$$0 + 1 = 01$$
$$1 + 0 = 01$$
$$1 + 1 = 10$$

The right-hand digit of the sum c is the "exclusive OR" of the values of a and b. It has value 1 if a or b is 1, but not both. The left-hand digit is the "AND" of a and b. It is 1 only if a and b are both 1. So that says we could build a circuit where the inputs a and b flip switches to indicate their 0 or 1 value, and the two digits of c would immediately "light up" at the speed of electricity. Instead of operating lights, the flow of electricity in the result then operates yet other switches, so that the arithmetic can cascade to perform arithmetic on numbers with many (binary) digits.

One type of switch that can be operated by electricity is called a "relay." A relay is a simple device, one made from ordinary iron and wire. If you wind the wire around a piece of iron and run electricity through the wire, the iron becomes an electromagnet and remains that way until the electricity is off. That electromagnet can pull on something else made of iron such that it mechanically closes or opens a switch. Compared to mechanical switching elements, relays are quite fast, but they are electromechanical and not electronic. In the early days of telephone technology, telephone companies used relays to route calls, so relays were a mass-manufactured part even by the 1930s. Howard Aiken used them in his Mark I computer. Konrad Zuse used inexpensive mechanical linkages in his first designs to represent binary numbers but later used electro-mechanical relays.

Relays are inexpensive but not very uniform in their response; a group of relays attached to a single source of electricity doesn't switch at the same time, which means a computer designer can only operate the system as fast as its slowest relay. What is worse is that relays are not very reliable, because on rare occasions the switch sticks in position after the electricity turns off. In a computer system that has many thousands of relays, the odds are good that at least one relay will fail.

An electronic switch moves only electrons, not masses of metal. The first device discovered that could accomplish this was the vacuum tube. The glowing tube in a neon sign has a low-pressure gas that conducts electricity between two electrodes, one at either end. If you create a nearly perfect vacuum, it is still possible to get electricity to flow, but the electrodes have to be closer together, and it helps to heat one of the electrodes to "boil" electrons out of it to jump across the vacuum. It is very much like the waterfall analogy, with electrons responding to the pull of electrical forces instead of water responding to the pull of gravity.

Like the waterfall analogy, it is possible to insert a "gate" that controls the flow. If the vacuum tube has a third electrode in the form of a screen placed between the other two, then its voltage can control how much current flows. Like the waterfall gate, closing a gate stops all flow; electrons and water will not flow "uphill" even when a huge downhill waits on the other side. Thus, a vacuum tube serves as a switching element. Because only electrons and not mechanical parts are moving, vacuum tubes can switch on and off in microseconds, and a vacuum tube is more reliable than a relay. They can still burn out, however, much like an incandescent lightbulb burns out.

In the early decades of electronic computing, vacuum tubes were by far the most costly components in a computer system. The invention of the transistor made it possible to replace vacuum tubes with small, solid-state devices. Today, the switching elements of computers are transistors that are "printed" (lithographed) by the billions onto a piece of silicon, so each transistor in an integrated circuit costs less than a millionth of a penny.

Appendix D | *Differential Equations*

Whereas everyone learns arithmetic, geometry, and some algebra in a general education, the next conceptual climb is a steep one that only those pursuing technical degrees usually undertake: calculus. Since much of the motivation for the early computers was to solve problems arising in calculus, this appendix gives an overview of the applications that give rise to calculus problems and explains why they are so difficult to solve using pencil-and-paper methods alone.

In elementary school, children learn the counting numbers 1, 2, 3, . . . , then fractions and decimals, then negative numbers and sets of numbers (like three-dimensional coordinates or statistical results). The concept that marks the transition to higher math is that what calculus shows us how to manipulate are not just numbers, but functions. A function is the operation performed on a set of numbers, like taking the cube root of x for all values of x between 3 and 7, or taking the cosine of x and adding 17 and then taking the square root of that whole expression. The actual value of x is not the focus, and neither is the numerical value that results from applying the function to any particular x. This can be disconcerting after experiencing a decade of math teachers demanding the answer to how operations change numbers into numbers. In calculus, the operations change *functions into functions*.

In the mid-1600s, two brilliant men independently invented the mathematics we now call calculus. Just as the question of who contributed most to the invention of the modern computer is the subject of argument, so is the question of who deserves the most credit for developing calculus. Isaac Newton in England and Gottfried Leibniz in Germany both made groundbreaking contributions but were not aware of each other's work.

Newton developed calculus as a way to describe physics in mathematical terms. For example, if a mathematical expression describes the position of an object as a function of time, what is the mathematical expression that describes the speed of the object? Determining speed from position means taking the "derivative" of the position function, also called "differentiating" the function. Differentiation is a calculus operation that has its own collection of memorized rules and methods just as elementary arithmetic has rules for multiplying many-digit numbers. The inverse question, that of determining the position if you know the speed, means taking the "integral" of the speed function, or "integrating" the function. In general terms, differential calculus is used to find the rate at which things change, and integral calculus is used to find how things accumulate, like the area or volume of objects described by functions.

Ordinary Differential Equations (ODEs)

As in the example mentioned above, differentiating the position function gives the speed function. Differentiating the speed function gives the acceleration function. A situation that often arises in physics is that an equation relates the position, the speed, and the acceleration. Since that equation involves differentials of a function (with respect to just one variable) as well as the function itself, it is an "ordinary" differential equation, or ODE.

Here are some examples of physical problems that are expressible as ODEs:

A rocket projectile accelerates as it burns fuel, but it also becomes lighter with time so that it takes less fuel to make it go faster. It slows with air resistance, some of which is proportional to the speed and some of which is proportional to the speed squared. The physical laws lead to ODEs that mathematicians can express with just a few symbols but that are very difficult to solve. Such calculations were of great interest to the computer developers of the World War II era, when hitting a target with a missile was a challenge involving a lot of trial and error. The intimidating and blackboard-filling math for this problem may be the source of the expression "it's not rocket science," since rocket science of this sort really *is* difficult.

As an asteroid moves through the solar system, it accelerates under the gravitational forces of the sun, planets, and other masses. Thus, the second derivative of the position (its acceleration) relates to the position by an expression that sums all those forces, giving rise to an ODE. Solving that equation is of great interest if the question is whether the asteroid might strike the earth in the near future.

A pendulum, or a mass hanging on a spring, moves according to an ODE. The more the mass moves away from equilibrium, the greater the acceleration in the opposite direction. This situation arises so often in physics that the ODE for it has a name: the harmonic oscillator equation.

Partial Differential Equations (PDEs)

Problems in physics are rarely so simple that they involve only a single equation involving one function that depends on one variable (like time). Consider the complexity of the airflow around an airplane wing, for example. Pressure, air speed, air density, and temperature all are functions of the position (in three dimensions) and the time, and those are just a few of the things that enter the equations that determine the lift and drag forces on the wing. Fundamental laws of physics say that the total energy, momentum, and matter cannot change with time. Each of those quantities is expressed with derivatives, and the fact that they are conserved creates a system of three PDEs that must be solved simultaneously. PDEs involve differentiation with respect to more than one variable, like both the time and the *x direction*.

One type of PDE problem is to find the steady state of a system. Suppose a room has a heater in one corner and an open window on the other side; what is the temperature at every point in the room? Mathematically, the problem is a PDE that involves differentiating the temperature in each of the three spatial dimensions. The temperature in the room at any point is the average of the temperatures in the immediate neighborhood of the point, except where the heater or window forces it to be a particular temperature. Another steady-state PDE problem is that of finding the shape of a trampoline when standing still somewhere on the mat. The depression of the trampoline at any point is the average of the depressions immediately around the point, except for the frame and under the feet of the person standing on it. For this kind of PDE, there is no need to consider time as a variable.

The other type of PDE involves time. Time-dependent PDEs can formulate how a physical situation evolves. In striking a note on a piano, for instance, a hammer hits the string, which causes complex sideways motion of the string as a function of both the time and the position along the length of the string. That problem is a close cousin to the harmonic oscillator problem described above for ODEs, except that both time and position are variables.

PDEs arise in many technical areas, not just physics. They can describe how populations of species grow and decline in an ecosystem; what the climate will be a century from now; how atoms bond to form molecules; how to design a suspension bridge to be strong with minimum materials; and how galaxies evolve over millions of years. They even find use in determining the best price for financial instruments, like put and call options. Economists use PDEs in macroeconomic theory. A famous remark by physicist Max Planck was that in his youth he considered going into economics but had to change to physics because the mathematics was too difficult.

Computers for Differential Equations

Differential equations are easy to express but usually fiendishly difficult to solve. At the beginning of the twentieth century, a handful of simplified examples were all that mathematicians could point to as amenable to pencil-and-paper analysis. The analytical solutions might work if the problem geometry was a sphere or a square plate or other idealized shape, but there was little hope of finding a solution, say, to the PDE that expresses the mechanical stresses on something in the shape of a wrench.

The approach that works with broad generality is to pick so many sample points in the function that the problem becomes one of working with lists of ordinary numbers, not functions. Using sample points gives the "discrete form" of differential equations, which are sometimes called difference equations because simple subtraction suffices to estimate the rate of change with respect to increments of time and space. For the piano string example, imagine that instead of a string, there are point masses evenly distributed along the length of the string that follow the simple rules of how masses behave when tugged on. This eliminates the calculus and gets us back to elementary arithmetic, but with a catch: to use enough points that the sampling is accurate requires a very large number of additions, multiplications, subtractions, and divisions. The sampling approach, or "numerical analysis" method, seems to offer the possibility of solving just about any problem that can be expressed as an ODE or PDE, but it begs for a way to do all that arithmetic at speeds far beyond what a human can do.

In the trampoline example, suppose the trampoline is square and sampled with a five-by-five grid. The amount the trampoline depresses at each grid point is approximately the average of the depression of the points around it. That leads to a set of twenty-five linear equations in twenty-five unknowns. Solving that type of system is what Atanasoff had in mind in designing his computer, since the total work to solve twenty-five equations is more than ten thousand calculations, intractable even with Marchant or Monroe desktop calculators. Atanasoff's design could solve such a system in about fifteen hours.

The ENIAC design suggests that ODEs were its main target, and missile trajectory calculation is the most commonly cited application for that computer. The ENIAC could store only twenty variables, but it could apply changes to them very quickly to simulate how a physical system might evolve through time, with the time sampled in discrete steps. Thus, the ODEs that describe a missile become a repeated procedure; at time 0, the missile is at a given position on the ground and experiences a given thrust. Arithmetic says how it accelerates as a function of time, if we ignore the fact that its mass is decreasing as it burns fuel and that gravity is pulling it into a curved path back toward the ground. At time 0.01 second later, the velocity and thrust and position and mass are sampled again and used to compute what it will do at time 0.02 second, and so on. Since the ENIAC could do thousands of calculations per second on its small set of variables, the calculation of the complete flight path of the missile could finish in reasonable time.

The progress in computer technology in the last seventy years has increased speed and storage by a factor of more than a trillion. This allows us to obtain close, high-resolution approximations of the solutions to a vast range of differential equations, not just the handful that can be solved with pencil-and-paper analytical methods.

Notes

Introduction

1 *MIT Inventor Archive*: "Inventor of the Week Archive," http://web.mit.edu/invent/iow/i-archive-a.html.

2 *"I had reached the Mississippi River"*: Mollenhoff, p. 157.

4 *"a practical limitation on the size of systems"*: Alt, p. 283.

Chapter One

11 *"to teach such branches of learning"*: Title 7, U.S. Code, Sec. 304. 2004 ed. Legal Information Institute, Cornell University, http://www.law.cornell.edu/uscode/html/uscode07/usc_sec_07_00000304----000-.html.

15 *"Hurrying toward his destination"*: Burton, p. 61. Tammara Burton is Atanasoff's granddaughter and her book is my main source of information about his childhood and personal life.

17 *"for their fundamental theoretical investigations"*: Nobel Prize Citation, 1977, http://nobelprize.org/nobel_prizes/physics/laureates/1977/press.html.

17 *"If you had been here in the first half of the semester"*: Mollenhoff, p. 26.

17 *"There were perhaps twenty-five graduate students in the class"*: Ibid.

19 *"He appeared to lack the patience necessary"*: Hodges, p. 38.

20 *"It was all the same thing to him"*: Ibid., p. 9.

20 *"It really is a gas engine"*: Ibid., p. 13.

21 *"Alan had no friend"*: Ibid., p. 23.

Chapter Two

24 "*can be anything: a distance*": Mollenhoff, p. 29.

24 "*in essence a variable-speed gear*": Hartree, quoted in Barnet, paragraph 12.

26 "*The advantages of the method*": Atanasoff and Brandt, abstract, p. 83.

26 "*the properties of vacuum tubes*": Welch, http://ed-thelen.org/comp-hist/TheCompMusRep/TCMR-V12.html.

27 "*a power supply and electric motor*": Ibid.

28 "*Don't worry about people stealing your ideas*": "Howard Hathaway Aiken," http://www.answers.com/topic/aiken-howard.

30 "*when the family's enormous vegetable garden*": Burton, p. 86.

31 "*I had been forced to the conclusion*": Ibid., p. 89.

34 "*represented an elegant and powerful symbolism*": Hodges, p. 112.

35 "*was not only a matter of abstract mathematics*": Ibid., p. 107.

Chapter Three

36 "*I have traced my ancestry back*": Zuse, p. 1.

38 "*Given my many detours*": Ibid., p. 21.

38 "*on all sides now*": Ibid., p. 30.

39 "*The psychological effect*": Ibid., p. 31.

39 "*When I began to build*": Ibid., p. 34.

39 "*which took money*": Ibid., p. 35.

40 "*pasted the paper*": Ibid., p. 36.

40 "*It took up almost the entire living room*": Ibid.

41 "*I don't want to discourage you*": Ibid., p. 42.

41 "*To construct large and expensive computing machines*": Ibid., p. 43.

43 "*I was in such a mental state*": Mollenhoff, p. 157.

43 "*When I finally came to earth*": Burton, pp. 34–35.

44 "*For fifteen days I strove*": Andreasen, p. 43.

45 "*The changes of travel*": Ibid., p. 44.

45 "*most of the time that we speak*": Ibid., p. 78.

46 "*I would hypothesize*": Ibid.

49 "*I chose small condensers*": Mollenhoff, p. 35.

Chapter Four

53 "*I . . . was of the opinion*": Zuse, p. 38.

54 "*It is not true*": Ibid., p. 55.

55 "*We did not dare*": Burton, p. 100.

57 *"It could just add and subtract"*: Ibid., p. 102.

60 *"The idea would be"*: Hodges, p. 141.

61 *"should interfere as little as possible"*: Leavitt, p. 136.

62 *"I was in Berlin"*: Flowers, "D-Day at Bletchley Park," pp. 81–82.

62 *"Thomas Harold Flowers"*: "Tommy Flowers—Technical Innovator," http://www.bbc.co.uk/dna/h2g2/A1010070.

Chapter Five

68 *"was the right person"*: Hodges, p. 181.

69 *"the geese who laid"*: Roberts, p. 348.

69 *"by the end of 1939"*: Ibid., p. 37.

71 *"What do you mean"*: Zuse, p. 58.

72 *"performed flawlessly"*: Ibid., p. 61.

73 *"It was a jaw-dropping accomplishment"*: Gustafson, personal communication, April 5, 2010.

74 *"Available were unskilled"*: Zuse, p. 65.

75 *"What should I be doing now?"*: McCartney, p. 30.

78 *"used vacuum tube circuits"*: Ibid., p. 36.

80 *"would send problems over"*: Gustafson, interview, February 22, 2010.

81 *"masked the unnerving sound"*: McCartney, p. 41.

81 *"If you're going to come"*: Ibid., p. 42.

82 *"Is there any objection"*: Burton, pp. 126–27.

83 *"Our attorney has emphasized"*: Ibid., p. 128.

84 *"Notorious for his idiosyncrasies"*: Wansell, http://www.dailymail.co.uk/news/article-1212910/How-Britain-drove-greatest-genius-Alan-Turing-suicide--just-gay.html.

85 *"Before the war"*: Hodges, pp. 214–15.

85 *"the operation of fifteen U-boats"*: Ibid., p. 222.

Chapter Six

88 *"his unusual imagination"*: Burton, p. 134.

89 *"an electronic device"*: Ibid., p. 138.

89 *"None of us had much confidence"*: McCartney, p. 51.

90 *"size, destinations, and departure times"*: Roberts, p. 367.

90 *"The Admiral at Halifax"*: Hodges, p. 261.

91 *"they found their outlook"*: Ibid., p. 251.

91 *"A machine could be designed"*: McCartney, p. 48.

93 *"Eckert acquired some mice"*: Ibid., p. 76.

95 *"He looked Atanasoff in the eye"*: Burton, p. 144.

95 *"We had a tube fail"*: Randall, http://www.computerworld.com/s/article/
print/108568/Q_A_A_lost_interview_with_ENIAC_co_inventor_J._Presper
_Eckert.

96 *"Even as I was putting it together"*: Zuse, p. 71.

97 *"So, of course, when after weeks or months"*: Ibid., p. 76.

97 *"hardly anyone could imagine"*: Ibid., p. 77.

98 *"If Aiken and my father had had revolvers"*: Welch, http://ed-thelen.org/
comp-hist/TheCompMusRep/TCMR-V12.html.

103 *"Despite the fact"*: Copeland et al., p. 2.

103 *"Colossus was a special-purpose machine"*: Flowers, "Colossus," p. 96.

105 *"When I came to put them together"*: Roberts, p. 469.

105 *"Hitler had sent Field Marshall Rommel"*: Flowers, "D-Day at Bletchley
Park," p. 80.

106 *"The result was a defeat"*: Ibid.

106 *"even up to 26 June"*: Roberts, p. 470.

106 *"If I had . . . spent the war interned"*: Flowers, "D-Day at Bletchley Park,"
p. 82.

106 *"It is regretted that it is not possible"*: Good and Timms, http://www.ellsbury
.com/tunny/tunny-000.htm.

107 *"You'd be working on a problem"*: I. J. Maskell, http://c2.com/cgi-bin/
wiki?TommyFlowers.

108 *"Flowers received very little remuneration"*: Ibid.

Chapter Seven

111 *"More steerage-class Jewish families"*: Macrae, p. 42.

111 *"he was one grade below me"*: Marton, p. 41.

111 *"Before he finished high school"*: Macrae, p. 71.

111 *"He joined in class pranks"*: Ibid., p. 41.

112 *"From all over the globe"*: Marton, p. 64.

114 *"by his first question"*: Macrae, p. 281.

115 *"an internal summary of their work"*: McCartney, p. 118.

115 *"Johnny grabbed other people's ideas"*: Macrae, p. ix.

116 *"The primary memory would be fairly small"*: Ibid., p. 309.

118 *"Dr. Schreyer was able"*: Zuse, p. 79.

119 *"Today when I look back"*: Ibid., pp. 87–88.

119 *"Hitler is said to have replied"*: Ibid., p. 81.

120 *"The stairway was too narrow"*: Ibid., p. 92.

121 *"For fourteen days we fled along the front"*: Ibid., p. 93.

121 *"go over to the Americans"*: Ibid., p. 94.

121 *"And when the Allied troops"*: Ruland, Von Braun, "Mein Leben fur die Rahmfahrt," quoted in Zuse, p. 94.

122 *"a large computing machine"*: Zuse, p. 97.

122 *"This environment did anything"*: Ibid., p. 103.

123 *"although we could have taken over"*: Ibid., p. 108.

124 *"the innovation and progressiveness"*: Ibid., p. 109.

126 *"With no administrative or executive powers"*: Flowers, "Colossus," p. 83.

126 *"exacerbated, and . . . even provoked"*: Flowers, "Colossus," p. 83.

128 *"almost as big a deal"*: Gustafson, personal communication, April 6, 2010.

128 *"supplied detailed circuit design"*: Copeland, "Colossus and the Rise of the Computer," p. 109.

129 *"The code he suggests is"*: Hodges, p. 352.

129 *"It is clear that"*: Gustafson, personal communication, April 2010.

130 *"were widely at variance"*: Hodges, p. 353.

Chapter Eight

132 *"all people who wish to continue as employees"*: McCartney, p. 160.

132 *"Well, the record is clear"*: Stern, interview with Irven Travis, p. 18.

133 *"perfect[ing] them in more detail"*: McCartney, p. 138.

133 "Mauchly was a dreamer : Burton, p. 160.

135 *"Mauchly was assigned the patent work"*: Cox, interview, February 22, 2010.

138 *"It was one room in a Victorian building"*: Copeland, "Colossus and the Rise of the Modern Computer," p. 111.

139 *"The Sixth Army Group"*: Colley, p. A27.

140 *"every [press] release"*: Clark, p. 26.

140 *"the university [of Manchester]"*: Hodges, p. 406.

142 *"that his decision was influenced"*: Copeland, et al., p. 187.

142 *"with the Russians"*: Marton, p. 183.

142 *"all those sitting around"*: Macrae, p. 333.

Chapter Nine

143 *"had met with the Pentagon"*: McCartney, p. 147.

144 *"The application was broad and unfocused"*: Ibid., p. 148.

145 *"the Princestitute"*: Macrae, p. 299.

147 *"People thought he was walking away"*: Cox, interview, February 22, 2010.

149 *"He could not handle a screwdriver"*: Macrae, p. 371.

152 *"I have a great deal of affection"*: Kaplan, interview with John Atanasoff, August 28, 1977, p. 13.

152 *"In many ways"*: Hodges, p. 438.

153 *"transformed his body"*: Wansell, http://www.dailymail.co.uk/news/ article-1212910/How-Britain-drove-greatest-genius-Alan-Turing-suicide-- just-gay.html.

Chapter Ten

155 *"became paranoid"*: Cox, interview, February 22, 2010.

157 *"There may have been similar systems"*: Eckert, "A Survey of Digital Memory Systems," *Journal of the Institute of Radio Engineers*, October 1953, reprinted in Burton, p. 165.

157 *"he had heard rumors"*: Mollenhoff, p. 83.

157 *"If you will help us"*: Burton, p. 165.

159 *"Now in the United States"*: Zuse, p. 114.

159 *"still did not completely trust"*: Ibid., p. 115.

160 *"screaming in horror"*: Rhodes, personal communication, April 2010.

161 *"I did not want to spend the rest of my life"*: Kaplan, interview with John Atanasoff, August 28, 1977, p. 19.

161 *"Retirement mellowed Atanasoff very little"*: Burton, p. 175.

163 *"At Harvard they were still completely convinced"*: Zuse, p. 116.

163 *"We had exactly a half an hour"*: Ibid., p. 121.

163 *"Many a night"*: Ibid., p. 122.

164 *"An electrical computing machine"*: "Machine Remembers," *Des Moines Tribune*, January 15, 1941, reprinted in Mollenhoff, p. 163.

165 *"An interesting sidelight"*: Ibid., p. 99.

165 *"I am not sure what Dr. Atanasoff told you"*: Clifford Berry, quoted in Mollenhoff, p. 99.

167 *"left him in substantial pain"*: McCartney, p. 206.

167 *"When I told a physician what I knew"*: Berry, p. 361.

167 *"huge impact on Atanasoff"*: Cox, interview, February 22, 2010.

168 *"Atanasoff-Berry Computer"*: R. K. Richards, *Electronic Digital Systems* (New York: Wiley, 1966), quoted in Mollenhoff, p. 103.

168 *"The ancestry of all electronic digital systems"*: Richards, *Electronic Digital Systems* (New York: Wiley, 1966), quoted in Burton, p. 181.

170 *"Studying Atanasoff's memorandum"*: Mollenhoff, p. 111.

172 *"If I had known"*: Burton, p. 190.

Chapter Eleven

174 *"I just wasn't sophisticated enough"*: Robert Mather, quoted in Mollenhoff, p. 118.

174 *"I'm not sure we could have reconstructed the ABC"*: Gustafson, personal communication, April 2010.

175 *"a rather delightful fellow"*: Sam Legvold, quoted in Mollenhoff, p. 119.

175 *"The center portion of this letter"*: Mollenhoff, p. 120.

177 *"that when you got into administrative work"*: Ibid., p. 126.

177 *"had practically accused me of plagiarizing"*: Mauchly, quoted in Mollenhoff, p. 126.

177 *"Dr. Mauchly came to Ames"*: Mollenhoff, p. 127.

178 *"Do you contend that I read the book?"*: Mauchly, Dodds, and Atanasoff, quoted in Mollenhoff, p. 127.

178 *"The 827 patent"*: Ibid., p. 128.

178 *"Our lawyers don't want me to remember anything"*: Ibid., p. 130.

178 *"Mr. Dodds, in the face"*: Ibid., p. 129.

179 *"that Dr. Mauchly was"*: Atanasoff quoted in Mollenhoff, p. 131.

181 *"perform all kinds"*: Ibid., p. 138.

181 *"He made a huge mistake"*: Ibid., p. 187.

181 *"little computing device"*: McCartney, p. 187.

183 *"boiled down to"*: Ibid., p. 189.

185 *"I'm thinking about the condensers"*: Mollenhoff, p. 158.

186 *"the box would then yield"*: Ibid.

187 *"He seemed to follow in detail"*: Atanasoff, quoted in Mollenhoff, p. 165.

187 *"Immediately after commencement here"*: Mauchly, quoted in Mollenhoff, p. 167.

190 *"computing machines may be conveniently classified"*: Ibid., p. 191.

193 *"consumed over 135 days"*: Ibid., p. 201.

193 *"that there is no difference"*: Honeywell, Inc., quoted in Mollenhoff, p. 203.

193 *"Between 1937 and 1942"*: Section 3 of Judge Earl Larson's opinion in *Honeywell, Inc. vs. Sperry Rand Corp., et al.*, October 19, 1973, section 4, quoted in Mollenhoff, pp. 265–67.

194 *"as a result of this visit"*: Ibid., section 18, quoted in Mollenhoff, p. 267.

194 *"work on the ENIAC"*: Ibid., p. 213.

Chapter Twelve

195 *"In the 1980s"*: Epstein, http://www.k9ape.com/publicservice/Who%20Invented%20The%20Computer.html.

197 *"Scott struggles hard on the Atanasoff saga"*: JBartik, http://www.amazon.com/ENIAC-Triumphs-Tragedies-Worlds-Computer/product-reviews/0425176444/ref=cm_cr_pr_link_next_5?ie=UTF8&showViewpoints=0&pageNumber=5&sortBy=bySubmissionDateDescending.

197 *"Jean Bartik was a fountain of information"*: McCartney, p. 253.

198 *"Vincent . . . wants me to walk"*: Iva Atanasoff, quoted in Burton, p. 266.

198 *"One fourth of the time"*: Ibid.

198 *"I hear them"*: John Atanasoff, quoted in Burton, p. 268.

199 *"Atanasoff's principles"*: Arthur Burks and Alice Rowe Burks, quoted in Burton, p. 257.

199 *"for his invention of"*: Citation, 1990 Medal of Technology, quoted in Burton, p. 269.

200 *"The ABC replica took three years"*: Gustafson, interview, February 22, 2010.

202 *"Mauchly was the only person"*: Cox, interview, February 22, 2010.

Bibliography

Books

Alt, F. L. "A Bell Telephone Laboratories Computing Machine." In *The Origins of Digital Computers: Selected Papers*, edited by Brian Randall. New York: Springer-Verlag, 1973.

Andreasen, Nancy. *The Creative Brain*. New York: Plume, 2006.

Burks, Alice Rowe. *Who Invented the Computer?* Amherst: Prometheus Books, 2003.

Burks, Alice R., and Arthur W. Burks. *The First Electronic Computer: The Atanasoff Story*. Ann Arbor: University of Michigan Press, 1989.

Burton, Tammara. *World Changer*. Sofia, Bulgaria: Tangra Tannakra Publishers, 2006.

Clark, Lloyd. *Anzio: The Friction of War; Italy and the Battle for Rome 1944*. London: Headline Review, 2006.

Copeland, B. Jack. "Colossus and the Rise of the Modern Computer." In *Colossus: The Secrets of Bletchley Park's Codebreaking Computers*, edited by B. Jack Copeland et al. Oxford: Oxford University Press, 2006, pp. 101–15.

Copeland, B. Jack, et al., eds. *Colossus: The Secrets of Bletchley Park's Codebreaking Computers*. Oxford: Oxford University Press, 2006.

Flowers, Thomas H. "Colossus." In *Colossus: The Secrets of Bletchley Park's Codebreaking Computers*, edited by B. Jack Copeland et al. Oxford: Oxford University Press, 2006, pp. 91–100.

Flowers, Thomas H. "D-Day at Bletchley Park." In *Colossus: The Secrets of Bletchley Park's Codebreaking Computers*, edited by B. Jack Copeland et al. Oxford: Oxford University Press, 2006, pp. 78–85.

Ginzburg, Ralph. *100 Years of Lynchings*. Baltimore: Black Classic Press, 1988.

Hodges, Andrew. *Alan Turing: The Enigma*. New York: Simon & Schuster, 1983.

Leavitt, David. *The Man Who Knew Too Much: Alan Turing and the Invention of the Computer*. New York: W. W. Norton & Co., 2006.

Macrae, Norman. *John von Neumann: The Scientific Genius Who Pioneered the Modern Computer, Game Theory, Nuclear Deterrence, and Much More*, 2nd ed. Providence, RI: American Mathematical Society, 2000.

Marton, Kati. *The Great Escape: Nine Jews Who Fled Hitler and Changed the World*. New York: Simon & Schuster, 2006.

McCartney, Scott. *ENIAC: The Triumphs and the Tragedies of the World's First Computer*. New York: Walker and Company, 1999.

Mollenhoff, Clark R. *Atanasoff: Forgotten Father of the Computer*. Ames: Iowa State University Press, 1988.

Roberts, Andrew. *Storm of War: A New History of the Second World War*. London: Allen Lane, 2009.

Sawyer, R. Keith. *Explaining Creativity: The Science of Human Innovation*. New York: Oxford University Press, 2006.

Zuse, Konrad. *The Computer—My Life*. New York: Springer-Verlag, 1993.

Articles

Atanasoff, J. V., and A. E. Brandt. "Application of Punched Card Equipment to the Analysis of Complex Spectra." *Journal of the Optical Society of America* 26 (1936): 83–85.

Barnet, Belinda. "The Technical Evolution of Vannevar Bush's Memex." *Digital Humanities Quarterly* 2, no. 1 (2008): para. 12.

Berry, Jean. "Clifford Edward Berry, 1918–1963: His Role in Early Computers." *History of Computing* 8, no. 4 (October 8, 1986).

Blannin, Alan. "Thomas Flowers." *Daily Telegraph*, November 14, 1998.

Colley, David P. "How World War II Wasn't Won." *New York Times*, November 22, 2009, p. A27.

"Machine Remembers." *Des Moines Tribune*, January 15, 1941.

Turing, Alan. "Systems of Logic Based on Ordinals." *Proceedings of the London Mathematical Society* 2, no. 45 (1939): 161–228.

Wansell, Geoffrey. "How Britain Drove Its Greatest Genius Alan Turing to Suicide . . . Just for Being Gay." *Daily Mail*, September 12, 2009.

Welch, Gregory. "Howard Hathaway Aiken: The Life of a Computer Pioneer." *The Computer Museum Report* no. 12 (1985). Accessed online at http://ed-thelen.org/comp-hist/TheCompMusRep/TCMR-V12.html.

Web

Epstein, Sheldon. "Review: *Who Invented the Computer? The Legal Battle That Changed Computer History.*" 2003, http://www.k9ape.com/publicservice/ Who%20Invented%20The%20Computer.html.

Good, Jack, Donald Michie, and Geoffrey Tims. "General Report on Tunny." GCHQ, 1945. Released to the Public Records Office, 2000, HW 24/5 and HW 25/5. Available online at http://www.ellsbury.com/tunny/tunny-000.htm.

"Howard Hathaway Aiken." Answers.com, undated, http://www.answers.com/ topic/aiken-howard.

"Inventor of the Week Archive." Lemelson-MIT Program at MIT, September 2008, http://web.mit.edu/invent/iow/i-archive-a.html.

Jbartik, "Worthy Effort, but Not the Definitive Work on Subject [*sic*]." Amazon .com review, July 22, 1999, http://www.amazon.com/ENIAC-Triumphs-Tragedies-Worlds-Computer/product-reviews/0425176444/ref=cm_cr_pr_ link_next_5?ie=UTF8&showViewpoints=0&pageNumber=5&sortBy= bySubmissionDateDescending. Retrieved March 4, 2010.

Randall, Alexander V. "Q&A: A lost interview with ENIAC co-inventor J. Presper Eckert." *ComputerWorld*, February 14, 2006, http://www.computerworld .com/s/article/print/108568/Q_A_A_lost_interview_with_ENIAC_co_ inventor_J._Presper_Eckert.

"Tommy Flowers—Technical Innovator." BBC/ h2g2, April 8, 2003, http://www .bbc.co.uk/dna/h2g2/A1010070.

Interviews and Personal Communications

Atanasoff, John V. Interview conducted by Bonnie Kaplan, August 28, 1977, for the Computer Oral History Collection, Lemelson Center for the Study of Invention and Innovation, Smithsonian National Museum of American History. Repository, Archives Center.

Cox, Kirwan. Author interview, February 22, 2010.

Gustafson, John. Author interview, February 22, 2010.

Gustafson, John. Personal communications, March and April 2010.

Rhodes, Richard. Personal communications, April 2010.

Travis, Irven. Interview conducted by Nancy Stern, October 21, 1977, for the Charles Babbage Institute, The Center for the History of Information Processing, University of Minnesota, Minneapolis, p. 18.

Index

About the Author

Jane Smiley is the author of fifteen works of fiction for adults and young adults, including the Pulitzer Prize–winning *A Thousand Acres*, and four works of nonfiction. *Private Life*, her most recent adult novel, was published in 2010 to critical acclaim. Inducted into the American Academy of Arts and Letters in 2001, she received the PEN USA Lifetime Achievement Award for Literature in 2006. She lives in northern California.

BEYOND
TRAGEDY